How To Rebuild and Restore
FARM TRACTOR
ENGINES

Spencer Yost

MBI Publishing Company

Dedication
To my son Parker and my daughter Elisha.
Your lives and beauty are proof that God's most precious gifts
are given to parents in the form of children.

First published in 2000 by MBI Publishing Company,
729 Prospect Avenue, PO Box 1, Osceola, WI 54020-0001 USA

The information in this book is true and complete to the best of our knowledge. All recommendations are made without any guarantee on the part of the author or Publisher, who also disclaim any liability incurred in connection with the use of this data or specific details.

We recognize that some words, model names and designations, for example, mentioned herein are the property of the trademark holder. We use them for identification purposes only. This is not an official publication.

MBI Publishing Company books are also available at discounts in bulk quantity for industrial or sales-promotional use. For details write to Special Sales Manager at Motorbooks International Wholesalers & Distributors, 729 Prospect Avenue, Osceola, WI 54020-0001 USA.

Library of Congress Cataloging-in-Publication Data
Yost, Spencer
    How to rebuild & restore farm tractor engines /
    Spencer Yost.
        p.   cm.
    Includes index.
    ISBN 0-7603-0661-3 (pbk. : alk. paper)
    1. Farm Tractors—Maintenance and repair. 2. Farm Tractors—Motors. 3. Internal combustion engines—Maintenance and repair. I Title.
    TL233.2.Y67 2000
    629.28'752—dc21   99-087764

On the front cover: A rebuilt engine is an important part of the complete restoration on this 1941 Case SC, owned by Evan Traxler. *Jeff Hackett*

On the back cover: Left: Parker Yost laps the valves on a Ford 8N four-cylinder engine. ***Top right:*** Gail Abbott's 1957 Farmall 450. *Jeff Hackett* ***Bottom right:*** John Deere AR. *Andy Kraushaar*

Edited by Steve Hendrickson
Designed by Bruce Leckie

Printed in the United States of America

CONTENTS

ACKNOWLEDGMENTS

It is impossible to write a book without the help, guidance, dedication and generosity of many, many people. During the short time line of a book project, it is impossible to buy six or eight tractors, buy the parts, and rebuild the engines yourself. You must find other folks who are rebuilding their engines, help them, and in the process, photograph the engine rebuild. The owners of the engines photographed for this book are the real heroes of this project, and to them I am eternally indebted. They gave much, expected nothing in return, and were patient and dependable on every level. I would like to take the time to individually thank them here:

My wife and best friend, Rita: Without her amazing support, editing, and love, I would have failed at this project.

John Davis: John owns two of the engines rebuilt in this book; the Case CO and the Farmall F-20. His willingness to rebuild his engines around my schedule and his family's hospitality during my many visits were way beyond kind and helpful—they were fundamentally important to completing this book. In addition, John and his wife, Kirsten, have become friends of ours—a friendship my wife and I value and enjoy.

Paul Bazzetta: Paul is a good friend who has provided me many gifts in my life, including an extra hand with the Ford 8N engine that was rebuilt and photographed for this book.

Tom Teague, Bill Ganoway, and Judy Leonard: Tom owns the John Deere B engine that you see rebuilt in this book. His reputation in collecting circles is legendary, and the legends still don't do justice to his generosity. I owe Tom much, the least of which is the thanks I include here. Besides being a great friend, *Bill* helped me with the John Deere B engine rebuild, and is one of the most knowledgeable mechanics and John Deere collectors I have ever met. Bill has probably forgotten more about John Deeres and engines than I will ever know. *Judy* is the glue that holds Tom's tractor collection together, and coordinates all of our activities and documentation regarding Tom's tractor collection. Without her neither Tom, Bill, or I would ever know if we were coming or going, and I am indebted to her for this work and her kind friendship.

Dick Harrold: Dick is the owner of the Allis WC engine you also see rebuilt in this book. As with John Davis and his family, the kindness and hospitality of Dick and his family, and their willingness to work around my schedule, was nothing short of amazing. Because of a tight schedule, Dick and I worked a very long, hard 10 hours on his engine with barely a break. Not many folks would do this for an author, but Dick did, and I appreciate it.

Geoff Gauger: Geoff photographed the rebuild of a Farmall A engine (the tractor is owned by Paul Bazetta), and those photos were to be included in this book. Because of a failure within the United States Postal Service, the film and photos he so diligently set up and shot were lost forever. That doesn't diminish my appreciation for his efforts and hard work, though. Thanks, Geoff.

Larry Dotson: For providing the material on bearing materials.

The men and women of the Antique Tractor Internet Service mailing lists and web site: The more than 1,700 folks who subscribe to these mailing lists, and the thousands more who visit the web site every day, are an unfaltering fountain of knowledge, guidance, and direction. Much of what I know about antique tractor engines was learned through them. Without their amazing collective wisdom, this book would have been impossible. Come visit us at www.atis.net

Central Fuel Injection: For providing photographs and assistance for the sections on diesel fuel injection.

Lee Klancher and Steve Hendrickson, my editors, and their staff: Lee, Steve, and their staff have shown me patience above and beyond the call of duty. Their support when I was unsure of myself or the quality of my writing has always made a fundamental difference in my motivation and capabilities. I also thank them for such wonderful and professional layout work. Steve also provided the photos for creating double flares in oil and gas lines. Last, but not least, I thank them for their abiding faith in me.

To friends and family: They sacrificed much while I wrote this book.

Photo Lab of Winston-Salem, NC: For quick, professional black and white film and print developing that helped make the photography in this book as painless as possible.

Jerry Cox: For being a great friend and mentor.

Jake Brewer: For answering so many of my pesky questions, especially the ones on diesel fuel injection systems.

All my friends and neighbors at the Rust and Dust Club: in Pfafftown, North Carolina, for putting on the Rust and Dust Show and being so kindly supportive of my work.

As you can see, the antique tractor hobby is nearly awash with people whose neighborly help and selflessness is boundless—qualities we all would do well to emulate. I can't think of a single time in this project, or in my life for that matter, when I wasn't greeted by kindness, generosity, wisdom, and advice from other tractor collectors. Because of this, their collective wisdom couldn't help but find its way into this book. I am indebted to all these people for their contributions. Their example has taught me much, given me much.

INTRODUCTION

During every tractor restoration, everyone reaches milestones that are incredibly fulfilling. Without a doubt, one of the most significant is hearing your formerly worn, stuck or broken engine—the same engine that everyone said wouldn't ever run again—bark to life and run as it did coming out of the showroom. My first engine rebuild was a motorcycle engine. I was 15 and inexperienced, and had no real direction other than a few books and a shop teacher who answered a few questions. Looking back, it's a miracle the engine ran; but it did and I, quite frankly, was prouder than I probably had a right to be, and certainly prouder than I had ever been of myself. It was a difficult puzzle, one that was important to me, and I solved it. That's an accomplishment anyone can relate to, and one that I hope I can share with you in this book. With each engine, that feeling of accomplishment returns. I still get every bit as excited when a newly rebuilt engine cranks up and runs.

Getting to that point is often the culmination of a lot of work, planning, learning, growing, dedication, and ultimately, commitment. It's no small feat to bring an engine back from the grave. This book will show you through the entire process, all the way to the other side of engine restoration, because the world is littered with engine rebuild projects that were started and never finished. I have endeavored to create a book that is not only full of the advice and guidance you need to professionally restore an engine, but a book that is readable, likable, and motivational. It will serve as a guide through the trials and tribulations you are sure to endure.

Take the time—right now—to contact the vendors in the back of the book and get a copy of the service and the parts manual for your tractor. There is no more important advice I can give you. The service and parts manuals have all the details, quirks, and nuances for your specific engine, and more important, the specifications that are imperative during the rebuild. You cannot, under any circumstance, rebuild an engine well without these manuals. Please purchase them now, before taking a wrench to your engine.

If it were possible to rebuild an antique tractor engine by using the manuals alone, there would be no need for how-to books. Service manuals are, without exception, written for experienced, professionally (and factory) trained technicians who only need a few details and specifications to help them rebuild an engine. If fact, just a quick scan of most service manuals will find the dreaded phrase "…disassembly is self-evident," or my personal favorite, "crankshaft and bearing service does not deviate from normal professional procedures." If we all knew what a "normal professional procedure" was, or if the disassembly really was self-evident, then the manuals would suffice. Of course, the manuals don't suffice because we are not professional mechanics. That is where this book picks up the slack. This book will tie together all the conceptual and organizational issues and elaborate on the procedures the manuals already assume you know how to perform. In fact, except in the most ridiculously simple circumstances, you'll see very few assumptions about specific procedures or your skill level.

Of course, there are some minor prerequisites you should have. For example, I can't believe you would be interested in rebuilding an engine if you have never changed oil, timed an engine, or changed spark plugs. In short, I assume you have some general mechanical skill. I also assume you have a tool collection or are willing to acquire one, and that you're willing to acquire some of the special tools needed. I also assume you understand how to use must common hand tools, including measuring tools, such as micrometers, calipers, and dial calipers.

Likewise, you should have a basic understanding of how a four-cycle engine works. However, I also assume you don't mind taking a small walk on the conceptual side, so I cover theories and ideas that are not commonly known or understood. These discussions should help you complete a successful and competent engine restoration.

Unlike a service manual, this book will not dwell on details of specifications, but on skills and procedures. The upside of this is I will not bore you with the details and specifications of 20 different antique tractor engines. The downside is that one of those 20 engines is your engine, and you won't find the specifics here. That's where the service manual comes in.

In short, this book will give you the basic skills you need to rebuild any antique tractor engine, regardless of its age or manufacturer.

GETTING STARTED

SETTING GOALS

It's no secret that your expectations for the finished engine determine how you should approach your rebuild. In addition, factors such as time, budget, and the engine's condition will also influence your approach. Therefore, the first step in a rebuild doesn't involve a wrench, it involves a cup of coffee, a chair, and some time to think through your motivations for wanting to do a rebuild. Maybe you want to get a running engine to run better, or repair a stuck engine, or maybe the rebuild is one step in a complete tractor restoration. Whatever your reasons and motivations, it is important to understand them.

After determining your motivations, you need to understand what you want to have when you are finished. In your mind's eye, do you see a sparkling, freshly painted engine that runs like a sewing machine, and never falters? Then

A nice antique tractor, such as this one, deserves an engine rebuild rather than relegation to the scrap yard or fence row. As this tractor carries a lot of sentimental value to the owner, the goal was to have an engine that is as good as new. To provide it, I performed a very thorough engine restoration, something I call a remanufacture. The restoration of this tractor engine is one of several featured in this book.

you have very high expectations, and you'll need most everything in this book, and then some. But maybe all you want is for the engine to stop blowing smoke when you reinstall it. In this case, you will not need to follow every procedure outlined in this book.

OUTLINE OF A TYPICAL REBUILD

There is no such thing as a typical rebuild, but there are groups of steps that everyone follows. These groups stay the same, but the steps within the groups may vary by mechanic or by project. Nevertheless, this will give you an idea as to an engine restoration process.

Engine Access: This includes cribbing and chocking the tractor, removing the front end if necessary, and other

---

MORE POWER!

COMMONSENSE PERFORMANCE MODIFICATIONS

Safety should be your Number 1 priority when you modify an engine. Tractors generate enough torque to flip themselves over. Tractors whose performance has been modified simply flip over much more easily and quickly, making them especially deadly. Be incredibly careful operating any tractor with an engine modification. If you're participating in a tractor pull, never enter the pulling track with a modified tractor without adding wheelie bars and other safety devices. Please approach any planned modification with common sense and guidance from a local performance machine shop or from other competitive pullers.

> ### TIP
> **Engine rebuilding can't be rushed. Workmanship will suffer, and if you view this as a hobby, haste robs it of all the fun.**

steps needed to gain access to the engine for removal or in-frame restoration.

Engine tear-down: This includes all disassembly steps necessary to begin parts inspection and replacement.

Engine inspection: Probably the most important group of steps, these procedures measure and inspect the components to see if they still meet standards and tolerances for continued use. This includes the entire engine, including the sleeves, block, head, other castings, and all moving and nonmoving parts. The inspection tells you which parts need to be replaced, machined, or repaired.

Final decisions and parts acquisition: Depending on cost and other factors, this may be where you abandon the rebuild, deciding instead to find a replacement engine or to sell the tractor for parts. For example, major block cracks may signal the need for a new block . . . or a new project. If you decide to move forward, this is when you start finding parts for the tractor.

Final disassembly: This includes removing any parts that were left in to facilitate engine removal or inspection. For example, sleeves are inspected and measured while in place and only removed if they need replacement. This is where freeze plugs, oil galley plugs, and so forth are removed.

Engine cleanup: All parts are thoroughly soaked, cleaned, then oiled to prevent rust. Parts that need to be professionally cleaned, such as the engine block, are taken to professionals.

Machining: Any machine work that's needed is done now. This includes boring, milling, general minor repairs, and welding.

Assembly: After most of the parts have been acquired (all major parts should be in hand), everything has been cleaned and any repairs and machining have been completed, the engine can be put back together. This is the part that folks think of when they think of rebuilding an engine, but this usually is the shortest and simplest part of a rebuild.

Installation and testing: The engine is closed up (after final quality checks are done), and is hand cranked to check for any binding or tightness. Then, the engine's oil galleys are primed with oil and the engine is installed in the tractor.

REBUILDING: WHAT DOES IT MEAN?

A typical rebuild includes inspecting and repairing/replacing all of the most important components and systems on the engine. However, a rebuild can reuse any parts that pass inspection, even if they are slightly worn—especially expensive or hard-to-find parts. Someone that simply wants their tractor to start more reliably and use less oil might be happy with a minor rebuild, something I call *refurbishing* an engine. Someone who needs to rely on a tractor for productive work, or whose tractor's engine is in very poor shape, will probably perform an extremely thorough rebuild, something I call *remanufacturing*. In short, there are several levels of rebuilds. In fact, if you restore enough antique tractor engines, you'll find a need for every level of rebuild.

I decided not to be dogmatic about using these terms. Instead, throughout the book I use the terms "restore" and "rebuild" interchangeably, regardless of how thoroughly you rebuild your engine. When I use the word restore, it usually refers to your tractor's restoration or your engine's complete restoration. When I use the term "rebuild," it usually refers to the engine project itself and the specific procedures.

SAFETY

Anyone about to rebuild an engine needs to have a basic set of safety equipment and know how to use it. A fire extinguisher is a must (one that will handle all types of fires) and a phone should be nearby for emergencies. A well-stocked first aid kit should be in the shop at all times.

Probably the most important component of safety is a clear head and a keen awareness of what is going on around you at all times. Working on an engine requires concentration and focus, and often while doing this work we miss clues that something is amiss. For example, a tractor might be slowly slipping off of a jack stand, but if you are busy and intently focused, you might not realize the situation is becoming dangerous. Looking up from your work from time to time, maybe stretching and looking over the situation, promotes safety and helps to minimize small pains and cramps that come from working in one position too long. A healthy attitude and a clear head improve shop safety.

ORGANIZATION

The organized mechanic never loses that important bearing, never forgets where a part went, has all the records associated with his work so he can make warranty claims,

> ### TIP
> **Novices should spend a lot of time investigating each new step, talking with experienced neighbors and friends. The more you know, the more you'll enjoy it and the safer you'll be.**

and never trips on tools and parts carelessly left beside his engine. Sounds like a worthwhile goal, but most of us fall a little short. I can be worse than most in this category, and don't want to leave you with the impression that I am organized. In fact, I can be very disorganized, especially when things are going fast and furious during a rebuild. After losing and stepping on expensive parts and tools and losing time because I didn't take notes, I have learned to slow down and learned some organizational techniques necessary to a successful rebuild. Here are some of the techniques I have learned the hard way . . . and a few other organizational traits that I need to learn.

- Each part you remove must be stored in a box or plastic bag (self-locking plastic bags and permanent marker are always in my tool chest).
- Keep each new part clean and in a box until you use it.
- Have a system to keep parts and tools organized while you work.
- Have the area well lighted.
- Plan ahead so you have everything you need to do that day's work. I hate wasting valuable tractor time running errands to parts stores, etc.
- Keep all tools clean and in good repair.
- Use drop cloths to cover work that will be unattended for any length of time.

Organization and cleanliness go hand in hand. While I am not very organized, I make sure my engine stays clean during the rebuild process. I do this two ways. First I do the rebuild in areas where I don't expect dust. Second, I keep the engine covered when I am not working on it, and I constantly keep an eye out for dirt and dust in the engine. Engines rebuilt in dirty environments have a greater risk of failure. That's not to say every horse barn rebuild will fail, and I am not saying every engine rebuilt in a clean room worthy of a professional race team will be perfect.

Finding parts for the restoration can be difficult, or it can be as easy as going to the Ford/New Holland dealership and buying a complete engine kit. The kit, seen here, comes with everything you need.

Organization during restoration is important. How you organize parts, tools, and procedures is up to you; the methods you use aren't important, as long as you use some kind of system. Here push rods are stored on a wood rack and numbered.

But at the least, I suggest rebuilding your engine in a room with a concrete floor. Minimize dust and dirt while the engine is open, for example, by wet mopping the floor instead of using a broom. Don't do jobs that produce dust while the engine is open, such as metal fabrication. (Grinding welds around open engines is especially bad!) Cleanliness is next to godliness when rebuilding engines.

FINDING PARTS

Finding parts is often one of the most time-consuming processes during a rebuild. For example, pistons for 50-year-old agricultural engines aren't lying around in every auto parts store. Most rebuild parts are bought from tractor dealers, specialty suppliers, swap meets, antique tractor graveyards, and other collectors in the hobby. Many current dealers such as John Deere, New Holland/Case, (International, Case, Farmall, Ford and many interchangeable parts for Ferguson), and AGCO (Allis-Chalmers and others) are usually helpful finding parts. Swap meets are a great source of reasonably priced parts, especially considering you can often trade or barter for these parts. Antique tractor graveyards are my favorite place to visit and are a great source of difficult-to-find items.

Which parts source you use depends on what class of part you need. There are three classes of parts: New (either reproduction or rebuilt parts), Used, and New Old Stock, NOS for short. NOS means the part was made by the original equipment manufacturer as a replacement or repair part when the tractor was not considered obsolete. NOS parts come from specialty suppliers, swap meets, other collectors, and tractor dealerships. New parts can be purchased from specialty suppliers, auto parts stores and dealers. If you need or want a used part, a tractor graveyard or another

Safety above all else! Always be aware of the circumstances you are working in.

collector is your best bet. Regardless of where you start, look to the appendices of this book for a list of suppliers.

SKILLS

You must master some basic skills before beginning any rebuild. The three most common skills we need to review are measuring, gasket making, and fastening. Simple? You bet. Often done improperly? Right again. Lots of things will go wrong if you don't measure correctly, seal correctly, or fasten correctly. It doesn't take much imagination to envision what would happen if a head bolt were not tightened correctly, a measurement was not made correctly, or an oil pan gasket were not made or installed correctly.

Measuring Parts

The key to measuring parts is to use the right tools, to measure the part where the manual dictates, and when in doubt, to take the reading several times and use an average. For example, bearing thickness measurements must be made with a micrometer. Don't use a caliper. If the manual says to measure 1/2 inch from the head of a pin, don't measure 3/4 inch from the head. It's often difficult to accurately measure the end play of tapered bearings. Take the measurement three times, setting up the dial indicator and base from scratch each time, then average the results.

One of the more important skills to master while rebuilding an engine is taking accurate measurements. Accurate measurements are easy if the surface is flat, but what if the surface is curved, such as this bearing shell? As this picture shows, simply add a steel rod of a consistent, known diameter, and then subtract that diameter from the final measurement. A little thought and common sense helps overcome little obstacles such as this.

Making Gaskets

Fortunately, most of the gaskets your engine needs will probably be available. But even in the best-case scenario, there is usually a gasket or two you must make. In the worst case, you'll have to make virtually all of them. Gasket making is both an art and a science. The science involves being very accurate and faithful in the reproduction and the cutting. But the art involves using the right materials, knowing when gasket thickness matters, and choosing and using the correct sealants. While a little common sense goes a long way, the consequences of doing it wrong are disproportionately large, compared to the simplicity. For example, if you would like to see how low your oil pressure can go, use a thick gasket on an oil pump bottom plate.

Here are some rules of thumb for gaskets:

- Gaskets should never be applied "dry." They should be installed with some type of sealant. The exception is the head gasket, which can be applied dry, or with a light coat of flat black paint. Others have used a high-temperature copper sealant with success, but I was always taught to stay away from them when installing a head gasket.
- Assume gasket thickness matters, and look to the part for clues as to what difference thickness would make. In some cases, gaskets act as a shim and maintain proper distances.
- Use high-temperature sealant for any gasket that involves the block (for example, the front cover or water pump gaskets). Otherwise, thinner sealants that are easier to work with can be used.
- Use gasket punches and a sharp knife to cut new gaskets. Rough, torn edges invite leaks.
- To save money, buy gasket materials in large rolls rather than small sheets.

Fasteners

Choosing, using, and tightening fasteners involves more skill and judgment than meets the eye. There are four things to consider when installing and tightening a fastener: What type of fastener should I use? How hard should the fastener be? How tight do I install the fastener? How do I lock the fastener in place?

Choosing the right fastener in your engine rebuild is usually easy: Simply reuse the type of fastener that came out of the engine. Many fasteners, like head bolts and

Lock or rope off your work area if it's dangerous—if, for example, you have a tractor up on jacks. Kids may climb on unstable machinery.

TABLE OF TYPICAL BOLT TORQUE VALUES:

Below is a table of typical torque values for various grade and size bolts. The actual torque value may be different for each circumstance. Always use the torque values specified in your service manual. If there are no values specified, use this table. Below the table is a list of assumptions, which are of particular importance. If the fastener you are tightening does not fall within these assumptions, alter the torque value. For example, if the two parts being joined by the fastener are made of soft material, you may need to use a slightly lower torque value.

The information was gleaned from various sources, but I relied heavily on data found in the archives of the antique tractor mailing list found at my web site, Antique Tractor Internet Service (www.atis.net). A message from Guy Burnham contained in the 1995 archives was of particular help.

Bolt Or Stud Diameter (Inches)	Type 1 Studs	Type 1 6" in length or less	Type 1 greater than 6" in length	Type 5 All	Type 8 In Cast Iron	Type 8 All Others
1/4	5–6	6–7	4–4	9–10	11–13	13–14
5/16	12–13	11–13	7–8	18–20	22–25	25–28
3/8	21–24	21–24	13–14	33–37	41–46	45–50
7/16	35–38	35–38	20–23	53–60	65–74	75–85
1/2	52–58	52–59	31–35	80–90	100–112	115–130
9/16	70–80	75–85	45–51	115–130	145–160	165–185
5/8	98–110	104–117	62–70	160–180	200–225	225–255
3/4	174–195	185–205	110–125	285–320	355–400	400–450
7/8	280–315	180–200	180–200	460–575	570–640	645–725
1	420–470	265–300	265–330	685–720	855–960	970–1090
1 1/8	595–670	380–425	380–425	850–950	1210–1360	1375–1545

Torque ranges are in lb.-ft.

Type 1 = SAE Grade 1 or 2 = no radial lines on head
Type 5 = SAE Grade 5 = 3 radial lines on head
Type 8 = SAE Grade 8 = 6 radial lines on head

Assumptions:
Surface finish is oxide coated, oil quenched, or bright.
All thread surfaces are clean and lubricated with SAE-30 engine oil or equivalent.
Joints are rigid, with no gasket or compressible material in the joint.
When reusing nuts or bolts, use minimum torque value.

engine mounting bolts, should always be replaced, due to their condition or importance. Otherwise, simply judge the condition of the original to decide whether it can be safely reused.

When replacing fasteners, you obviously must match length, head type, thickness, and thread pitch. You must also match hardness. Be sure to use hardened steel bolts where hardened bolts were used in the past. Unlike modern bolts, though, the hardness of older bolts is usually not marked on the bolt head. Older hardened bolts are usually darker in color than other bolts, and they will scratch a modern Grade 5 bolt. Replace older hardened bolts with a modern Grade 8 bolt. When in doubt, use a Grade 8 bolt. The only exception to that rule, are shear bolts and pins. A shear fastener is designed to fail where your safety could be compromised if it didn't.

Tightening a fastener properly requires that you understand what happens when you tighten a bolt. A properly tightened bolt pulls two parts together, and then it is tightened a little further to stretch the bolt. This stretch is called "preload" and is very important. Torque specifications that come with your antique tractor manuals will tell you exactly how tight to tighten important bolts; these recommendations should be followed. The tool for this procedure is a torque wrench, which is discussed later in this chapter. If you can't find torque specifications, the table in this chapter will guide you in tightening bolts correctly. Remember, these recommendations assume the bolt has a

The whitish corrosion on this bolt shows what happens when a steel bolt is used in an aluminum housing. Over the years, differing metals in close contact will often corrode like this. The best way to prevent it is to use a thread sealant. It will help prevent corrosion and help stop leaks and lubricate the bolt for final tightening.

light coat of lubricant or sealant, the parent materials are sturdy and not soft, and the bolts are new. Other circumstances require different torque values.

Locking the fastener in place is sometimes imperative, sometimes a good idea, and sometimes overkill. In some assemblies, such as crankshaft assemblies and steering components, castellated nuts with cotter pins ensure the nuts will never come off.

Other times, thread sealants are a good idea. Head bolts and studs often protrude into the block's coolant jacket. You should use a thread sealant on these fasteners for two reasons: First the corrosive effect of the coolant will make the bolts difficult to remove. Second, without sealant you will have a greater risk of a coolant leak around the head studs or bolts. In addition to thread sealant, there are different grades of thread-locking compounds that "glue" bolts and fasteners into place. These products should not be used in most restorations. If you do use them, don't use the locking compounds that permanently install the bolt, requiring that later the bolt be drilled out.

Pets or children (yours or your neighbor's) may find their way to dangerous chemicals. Keep all dangerous chemicals behind lockable doors.

TIP

Modern bolts have their hardness marked on them. To determine the hardness, count the radial slashes on the head and add two. For example, a modern Grade 5 bolt will have three slashes on the head.

Various types of lock washers are available as well. They should be used anywhere lock washers were used before, or whenever you suspect the fastener may be loosened by vibration or other forces.

SUBCONTRACTING WORK

Often you will need to subcontract certain parts of your engine rebuild to professionals. The most common example of this is machining the engine parts before assembly. Other examples might include sleeve pulling and pressing, crankshaft and bearing inspection and restoration, and similar work. Regardless of what jobs you farm out, you'll need to find reputable shops. Your local mechanic can do most general mechanical procedures (sleeve pulling, installing crankshafts) for you, and he can give you references for machine shop services. If you belong to an antique tractor collector's group, many members there will be able to provide references. Another source of trustworthy references is your local full-service automotive parts business.

Without any specific recommendations from these sources, I use the following old saw to find a reputable shop: "Professionals look and act like professionals." I prefer to see a shop with a clean, professional appearance that employs people with a friendly, professional demeanor. Most really good shops run tight ships and you find those attributes there. Other evidence of competence is continuing research and education, investment in the latest tools, and professional affiliations. These things point to a real commitment and love for their profession, which usually translates to top-quality work and fair business practices. On-site visits are required; be sure to look at a couple of shops before trusting your antique tractor engine to one of them.

NECESSARY TOOLS

Probably the first question on every novice rebuilder's mind is: What tools do I need? The next is: How much do I have to spend? Fortunately when it comes to tools, rebuilding antique tractor engines allows us a little more free rein than newer higher-precision engines, and our tool needs are modest, compared to many modern shops. You will have to invest in a small set of tools, however, and your checkbook may be tested more by tool purchases and rentals than it will by parts purchases.

While typical hand tools are all that is needed for disassembly/assembly during engine restoration, you'll find time savers, such as this crank handle socket wrench, a big help. Other handy tools include retaining ring pliers, punches, drifts, two or three different types of mallets and ball peen hammers, and a nice selection of cheap screwdrivers—the kind you don't mind grinding new blade profiles into.

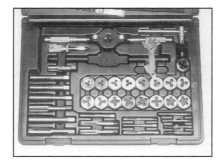

A tap and die set is almost a must for engine restoration. It is the only way to save bolts and nuts that were damaged during removal. In addition, many bolts and nuts have enough grime and rust to warrant a thorough cleaning with a tap or die. This process is called "chasing" the threads.

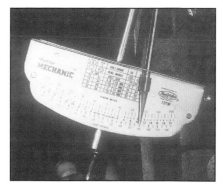

Torque wrenches must be used to properly tighten certain bolts found on an engine. This type is known as a "pointer" torque wrench. While not as accurate as the "click" type, it is sufficiently accurate for most work on antique tractors.

Basic Toolbox

The basic tool box consists of all the tools and supplies you already use to maintain your tractor. This includes typical hand tools such as wrenches, screwdrivers, pliers, and the like. Socket wrench sets are mandatory, and you will need two sizes: the standard 1/2-inch drive set and a 3/8-inch drive set. You'll also find an air wrench and a 3/4-inch socket wrench set pretty handy too. I suggest that you also have a good set of combination wrenches, which have a box end and an open end. A combination wrench set whose closed ends are offset is especially helpful. These wrenches are the most versatile, and they come in very handy.

Don't forget about torque wrenches. While precision tightening is not required by 90 percent of the fasteners on a tractor, there are circumstances that do require proper tightening, such as cylinder head fasteners. While the torque values are important, the most important aspect to head fastener tightening is consistency. They must be tightened alike to minimize future head warping, coolant and oil leaks, or blown head gaskets. No matter how experienced you are at turning a wrench, there is no way you can consistently tighten 12 or more fasteners to the same torque value by feel alone. A torque wrench that measures from 25 to 150 foot-pounds is a must.

There are several styles of torque wrenches to consider. The "click"-type torque wrenches are best and most accurate. These wrenches usually have a vernier-style dial that you set to a specified torque. When you reach that torque value, the wrench makes an audible "click" that signals you to stop pulling. The other, older-style torque wrench

Never use a hardened bolt in place of a shear pin!

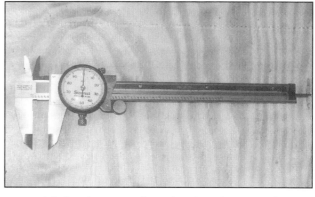

A Vernier dial caliper that measures from 0 through 6 inches is a must for engine restoration too. This one has a dial gauge for reading the measurement. Tenths of an inch are read from the frame of the caliper, while the hundredth and thousandth places are read from the dial.

A dial gauge is imperative when measuring some types of end play, such as valve rotor gap clearances and tapered bearing clearances. A dial gauge is used with a magnetic base (not shown) and an articulated mounting arm to position the gauge.

involves a stationary index pointer that points to a gauge. The gauge moves with the wrench handle as the handle bends with the force you are applying. This type wrench will do in a pinch, but it's not quite as accurate. As for size, I recommend a 1/2-inch drive torque wrench.

Measuring is a very important part of engine rebuilding. Necessary measuring tools include a micrometer than measures from 0 to 1 inch, a caliper than measures from 0 to 6 inches, a cylinder bore measuring gauge, feeler gauges, a spark plug gap tool, and a steel rule. The steel part is important, as the rule will also serve as a straightedge at times, and wood or plastic rules aren't accurate straightedges. These tools can occasionally be rented, and most are expensive if you buy high-quality versions. Top-notch brands, such as Starrett, are safe bets for quality, heirloom-grade tools, but other trusted brands from reputable outlets such as Sears (Craftsman), Mac, and Snap-on are reliable and accurate.

Tools Specific to Rebuilding

Tools specific to engine rebuilding abound, and many are necessary. An example would be a ridge reamer. This tool

To install the pistons, you will need a piston ring compressor. This compresses the rings and keeps them out of harm's way while the piston enters the bore during installation. Be sure to oil the piston, rings, and compressor well when using this tool.

has no manual counterpart that is as safe, effective, and accurate. You must buy or rent one of these. Some tools are available because they are easier than many manual improvisations, but are not more effective. An example is a piston ring groove cleaner. These tools make easy short work of cleaning piston ring grooves, but the widely used shortcut of using an old piece of a piston ring cleans the groove just as well. It's just slower and harder. Here is short list of tools, used only with engine rebuilds, that you will have to make, buy, or rent: ridge reamer, piston ring groove cleaner, cylinder hone, sleeve puller, piston ring compressor, and valve spring compressor.

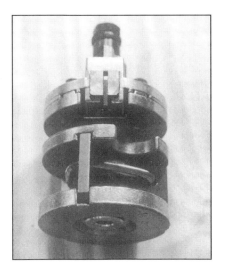

A ridge reamer such as the one shown is used to remove the unworn metal, known as a ridge, from the top of the engine bores before piston removal. Before reaming the ridge, take a diameter measurement of this unworn portion. You'll need this original-bore diameter measurement to accurately assess bore wear and to determine the original bore diameter.

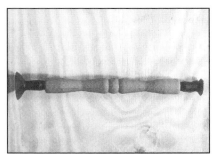

A valve lapping tool is attached to the top of a valve with suction force. This allows you to spin the valve back and forth, with an abrasive lapping compound on the valve face. This creates mating surfaces on the valve and valve seat that are smooth, even, and clean. A child's suction cup arrow works in a pinch.

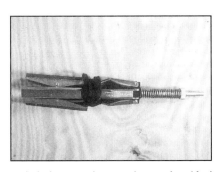

A cylinder hone is used to create the piston fit and final finish of a sleeve or bore. The hone is moved up and down through the bore while it is being spun by a drill. Use a 50/50 mixture of kerosene and diesel fuel as a lubricant, flushing fluid, and coolant. Some service manuals will require that the cylinder be honed without a lubricant. If yours does, you can still use the mixture for most of the job, then finish up the honing dry as the manual specifies. The stones usually need to be replaced after just a few engines.

These pictures illustrate some other tools that are handy for restoring an engine. A gasket scraper makes short work of removing gasket and gasket sealant residue, without damaging the metal surfaces.

A dwell meter will come in very handy when it comes time to set the points and timing on your tractor's engine. This will make your first engine firing much easier.

A multimeter, such as this, come in handy for all kinds of electrical work, from setting a magneto to testing switches and circuits.

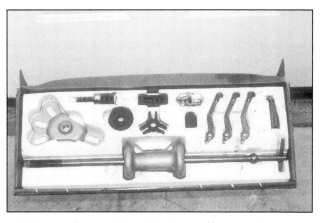

A pickle fork is the only reliable way to separate tie rods without damaging them. Make sure the pickle fork is properly sized for your steering components.

A slide hammer pulls gears, pulleys, pilot bushings, and bearings easily and without damage. Larger special-use pullers may also be needed for more specialized jobs.

Just remember that many of the tools I mention may have a common-sense improvisation you may use to save money. I'll mention these throughout the book, so don't rush out to buy these tools until you need them.

There is a long list of tools you will use on this project that you will need to beg, borrow, or buy, but these tools can be used with other projects, and their purchase can be justified for multiple uses: seal puller, hub puller, gear puller, gasket scraper, ball peen hammer, drifts, sledge, and a tube flaring set capable of creating double flares.

Again, don't rush out and buy these tools until you need them. Some, such as pullers, are available for rent.

You can also improvise to minimize the cost of tools. I am not a tool snob who thinks you need to have a gleaming set of industrial-grade tools to rebuild an engine. But I will say that any shortcuts you make on tools may compromise your safety or, at the very least, your sanity. Seriously consider borrowing, buying, or renting the right tool before starting into a procedure with an "almost-right" tool.

Engine Stands and Hoists

Engine hoists and stands may or may not be necessary, depending on the design of your engine or the extent of your rebuild. Some engines, if you are only doing a minor rebuild, will not need to be removed from the tractor. Other engine designs even allow you to remove the crankshaft while the engine is on the tractor. Therefore, do not assume you must remove the engine until you have made some decisions and done some partial disassembly with the engine in place. You may not even need an engine stand or an engine hoist.

TIP

Auctions and yard sales are excellent places to acquire tools. Tools found this way are often barely used, and the price is a fraction of new.

Some engines can be completely restored without removing the engine from the tractor. This John Deere B shows how the block can be slid forward after you remove the mounting nuts, three of which can be seen here near the center of the picture. As part of your research and planning, decide how much disassembly is needed before you start the restoration.

If the restoration is more than a minor refurbishing, you'll need an engine stand. You will probably need to purchase one, as the engine will remain on the stand for quite some time, making rental costs difficult to justify.

TIP

You don't need a special shop to rebuild an engine. Any spot in your garage, shed, or barn will suffice. Just make sure that the basic space, cleanliness, and safety issues are addressed.

If you decide the engine block must be removed, then you will probably need an engine hoist, and you will need an engine stand. Hoists are optional in the case of small engines, as they can be removed with the help of a friend or two. Most antique tractor engines require a hoist for removal, though. Fortunately, a hoist is used just two times during a rebuild—for removal and assembly—so you can rent one by the hour or day and save quite a bit of money.

A hoist should be rated to the weight of your engine. The common 3- to 8-ton hoists are sufficient, but remember these ratings are often with the arm fully retracted. If you are unable to get your hoist close to the engine and must extend the arm, the lift capacity of the hoist diminishes with each inch of extension. When in doubt, get the bigger hoist.

Engine stands are a bit different. Engines remain on the stand for a long period of time, so renting is usually out of

To mount the block to the stand, line up the stand's arms to the holes used to mount the engine to the tractor. If possible, align the engine's center of gravity to the pivot tube to make turning the engine easy and safe.

Here, lining up the arms required a bit of ingenuity. Only three arms are used, and the third arm is turned upward to mate to the high center engine mounting bolt hole. This was safe with this light engine, but be aware that all four arms will be needed on an engine that weighs more than a few hundred pounds. If lining up the arms is impossible, use a stout steel plate as an adapter.

To ensure that the engine is safely attached to the stand, use hardened steel bolts and washers. Many engines use blind holes for mounting bolts. In this case, use mounting bolts that are exactly the right length to reach all the way to the bottom of the holes. This will mount the engine as securely as possible.

TIP

Buy your engine stand, and rent your hoist.

the question, and I recommend buying one. For small to medium engines, such as Massey Harris Ponies, Farmall Cubs, and Case V series tractors, stands rated for 750 pounds are sufficient. The larger stands rated to 1,250 pounds are required for John Deere Ms, Farmall Hs, and the like. Farmall 500 series tractors, the larger New Generation John Deere tractor engines, and the larger Caterpillar diesel engines require even stouter engine stands.

Just a quick note on John Deere horizontal two-cylinder engines: While the block is often removed for milling and boring operations, these engines are not well suited to stand installation. Just remember to take the time to disassemble the tractor as far as possible to facilitate easy, safe access to the engine.

To fit the engine to the stand, you line up the arms of the engine stand with the threaded holes that mount the engine block to the bell housing. There are typically no other holes to use, but in some cases there may be other holes, such as starter mounting holes, that exist. Do *not* use these smaller auxiliary holes, as they are not designed to withstand the stress and weight of the entire block! In some cases, you may have to make an adapter plate to mount the engine stand. This plate should be a stout steel plate, 3/8-inch steel or better, with holes drilled into it that match both the engine and the stand's support arms. When mounting the engine to the stand, align the block's center of gravity with the stand's pivot tube. This will make turning the engine over much easier and safer.

CRIBBING AND SHUTTLING EQUIPMENT

Rebuilding an antique tractor engine often requires that the tractor be supported (cribbed) and moved (shuttled) with some or all of its wheels or axles detached. Supporting and moving large, heavy, and unstable assemblies and partial assemblies can be dangerous, so take great care when designing and building cribbing and shuttling systems. Cribbing involves building a criss-crossing (log cabin style) lattice work of rough-sawn timbers that supports part of the tractor while other components are removed and being worked on. For example, it's often necessary to remove the front axle of the tractor to remove the engine. This requires you to build cribbing that supports the midframe section of the tractor. There are several reasons that rough-sawn, large-dimension lumber is the ideal choice for cribbing material: Rough-sawn lumber resists sliding, it distributes loads well, it is inexpensive, and if it fails, it

PERFORMANCE TIP

Just swap engines if greater horsepower is needed. M&W, Funk, and others made performance modification kits and engine adapter kits to help swap engines, or use components from a larger engine in your engine. Remember there is always a limit to what you can do with any given engine. A bigger engine may be just the ticket.

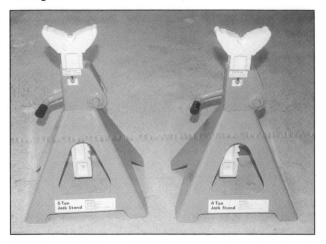

To hold large pieces of the tractor while the engine is removed, use jack stands or cribbing. This pair of 6-ton jack stands will handle any but the very largest assemblies of antique tractors. Eight- or 10-ton jack stands are available for really big projects.

Here's a good example of wood cribbing, holding up the front end of an Allis WC. This wood cribbing is very stable, and in some cases safer than jack stands. Rough-cut lumber works best for cribbing, as the timbers are less likely to slip.

doesn't often fail quickly in a catastrophic manner. This gives people nearby a chance to escape.

Shuttling a partially disassembled tractor is tricky and dangerous, and I highly recommend that you park the tractor in a spot you can leave it throughout the entire restoration. Unfortunately, many of us have small shop spaces, and often the frame of the tractor has to be moved a short distance, perhaps to make room or move the tractor to an outside area for steam cleaning. When shuttling tractors, the cribbing system must be designed to handle dynamic loads. That means your cribbing will have to be much stronger than normal, and timbers must be fastened to each other. At the bottom of the cribbing, you'll need to install

PERFORMANCE TIP

The rear end of your tractor may not be able to handle the increased torque and horsepower of your modified engine. A rule of thumb is the rear end is overdesigned by about 10 to 15 percent. Of course, this is just a rule of thumb, as many rear ends can handle all the performance improvements you can muster, while others couldn't even handle the engines that came with the tractor. Please know that any flaw in your drive train will probably fail catastrophically if you enhance your engine. Be sure of your tractor's drive train health before starting performance improvements.

at least four heavy-duty drop-down casters rated to handle the load of your tractor, plus 10 percent. Retractable casters have a strong steel housing that the caster retracts into when it's not in use. The casters can be pushed down and locked to move the load. Lockable casters may be used too, but they are not quite as safe as retractable casters.

When shuttling the tractor, use rope or chains attached to the tractor as "leashes" to pull the tractor into position. Do not pull on the cribbing! A second person with a leash can help steer. By using leashes, you are far enough away from the tractor to minimize the risk of injury, should the cribbing fail.

SHOP SPACES

A shop space can be anything, and doesn't have to be a formal or professional shop area. I can rebuild an engine in a space as small as 120 square feet, and have. The only requirement is a little space for parts storage, a little space for your tool chest, a little space for the engine or the front of the tractor, and about 50 square feet around the engine and the front of the tractor for movement. I find 250 square feet to be about right. This is the size of a small and inexpensive shed.

This shop area need not be fancy, large, or nice, but two things are important: You must have adequate lighting, and the area must be reasonably dirt- and dust-free. Good lighting reduces eyestrain, and it helps you notice problems and unusual wear you may miss in a dark and gloomy shop. Cleanliness is also much easier to maintain in a bright shop. Power is not a big concern, since most of the power tools you will need during a rebuild are normal hand tools

Shop spaces can be anything, from a special-use large building built for the purpose or a small garage, as seen here. Space requirements for engine building are modest. Here, Dick Harrold, owner of the Allis WC you will see throughout the book, is carefully removing main bearings from his engine.

that require a single 120-volt outlet. When combined with the lighting, all you would need is one or two 15-amp 120/110-volt circuits. This can be improvised by running two separate drop cords from another building, one for lighting and one for power tools and other appliances.

Obviously safety is the Number 1 priority whenever you are working around equipment. Every shop must have a complete first aid kit, although the small home-type kits usually are not acceptable in a shop. The likelihood of serious injury is greater in a shop than in a home, so a commercial first aid kit is more appropriate. In addition, a fire extinguisher designed to handle all types of fires (grease, electric, and paper) should be within easy reach. For complete protection, a telephone should be installed in the shop.

A couple of things to be aware of:

• Oily, smooth concrete floors are very slippery—and very hard when your head hits the floor.

• Oily rags may spontaneously combust if they are piled together. Keep them in a sealed metal can designed for this purpose, and always clean or dispose of rags frequently.

• Combustible fumes are heavier than air and congregate near the floor. That is why a dropped tool or cigarette can blow a shop to kingdom come, even when you barely smell the fumes of the solvent, paint, or fuel. For the same reason, fainting from fumes is a very real danger with space heaters that use fuel, such as kerosene heaters. The heater draws in the fumes, burns them, and adds carbon monoxide and other dangerous fumes. If you use a furnace in the shop, get a carbon monoxide detector. It could save your life.

• Ventilation and lighting go a long way toward ensuring your safety.

• Never get under a piece of equipment without checking and rechecking the support system.

• Safety is an approach, an attitude—not a recipe or step-by-step plan. Be aware, and be clear-headed at all times. Try to anticipate every safety problem before it comes up.

ENGINE REMOVAL

So you have reached the moment of truth. You've decided to rebuild your engine, you've done a little research, reading and planning, you've checked the tool box, set up some space in the shop, and parked the tractor. Before you just dig in and start tearing into everything, let's get a little organized.

SHOP ORGANIZATION

We talked earlier in the book about shop spaces, but now we'll talk specifically about the work area around the tractor. To be ready to rebuild an engine, you should have several things handy. You'll need several 5-gallon buckets with lids to catch draining fluids. A bag of absorbent material can be scattered on the floor below the tractor to contain and absorb fluid spills. Clay-based kitty litter works in a pinch, though the specialized products do a noticeably better job. Also, be sure you know how much fluid you are draining by referring to your service manuals. There is nothing messier and more frustrating than watching your 5-gallon bucket overflow because there were 6 gallons of the fluid you were draining.

It is also handy to have your tool box near the tractor. It helps to have a low, long, portable parts shelf for storing parts near the tractor. Another handy item is a small wooden wire spool, the same type your phone and cable companies discard every day. If you turn one on its side and install three or four wheels, you have a nice rolling bench to hold tools and parts.

While these engines are simple, there are still a lot of parts and pieces to keep up with. Staying organized saves you tremendous money, because the disorganized person loses expensive parts. You shouldn't even think about taking your tractor engine apart without having a permanent marker, small boxes, and plastic bags by your side. Every part that comes off needs to be identified and marked where it came from. I even try to bag and label everything that comes off the tractor. Why? First, parts are easily lost

TIP

Get your work area ready before starting engine disassembly.

if you don't keep them in a bag or box. You'll have to put them on a shelf or set of trays anyway, so you may as well package them and mark them.

I also found that guessing my way through a huge can of fasteners and parts that are jumbled together didn't work. As I assembled the engine, I inevitably wasted time, lost parts, and misused fasteners. Missing fasteners and parts results in preventable trips to the hardware store or tractor graveyard or time-consuming mail orders right at the worse possible time. To top it off, I then wondered if the missing parts were used incorrectly earlier in the assembly, and if they would ever cause a problem. These frustrating little roadblocks made me love Zip-Lok bags, the kind with white patches that let you write on them. For larger or sharper parts, use boxes.

Another way to stay organized is to make notes. I personally don't make extensive use of notes, other than labels on the parts bag or box, but many people make notes every time they work on the engine. That way any problems that have to be addressed during assembly can be noted to serve as a reminder. My favorite real life example was a stud. I realized after I removed it that it was in poor shape and not reusable. I threw it away, and promptly forgot about it. Several weeks later, during assembly, I was mysteriously missing one stud, and I spent half an hour searching for that one stud. I was sure it was lying around on the shelf or in one of the boxes. Then I finally remembered it was broken and I had discarded it. A simple 10-second note would have saved 30 minutes of searching. Repeat this process several times during an engine rebuild, and you quickly become a believer in note taking.

The first step of engine restoration is deciding to what extent you plan on rebuilding the engine, a decision that can't be made before a little investigative work. Here, John Davis drops the oil pan on his Farmall F-20, another tractor featured in this book.

Of course, how you organize your shop and rebuild is your business, but I will recommend that you do stay organized. You'll save lots of time and frustration, and you will be less likely to lose or damage parts—some of which are time-consuming and expensive to replace.

HOW MUCH OF A REBUILD IS NEEDED?

How to proceed with the engine tear-down and how far to go is a question I get a lot from first-time rebuilders. Like most answers to difficult questions, it depends on what you are trying to accomplish and what known problems the engines has. If the engine doesn't have any specific problems (other than general symptoms that an old engine shows), or if you are not trying to accomplish a complete remanufacture, then you might consider tearing down the engine just enough to access all the serviceable parts. In this case, you might simply remove all the auxiliary systems, including the radiator, manifolds, etc., and then remove the head. Then remove the oil pan and oil pump, loosening and removing the connecting rod bearing caps. The reasons for going no further is simple. You will probably just make a few cylinder, piston, and ring measurements, hone the cylinders, probably install a new ring and or piston set, and then close the engine back up.

If your engine is stuck, then unsticking the rings and pistons is your first priority. For this reason, you should not disassemble more than necessary to access the cylinders and pistons. Likewise, if the engine has specific problems that do not require engine removal to service, then you should only disassemble the engine far enough to address these problems.

Davis checks out the condition of the engine's bottom end. Bearing clearances are easily checked with the engine still in place.

If you want to completely remanufacture the engine, or if the engine had significant problems, such as bad oil pressure, then the engine will have to be completely torn down and reassembled.

In short, how far you disassemble the engine isn't a science, and no one can tell you what to do without seeing your specific circumstance. I recommend only going as far as necessary to correct your engine's problems, or to perform the rebuild you want. I think with some minor disassembly, followed by just 15 minutes of inspection and assessment, you can decide on a plan that serves you well.

EXTERIOR ENGINE COMPONENTS AND ACCESSORIES

Every engine has external components and accessories, such as magnetos, carbs, and water pumps. Which ones need to be rebuilt depends on a lot of things. Some systems, such as fuel and spark delivery (carburetor and magneto/distributor), should be refurbished at least every time significant engine work is done. Other systems, such as the water pump, should be at least partially disassembled, inspected, and cleaned every time the engine is rebuilt, regardless of the level of rebuild. Some other systems, such as engine-driven hydraulic pumps, governors, and oil

This Farmall F-20 has very little in the way of protective sheet metal or other assemblies to remove before beginning engine tear-down. The over-the-top steering shaft doesn't need to be removed for engine access or removal, but it is at head height and represents a constant source of pain if you don't remove it.

pumps, can be inspected and left alone if they weren't causing problems before the rebuild. Which systems you rebuild depends entirely on your goals and the condition of these accessories at the beginning.

RADIATOR

Every radiator, even if it isn't showing signs of leaks, should be pressure tested. Pressure testing involves building or finding a tank that can hold your radiator and enough water to submerge it. Then block the outlet and the inlet of the radiator with a rubber cork. In the inlet cork, drill a hole wide enough to fit an air-hose nozzle. Fit the nozzle in the cork and then submerge the whole assembly. Then

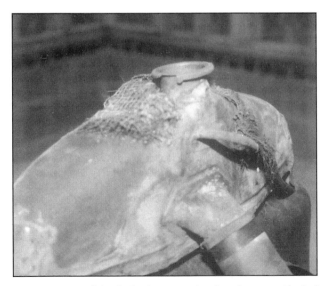

Engine restoration includes all related systems, such as the cooling system. This Ford 8N radiator still sports the original horsehair pad, which keeps the hood from rubbing or damaging the radiator. This top tank is in good condition, with no dents or gouges to be seen.

inject air, building pressure in the radiator to specification. Any leaks will show up as a trail of bubbles in the water. Be sure the test is consistent with the operating pressure of your radiator. Too much pressure can damage the radiator. Thermosiphon cooling systems found on many tractors usually only operate at a few psi. (If your engine doesn't have a water pump, it is a thermosiphon system.) Even the more modern antique tractors with water pumps often are only designed to operate at 5–7 psi. Therefore, make sure you or the radiator shop test the radiator at the proper psi. Some pinhole leaks will not leak at normal operating pressures but will appear at the pressure typical of modern engines (10–15 psi or more).

If your radiator is in good shape and it doesn't exhibit any tell-tale bubble trails, you are in great shape. If it has a few minor leaks, you may also be in luck, as these can often be repaired. If the leaks are serious or your radiator is damaged beyond hope, then you may have an expensive road ahead of you.

There are two major parts to a radiator: The tanks and the cores. Radiator tanks often are damaged, and finding accurate replacements is often extremely difficult and costly. This is especially true of the unstyled tractor, on which the radiator tanks often had the tractor maker's name cast into them. Salvageable used and NOS tanks for most models have long been gone. If your tanks are beyond repair, there is no substitute for calling dozens of salvage yards looking for good radiators.

The radiator cores can also be a problem. First, seek the advice of a good radiator shop. They can often solder and repair leaking radiator cores if the leaks are not major. If the leaks are irreparable but are restricted to just the core, you can have a new core made. Antique tractor radiators are typically an unusual size, and a custom core will have to be made. This is not cheap, but new cores usually work very well.

ENGINE ACCESS

Start the engine removal by removing all protective sheet metal, auxiliary systems, and components from the engine. You'll also need to remove the gas tank and disconnect fuel and oil pressure lines. Now is also the best time to remove items that may be damaged during engine removal, such as fan shaft assemblies, steering wheel shafts, and throttle linkages.

A few pieces that may interfere with engine removal are easily overlooked. An example is the starter. As you unbolt the engine, it may rotate slightly and bind against the starter's housing. I like to remove as much as possible while the engine is still on the tractor. It's easier then, and everything comes off during the rebuild anyway. Since your hoist will need attachment points, you should leave the head on, or at least leave the head studs in so you can reinstall the head long enough to remove the engine.

Draining all gasoline is an absolutely necessary first step for safe engine rebuilding. Draining the carburetor at this time is also a good idea.

Accessing the Engine

The first step of any engine removal is to take off any sheet metal panels, such as hoods, radiator grills, and related parts. Fasteners that hold these items in place are usually stuck tight, because they are exposed to the weather and, in the case of grills and radiator side plates, heat. In addition, they are often small and soft, and are frustratingly easy to break. Some of these fasteners will respond well to heat, penetrating oil and patience, but many don't, and the result is a broken fastener. In the excitement and rush of starting a project, breaking these bolts is common. Take your time and be careful.

Fuel Tank

Another item that usually needs to be removed at this time is the fuel tank. Be sure to carefully drain all fuel and store it or dispose of it safely. The tank is mounted to the frame of the tractor, and removal is typically self-explanatory. Be sure to remove the fuel line at the tank and at the carburetor, or the fuel filters, if the tractor is a diesel. Set the line aside, as it is easy to bend. Remove the tank and place a solution of tank cleaner, available at most local auto parts stores and at vendors listed in the appendix of the book, in the tank to soak. Completely cleaning the fuel system is an impor-

Engine restoration starts with sheet metal removal. Hoods, side panels, louvered panels, and radiator panels all need to be removed to gain access to the engine. Paul Bazzetta and his daughter Leanne show how the hood and front shroud of a Ford 8N can be removed all at once.

With the engine exposed, start removing all the auxiliary equipment, housings, and brackets from the engine. If the oil filter housing has a drain plug, it should be drained of oil first.

The wiring harness should be removed, one leg at a time. Use masking tape tags to mark each leg with its location before removal. Then, after all legs are removed, remove the entire harness whole, so you have a pattern for wire lengths and a reference for wire color and gauge when you replace the harness with new wiring.

Penetrating fluid is the antique tractor mechanic's best friend. From stubborn spark plugs to rusted bolts and nuts, you'll find plenty of opportunity to soak fasteners to make removal possible. If the fluid doesn't work, heat the part with a plumber's torch to help loosen it, after the volatile vapors of the penetrating fluid have had a chance to evaporate.

Engine access includes removing all tie rods, drag links, and other steering items. Jerry Cox is removing the front half of the stabilizer arm housing so that the stabilizer arm can be swung out of the way.

tant part of engine restoration. We cover that a little later in the book, but go ahead and start soaking the tank now.

Occasionally some tractor designs require you to remove other components before you have access to the engine. Some examples of these parts are steering shafts, hydraulic reservoirs, wiring harnesses, and fan shafts. Now is also the time to remove any other items that your tractor may have that are particular to it. Maybe someone in the past had welded on brackets. If you don't need or like the brackets, now is a great time to grind or torch the welds out and remove them. Some more examples include cultivator mounts, tools bars (small bars used for hitching implements up near the engine), or any implement still mounted under the engine on the front or midsection of the tractor.

Wiring Harness

The next thing to remove is the wiring harness. Before removing any part of the wiring harness, is it very impor-

tant that you disconnect the battery, if your tractor has one. To disconnect a battery, always remove the ground terminal first. Notice that I did not mention the polarity of the terminal to disconnect first. Antique tractors with batteries were almost always designed and built with positive ground electrical systems. That is completely opposite of modern equipment. To complicate matters, it was very common for misguided or uninformed owners and mechanics in the past to change the system to a negative ground system. Therefore, you must first determine, regardless of the polarity, which is the ground terminal. Fortunately, this is easy. Simply find the battery terminal whose cable does not lead to an electrical device. This cable will be connected to the frame (or some part that is connected to the frame). Disconnect this grounded cable from its terminal first, then disconnect the other cable.

When disconnecting the wiring harness, you should mark the end of each wire with where it came from. A

With the stabilizer bar removed, Cox uses a pickle fork to remove the drag link from the pitman arm. Remember to keep track of all nuts, cotter pins, and other pieces of hardware from these assemblies.

length of masking tape wrapped like a flag around the end of the wire makes a handy place to jot this information down. Do not, regardless of the condition of the harness, just pull and discard wire. The gauge (thickness of the wire) is important, and any original-looking wire should be saved so the gauge can be reproduced when you make up your new wiring. If originality is important to you, then keeping the wire will allow you to faithfully reproduce the color as well with your new wiring.

Oil Lines

Oil pressure lines should be removed next. Oil pressure lines usually run to some other areas of the tractor toward

TIP

Disassembly is a step-by-step affair. Take each step one at a time and don't go any further than is necessary for the level of work you are performing.

an oil pressure gauge. Very old antique tractors often only have some type of oil pop-up gauge that may be on the engine itself, but most tractors made after the Great Depression had gauges. Be sure to remove these lines from the gauges carefully, and then remove any other length of oil pressure line that may be damaged or get in the way during engine removal.

PULLING THE ENGINE

Removing the engine is one of the trickier aspects of engine rebuilding, and is certainly a dangerous one. These engines are typically incredible heavy, and often the remaining portion of the tractor is left unstable as well. Before removing the engine, make doubly sure that once the engine is removed, the tractor will be stable and will not fall or move from its supports.

Remove the engine with a hoist. Be sure to buy or rent a hoist capable of lifting the weight of the engine. I have a 3-to-8-ton hoist in my shop (its capacity is determined by how far I extend the boom), and this hoist has handled every situation without any compromise in safety. I have never rebuilt the very largest of antique tractors, but it should even handle those, especially if I remove the head, oil pan, and strip the engine down as far as possible first. There are smaller hoists available and I have used them, but I don't recommend them.

The hoist arm is attached to a heavy chain, which bolts to two brackets that you must bolt to the engine. An alternative to this is a load leveler, which I recommend. The load leveler has a hook or cleat that attaches to the hoist arm. The hook is attached to a block that has a stout

To set a tractor up on a jack, first you must lift it. Here a hydraulic floor jack lifts the tractor high enough to get a stout stand underneath it. Please remember that a hydraulic jack is not a substitute for cribbing or a jack stand. Hydraulic jacks can fail or drop slowly. Never use one as a permanent stand, and never get under a piece of equipment that is supported only by a hydraulic jack.

threaded rod running through it. The threaded rod is attached to a cross-member that's about 18 inches wide. At the ends of the cross-member are two hooks that you can bolt to brackets on the engine. By turning the threaded rod, you can adjust the hoist attachment point back and forth. The end result is an engine that's perfectly level as it's removed from the tractor.

Head bolts and studs seem to work best as bracket attachment points. The trick to hoisting safely is to try and visualize the balance point of the engine, and attach the brackets equidistant from this balance point. As you unbolt the engine from the torque tube, be aware the flywheel is heavy and will cause the engine to tilt backward, once it is clear of the tractor. When you rig your chains, keep this in mind.

Because of the weight of the flywheel and starter, if left on, I find that most in-line four-cylinder engines balance at a point under the Number 3 cylinder. This means I attach brackets near Number 4 and Number 2 cylinders. Also, engines are not balanced from right to left. Because of differing engine accessories, the engine may lean, or list, to one side, usually the side with the extra driven accessories such as a hydraulic pump. Engines without these acces-

sories usually lean toward the camshaft side. I find that if I offset the brackets toward the heavier side, this engine balance is close enough to safely manage any engine list once on the hoist.

Removing Structural Engines

Engines whose blocks are an integral part of the tractor frame require special care during removal. The tractor must be supported from below and behind the engine. You must then removal the entire front pedestal or axle before you can lift the engine away. Engines that are not an integral part of the tractor frame are easier to pull, as you can often leave the front end of the tractor intact.

The first step in removing a structural engine is to support the belly of the tractor directly behind the engine. Wood cribbing works best, but jack stands are acceptable. The trick here is to jack the tractor up so the front wheels have no weight on them, but they are not far off the ground. Double- and triple-check your work, making sure the tractor is stable. Begin by removing the axle and steering components that are bolted to the front of the engine and engine front axle supports. Many of these components are heavy and unwieldy, so make sure you have a helper ready to give

Here you see a jack stand well placed and secure under a tractor. The equipment is kept as low as possible and the stand is used on a hard flat surface. A second jack stand or a backup set of cribbing is an excellent idea if the equipment is to be supported over a long period of time.

This Ford 8N is jacked up and is ready for front axle removal. Keep the axle close to the ground to make removal as safe and easy as possible.

Secured by a hoist, the front axle is unbolted and ready for removal. With a friend's help, the axle assembly can be steadied as the hoist is pulled away from the tractor. Most axles can be pulled away as a complete assembly, as seen here.

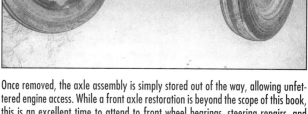

Once removed, the axle assembly is simply stored out of the way, allowing unfettered engine access. While a front axle restoration is beyond the scope of this book, this is an excellent time to attend to front wheel bearings, steering repairs, and adjustments.

you a hand. Your engine hoist will help hold and move heavy axle assemblies.

Once you have the front axle, radiator, grills, etc. removed, you remove the engine. As you unbolt the engine from the torque tube, the weight of the flywheel will cause the engine to tilt backward once it is clear of the tractor. When you rig your chains, keep this in mind.

Raise the hoist just enough so the chains are taut, but you don't want the hoist to lift the tractor. The engine must slide out and away from the drive shafts, and excessive upward force on the engine will make it difficult for the engine to slide out. After everything is unbolted and you have checked your supports again, start rolling the hoist so the engine is pulled straight out from the structural mem-

When everything has been removed, it's time to pull the engine from the tractor. In many tractors, such as this Ford 8N and Farmall letter series, the engine is a structural member. Because of this, the castings and oil pan are heavy, and a hoist will have to be used. Here the load leveler is hung from the hoist and chained to the engine. Before removing the engine mounting bolts, put slight tension on the lifting chains so the engine doesn't drop and bind them.

The engine is pulled free. After you remove the large lower structural members, which often also act as oil pans, it is ready to be prepped for engine stand installation.

After loosening the mounting bolts, pull the hoist outward, pulling the engine straight out from the midsection casting. Pulling the engine straight out is very important, as any slight deviation will bind the transmission input shaft against the clutch.

To remove these heavy items, lower the engine so it is very close to the floor and begin removing the bolts. With the engine close to the floor, the pan can drop after the fasteners are removed, and the engine can be lifted and pulled clear.

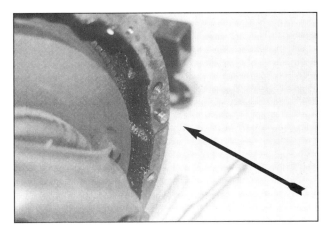

Another reason that pulling an engine straight out is important: alignment pins. These small pins align the engine to the transmission during installation. Too much lift by the hoist or a crooked removal will bind these pins in their holes.

Please note that the distance between the pan and the engine is exaggerated for photographic purposes. The amount of drop for the pan should be an inch or two at the most. Remember to keep hands and toes out from under the pan during this step!

Before mounting the engine to the stand, the flywheel must be removed, and a few other chores covered in the next chapter must be completed. Note that the front cover and auxiliary systems often found on or mounted to the front cover have been removed. That is also covered by the next chapter. Here the engine is mounted to the stand and ready for restoration.

ber it was bolted to. If you have difficulty pulling the engine straight out, start looking for reasons. I have accidentally left oil pressure lines connected before, and I can tell you from experience that the engine will not slide out if the oil pressure line is still attached! Whatever you do, do not pull or tug excessively—the tractor may be pulled off the cribbing or you may cause the cribbing to fail.

Removing Nonstructural Engines

If the engine is not structural, the job is a little more straightforward. You only need to remove enough of the front axle, steering assembly, and radiator assembly to provide clearance for engine removal. The tractor frame remains intact, and only the engine block needs to come off. Often the front of the engine is supported by a cross-member that is difficult to detach. It may be easier to detach the entire cross-member from the frame and remove it still attached to the engine. Then the attachment points between the cross-member and the engine are a little more accessible.

Just a quick safety reminder: If the tractor is cribbed, constantly check for signs that it may be falling off the cribbing. This is dangerous work, and constant surveillance of the support is critical. Remember that most antique tractors have a front axle that not only pivots with the steering

Double- and triple-check all supports and hoists before trusting any weight to either.

system, but also moves vertically. Never split the tractor in half (detach the engine and front end from the transmission) with the front axle still attached, unless this vertical axle movement is prevented with blocks or braces. The safest approach is to jack up the tractor, remove the front end, then remove the engine.

As I mentioned earlier, engines that are not structural can be removed with the front axle still in place. Just don't remove the engine and front end from the rear half of the tractor without accounting for vertical movement of the front axle.

ENGINE STAND INSTALLATION

Once you remove the engine, you must remove the flywheel before you can mount the engine to the stand. The flywheel is heavy, so you must have an extra set of hands to help here. Once the flywheel is removed, then you mount the engine to the stand. If you are in luck, the engine stand mounting arms will line up nicely with the mounting holes in the back of the engine block. If not, then you must make an adapter plate. To make an adapter plate, find a stout piece of plate steel (at least 3/8-inch thick) large enough to accommodate the pattern of holes needed for both the stand and the hole. First drill holes for the engine, then drill holes for the stand arms. Be sure to use the thickest bolts you can for the mounting, and I always use hardened bolts as well. After mounting up the engine, double-check your engine stand, plate, and engine to make sure everything is firmly attached.

At this point, you have the engine torn down, probably removed and mounted to a stand, and all your parts organized and handy. You should have the tractor stable, and even roped off if you think children may try to climb on the tractor when you are not around. Now comes the fun part, where you actually start tearing into the engine and begin the rebuild. Now is also a good time to rethink your strategies, inspect the tractor and engine more closely and make sure your current plans still make sense.

ENGINE DISASSEMBLY

The preparation and engine removal covered earlier are more work than most people imagine, and believe it or not, most of the hard work is behind you. Now comes the fun part, the part that makes the most difference and that yields results as you work. The understanding and familiarity you acquire now will help you troubleshoot engines the rest of your life. You avoid problems and answer questions when you turn a part and system inside out, trying to get a grasp on its purpose, design, and engineering. Enjoyment and learning come along the road to your destination, and are not the destination themselves.

In the previous section of the book, the engine has been disassembled, with many items removed and stored. But until now, the engine has remained closed, and its interior condition and problems have been unknown.

This little operator, Ben Davis, looks ready for an engine restoration. After completing the initial tear-down, his father is ready to open up this Farmall F-20's engine and begin the restoration. This engine will be restored "in-frame"; that is, the block will remain on the tractor while the engine is restored. While there are some limitations to this approach, (for example, the crankshaft can't be removed), enough work can be done to correct this engine's problems.

The mouse larder shown in the exhaust port is an example of the many surprises you might find when you open up your engine. Amazingly, the mouse built a nest in the head above an open valve.

Unfortunately, the mouse created quite a mess and nearly ruined one of the bores, as we found when the head was pulled. The moisture and droppings left behind by the mouse rusted the bore significantly, creating quite a bit of work to clean up.

This chapter was one of the most difficult to write, because the greatest variations among engine manufacturers are found in the auxiliary systems (magneto, hydraulic pumps, water pumps, etc.), clutch, flywheel, and engine access. These variations include the manner in which auxiliary systems are mounted, the way timing gears are accessed, and design and orientation of clutches and flywheels.

For example, on horizontal John Deere engines, the governor assembly serves as an engine access cover, and it drives the magneto or distributor and the fan shaft. This dif-

fers tremendously from a Farmall letter series tractor, on which the front cover is a structural part of the tractor. Older Farmalls and many third-party manufacturers have a very simple timing gear cover, while very old antique tractors have no real timing cover. Ford N series tractors mount the distributor to the front timing gear—something you see very rarely in other makes. If this isn't enough, the clutch/belt pulley of John Deere tractors differ drastically from the clutch and flywheel combination of most other engines.

I have tried not to delve into specific steps for specific models during this chapter. Unfortunately, the huge differences in design among timing gear and engine access covers and auxiliary systems require that I occasionally become specific as to certain makes during certain parts of this chapter. Primarily, I organize makes into two groups—horizontal engines and vertical engines. John Deere horizontal engines make up the first group, but all others, including the John Deere vertical two-cylinder tractors, fall to the latter group. My reasoning is simple—a vertical engine, regardless of make, shares a front cover design and

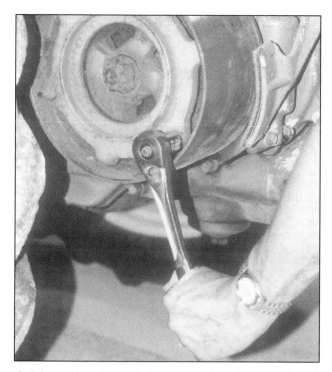

Clutch disassembly on a horizontal John Deere engine begins by removing the clutch cover (not shown), and then removing the castellated adjusting nuts that retain the pressure plate.

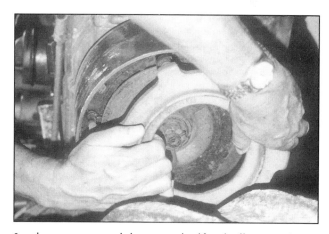

Once these nuts are removed, the pressure plate lifts right off, exposing the drive disc.

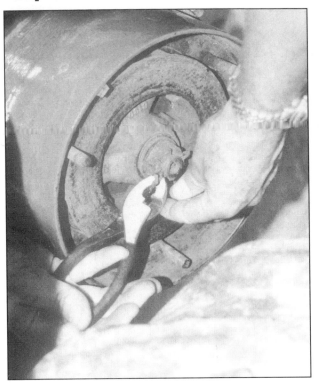

1 After the pressure plate is removed, the drive disc comes off. First, remove the cotter pin that retains the fastening nut.

2 Next, loosen the nut while preventing the crankshaft from turning. If it's stubborn, go carefully and use penetrating oil. Remember, this nut threads onto the end of the crank, and it would not be good to damage it!

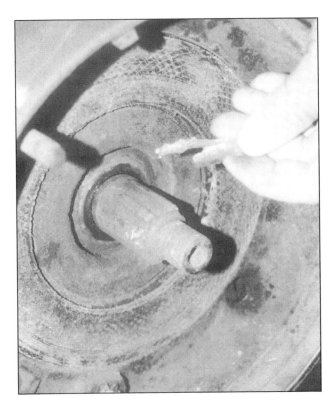

3 After loosening the nut, the drive disc is pulled off; in some tractors, it must be driven off with forcing screws or pullers. Upon pulling the drive disc, we found slivers of metal falling out from around the disc's hub. These slivers of metal are remnants of shim stock.

4 As the last picture shows, the drive disc extensively damaged the splines on the end of the crankshaft. This occurred because the disc hub was allowed to wear excessively, which damaged the crankshaft splines. To repair this, the previous owner had placed shim stock on the crankshaft and forced the drive disc onto the crankshaft. To repair this problem, a new drive disc with an undersized hub was purchased. This fitted tightly against the worn splines, allowing like-new operation. The undersized drive disc was purchased from Denglers. (See appendix.)

auxiliary system mounting. Likewise, John Deere horizontal engines are in a class by themselves and simply have to be addressed separately.

REMOVING FLYWHEELS AND CLUTCHES
Horizontal Engines

We'll first discuss removing the flywheel, clutch, and pulley on John Deere two-cylinder horizontal engines.

Removing the pulley/clutch assembly is fairly straightforward, and is covered well in most of the service manuals, but we'll highlight the main steps here: Remove the clutch cover, and then remove the clutch discs by loosening and removing the castellated adjusting nuts on the front of the clutch assembly. Be careful to find and observe registration marks on the crankshaft and main drive disk. (Not all John Deere tractors have these registration marks.) Next, pull the clutch drive disk. Most John Deere drive discs can be removed using two bolts installed into threaded holes in the drive disc. By tightening the bolts in an alternating fashion, you will pull this drive disk right out.

Clutch lever linkage needs to be disassembled and removed following drive disk removal. After removing the snap rings that retain the belt pulley bearings, most of the pulley assembly will pull out.

John Deere flywheels can be removed by first removing the starter and cables, and the flywheel cover assembly,

if your tractor has one. The flywheel is fastened to the crankshaft with a flange secured by mounting bolts. Once these bolts are removed, the flywheel slides off. Be sure to inspect the flywheel and crankshaft splines at this point for excessive play or damage. Your John Deere tractor is now ready for further engine work.

Vertical Engines

Removing the flywheel in a traditional vertical engine involves first removing the clutch. The clutch consists of

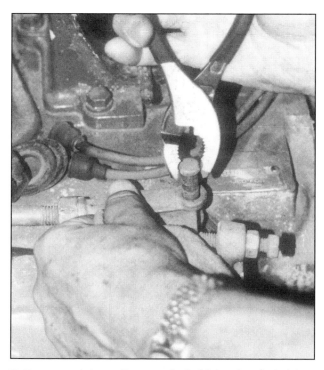

1 To continue with disassembly, remove the clutch linkage from the clutch lever by removing all pivot pins from the linkage. Remember to store and label them for reassembly.

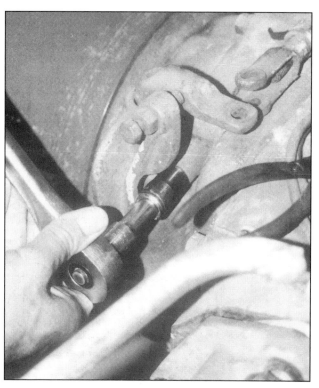

2 Next, unbolt the clutch lever housing from the timing gear cover.

3 Now you can slide the clutch lever assembly out.

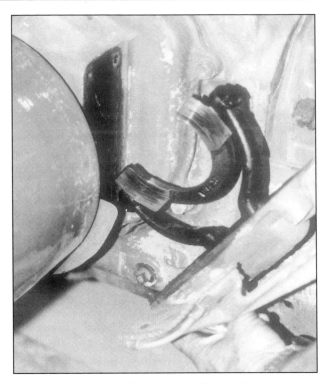

4 The clutch lever is now visible. It engages and disengages the clutch by moving the operating sleeve in and out.

5 At this point, some models require the removal of a snap ring to remove the belt pulley. After this, the belt pulley of a John Deere horizontal two-cylinder tractor will slide right out. This assembly is heavy, so be careful. The operating sleeve with its spiral grooves is visible here.

two primary components: The pressure plate and the friction plate. The pressure plate is bolted to the flywheel, while the friction plate is sandwiched between the pressure plate and flywheel. The friction plate is the component that drives the transmission's input shaft (also called a drive shaft). Before disassembly, measure the distance between the tops of the pressure plate fingers (the small adjustable levers on the pressure plate that look like "fingers") and some surface on the flywheel. You'll need this measurement to adjust the clutch if the pressure plate is rebuilt.

To make this measurement, I remove the clutch and flywheel from the engine, then bolt the clutch back on the flywheel on the bench. I then place the flywheel and clutch, with clutch pointing upward, on the bed of a shop press. I measure the distance between each finger and a strut that is on my press above the bed. This gives me a distance that is relative to the bottom of the flywheel, a surface that will not be ground during reconditioning. If your clutch has a pilot bushing that is driven into a blind hole in the flywheel, you will often be able to measure the distance between the bottom of this pilot hole and the fingers. In short, some imagination may be needed, but without too much fuss you should be able to measure the distance between the tops of the pressure plate fingers and some surface on the flywheel that will not be reground or polished during reconditioning.

To remove the clutch, unbolt the pressure plate from the flywheel. The friction disc should fall loose when the pressure plate is removed, so be sure to catch it. The friction plate may occasionally, on tractors that have sat unused for a long period of time, be rusted to the surface of the flywheel and will need to be pried off with a putty knife or gasket scraper.

Removing the flywheel requires loosening several bolts that attach the flywheel to the crankshaft hub. These fasteners are usually hardened steel bolts that either thread into holes in the hub or are fastened with nuts. Either way, there is usually some sort of locking device to prevent the bolt or nut from coming loose during operation.

Have a helper give you a hand during flywheel removal, as they are quite heavy. Visual inspection of the flywheel and clutch involves looking closely to identify any parts that are missing or broken, such as ring gear teeth, pilot bushings in the flywheel's center, or any clutch surfaces that are highly worn. Make a mental note to take a closer look at the flywheel to clutch mating surface after the clutch is removed (covered a little later). This surface should be smooth and free of rust, surface cracks, and other signs of heat and stress fractures. It should also be free of any significant scratches and striations (usually caused by clutch linings that were allowed to wear too far). Highly polished surfaces are a sign of an improperly adjusted clutch, a pressure plate with loose springs, or an operator who has allowed the clutch to "slip." Any evidence of these surface problems requires that the flywheel be resurfaced by a machine shop.

This is a typical flywheel-mounted clutch pressure plate assembly found on most vertical in-line four-cylinder tractor engines. The three levers seen in the center are known as clutch "fingers." These fingers accept an "inward" (toward the flywheel) movement from the clutch pedal linkage, which in turn depresses springs. This decreases the amount of force applied by the springs against the pressure plate, which in turn releases pressure on the pressure plate, disengaging the clutch.

Ring Gears

Ring gears often need to be serviced during a rebuild as well. When they shut down, engines stop in predictable, repetitive ways. This means the starter usually engages the ring gear at the same one or two locations. This in turn causes the ring gear to wear in those spots. This makes starter engagement noisy; and ultimately, the starter will fail to engage and spin the engine. If you find this type of wear, you will need to correct the problem. If the ring gear seems to be in generally bad condition, consider replacement. Most of the time, though, the ring gear can be rotated to move the worn spots away from their old locations. If there also seems to be excessive wear around the entire circumference, then the ring gear of many flywheels can be reversed, exposing fresh edges to the starter pinion gear.

This flywheel shows the type of surface abnormalities you may find after you remove the clutch from the flywheel. Light surface rust had formed between the clutch disc and the flywheel mating surface. If this rust becomes extensive enough, the disc will become "frozen" to the flywheel, preventing the clutch from disengaging. Also note the carrier bearing in the center of the flywheel. This needle bearing maintains alignment between the driveshaft (properly called a transmission input shaft) and clutch. This bearing is also sealed, and requires no maintenance or adjustment during an engine restoration. It is either reused, if good, or replaced.

The ring gear on this flywheel is in excellent shape, showing only slight wear at the front edges of the teeth. Often ring gears will have broken or missing teeth, requiring removal and replacement.

TIP

Crankshaft splines are commonly worn or damaged. Consult with a machinist and parts suppliers about repair or replacement as soon as you find this type of damage. The need to replace a difficult-to-find and expensive crankshaft may cause you to cancel the project or adjust its timetable.

Removing and installing the ring gear requires heat. First remove any set screws that may exist around the circumference. While occasionally you will find an antique tractor whose ring gear is installed with only set screws, the gear is usually also shrunk onto place. That means the ring gear is heated, then installed and allowed to cool. The ring gear shrinks when it cools, holding tightly onto the flywheel. To remove the ring gear, you first must clean the entire flywheel thoroughly with a rapid-drying, non-residue-forming cleaner, such as brake cleaner. Since you will be heating the ring gear to remove it, cleanliness if very important for safety. Wire brush or grind away any rust or marks that would interfere with the ring gear removal or installation. Clean again as necessary.

The next step, and the step that creates the need for diplomacy and negotiation with the person in your household responsible for cooking, is to place the flywheel in an oven preheated to about 400 degrees. Leave the flywheel in the oven long enough to thoroughly heat the ring gear, but remove it from the oven before the flywheel itself has time to heat and expand. About 5 to 15 minutes seems to work, depending on flywheel size. If your flywheel is large and will not fit in an oven, a heating tip on a torch will suffice, though having a helper work the ring gear off while you heat it is a requirement.

Working very quickly, remove the flywheel from the oven (or remove the heat source), and then drive the ring gear off the flywheel with a soft steel or brass drift. The ring should come off easily. If it doesn't, you have probably let the flywheel itself become too hot. In this case, the entire assembly must be allowed to cool completely, and the procedure then repeated. If this still isn't working, then you will need a hotter heat source. Patience and finding the "right" amount of heat are the keys to making this work.

Installation is the reverse of removal. This time, however, you will only heat the ring gear in the oven. To install, remove the ring gear quickly from the oven and drive it into place, being sure to rotate the ring gear as needed to move the worn areas away from the previous positions. You should also consider reversing the ring gear if it is possible. Also remember to line up the ring gear with the set screw holes if your flywheel uses set screws.

REMOVING CRANKSHAFT PULLEYS

To start, remove the nut or bolt on the end of the crankshaft that holds the pulley in place. To keep the crankshaft from turning while loosening the bolt, use an impact wrench. The blows from the wrench will loosen the nut without turning the crankshaft. If the crankshaft does turn, a helper with a V-belt cinched around the pulley can hold it. If no impact wrench is available, holding the flywheel can work, but have your helper wear gloves, as the starter ring gear has sharp edges. If no helper is available, the oil pan will have to be dropped and the crankshaft immobilized with a block of wood. If the engine is still on the tractor, putting the tractor in gear and setting the parking brakes may work too.

Behind the pulley is usually a thick, and sometimes slotted, washer. Keep this washer stored with the nut, and don't lose either. Both can be hard to find and if lost,

Removing the crankshaft pulley begins by removing the pulley fastener. Here it is a bolt that's notched to accept a crank handle for manual starting. With the engine open, it was easy to immobilize the crankshaft by placing a block of wood between the crankshaft and the engine block.

After fastener removal, the pulley is slid off the crankshaft. Often the pulley must be pulled from the crankshaft with a puller. Note the mating of the pulley notch and crankshaft key.

require a trip to the junkyard. One more item: While I have not worked on an engine with a reverse-threaded pulley fastener, I understand some are. After research, I can't find any engines to mention as an example, but I bring it up so you will know to check your service manual first for the thread pattern.

The crankshaft pulley needs to be pulled next, after the auxiliary systems are removed. Eight times out of 10, the pulley will remove easily enough with standard pulling tools. There is usually a felt dust seal behind the pulley, and this should be removed and kept with the pulley fasteners, washers and pulley. The oil seal behind all this is best removed after the front cover is removed, so wait until the cover is off.

If your crankshaft pulley is a pain to remove, be careful not to apply too much pressure. Crankshaft pulleys are often pressed into place, and are not "beefy" enough to handle the full force of some pulling tools. In addition, standard gear pullers pull with the anchor point in the middle of the pulley, which in this case is the end of the crankshaft. Since many engines use bolts as pulley fasteners, the puller anchors in the bolt hole. If you pull using this scenario, you will ruin the bolt hole in the end of the crankshaft. Use a thick steel "coin" or cap so when you anchor the gear puller, you will not damage the end of the crankshaft. If your pulley is held on with a nut, you may use the end of the crankshaft directly, but be careful not to damage the threads.

On the Allis WC engine you see pictured in this book, the crankshaft pulley broke its woodruff key and the crankshaft spun freely in the pulley's bore. Apparently, it went unnoticed for quite some time, because the pulley bore wore extensively. The previous owner "fixed" this by adding shim stock between the crankshaft end and the pulley bore, and simply jammed the pulley into place. This made removing the pulley impossible by hand. The engine had to be taken to a mechanic with a special puller that pushed against the front cover instead of the end of the crankshaft, as the force would have damaged the end of the crankshaft.

The lesson of this story applies to all engine rebuilding procedures: Use good-quality tools, and if it isn't working after giving the tool a complete chance at the problem, something is wrong. Sometimes "just one more turn" of the wrench may break something, so a bigger tool or a tool of a different design is needed. Sometimes it takes a professional. Don't risk life, limb, and parts trying to make something work that just clearly won't.

CLUTCH RECONDITIONING

To recondition your clutch, you have three components to worry about: clutch disc, the pressure plate, and the pilot bearing. I use these terms generically, and each component shows up in a wide variety of designs and names depending on the tractor.

The clutch disc is the component most likely to need attention. It carries the friction lining material, which wears over time. The pressure plate clamps the clutch disc to the drive assemblies. The pilot bearing may or may not exist on your tractor; its sole purpose is to maintain alignment between power sources and power shafts while the clutch is disengaged. On John Deere horizontal-engine tractors, the pulley bearings need inspection instead of pilot bearings.

In addition, clutches show up in a wide variety of other designs, including wet clutches and multistage clutches. Wet clutches are just as they sound: The disc runs while bathed in oil. Wet clutches are rarely seen in antique and classic tractors, and when they are found, they are used as part of live and independent PTO and hydraulic systems. They are never used as primary drive clutches.

The multistage clutches are also just as they sound: They operate in two distinct stages; each stage drives a separate power system, and each operates independently, depending on how far the operator disengages the clutch. If the clutch is fully engaged, then both systems are driven. If the operator partially depresses the clutch pedal, then one of the drive systems is disengaged. If the operator fully depresses the clutch pedal, then both drive systems are disengaged. This is a common design on classic tractors with live PTO or hydraulics; a continuously running PTO is different, and bypasses the clutch completely.

Clutch Discs

Restoring clutch discs is fairly simple. The job involves removing the old friction lining material and replacing it. While you can certainly do this yourself, there are a million good reasons not to. First, old lining materials contain asbestos, and removing it yourself is a significant health risk. New lining material may actually be NOS, which means it also may contain asbestos. Setting the rivets well

This clutch friction plate shows minor wear. Often the clutch disc will be so worn the rivet heads are exposed, allowing them to wear against the flywheel and pressure plate. The springs seen along the inner portion protect the clutch, engine, and pressure plate from shock loads presented by accidental or careless rapid engagement of the clutch.

TIP

Most flywheel ring gears require heat to remove. Using an oven can make short work of this, if you set the oven to 400 degrees and only leave the flywheel in there long enough to heat the ring gear without heating the flywheel. Large flywheels won't fit in most ovens; you'll have to apply heat with the heating tip of a gas welding set.

is critically important and unless you are a champ with a rivet hammer and anvil, I don't recommend using your clutch disc as a learning experience.

Many full-service automotive stores will send the clutch disc off to be relined. I recommend this approach and use it myself. Trying to line up material, exposing myself to asbestos, finding proper rivets, and spending the time to set rivets just isn't worth the $35 the last clutch disc cost me. Plus, the professionals leave me with a much better clutch disc.

Very old antique tractors may also use disc sizes and materials that are no longer made, so you may have no choice but to find the material yourself, though the automotive parts rebuilder may still set the lining for you. To find the material, making a lot of phone calls will be necessary. Start with your local sources of parts, including automotive shops, who often have great leads if they can't get something themselves, and then work your way through the appendix in the back of the book. Very old antique tractors typically used a clutch lining very similar to the woven material that old-style brake bands are lined with. Since this material is much more readily available, it can often be substituted if you can find pieces large enough. Modern reproductions of the material are safe, but be aware that NOS material will contain asbestos. You should not use this material, and giving it to the rebuild shop may be illegal, especially if you don't alert them to the presence of asbestos. Make sure you inquire as to asbestos content when you are buying NOS material. Unfortunately, the sellers themselves often do not know. You'll just have to assume asbestos is present unless you know otherwise.

After spending lots of time and money on the phone finding material, worrying about asbestos, removing old material, cutting and shaping, setting the rivets, and inspecting your work, you'll see why I recommend hiring this step out. It usually isn't horribly expensive, and frankly, pros always do a better job than most of us can.

In the center of the clutch disc is a hub that is either driven by a shaft, or that drives a shaft itself. Either way, the splines of the hub will show some wear. Hubs are not too expensive, and I recommend replacing them if the drive edges of the splines show wear. Some hubs are reversible, and you may be able to drill out the rivets, reverse the hub, and reset the hub with new rivets. If you hire out the lining of the clutch disc, having them replace the hub adds only a small amount to the total bill. They will also clean and coat the metal parts of the disc.

Pressure Plate

The clutch pressure plate may need some work as well. I use the term pressure plate to generically refer to the "action" part of the clutch. This assembly takes the travel produced by the clutch pedal or lever, and through a series of operating linkages moves a spring-loaded assembly onto, or away from, the friction plate.

While making generalizations here about rebuilding is difficult, you need to keep a few things in mind. All contact surfaces should be smooth, flat, and free of damage, marks, or scratches. Resurfacing these parts or replacing them is required if you find any of these problems. Most pressure plates are spring-loaded in some way, and these springs weaken over time. While you can test them, finding specifications for these springs to see if they are suitable for reuse is difficult. In the absence of specifications, about all you can do is remove them, measure their overall length, then pressure-test them and compare values.

To pressure-test clutch springs, you can hire a mechanic with a spring tester or you can use a simple shop press. Set an accurate scale on the bed of the press. Then set the spring on the scale, centered under the ram of the press. Lower the press until the spring is two-thirds of its unloaded length. Note the weight on the scale. Repeat this for each spring. Be sure to wear goggles during this test! Any spring that requires significantly less pressure than its mates to compress to two-thirds of its unloaded length should be replaced. While a total force may be specified in the service manual, you shouldn't compare your results unless your scale is extremely accurate or you've hired out this step to a shop with a spring tester. Comparing the results in a relative way among all springs is sufficient. Other than surfacing and spring replacement, there is little else to do with a pressure plate besides to clean, sandblast, and coat nonwear surfaces with a good-quality paint or no-rust coating. (Don't coat the friction surfaces.)

TIP

Unless your flywheel is in pristine condition, having it surfaced and balanced is always a good idea during engine restoration.

Clutch Bearings

Many tractors have thrust bearings, pilot bearings and/or bushings, or other bearings that must be inspected, cleaned, and lubricated at this time. Thrust bearings are usually used as, and referred to as, a throw-out bearing. Many clutches, particularly flywheel-mounted clutches, use a thrust bearing that actuates the clutch pressure plate. When sandwiched tightly between the heel of your hand and a hard surface, this thrust bearing should rotate very quietly, smoothly, and without any rubbing or grinding sensations. Replace the bearing if it has any of these problems.

Your tractor may also have a pilot bearing to maintain drive shaft alignment, or if your tractor has a clutch mounted on the belt pulley, there will be belt pulley bearings to inspect. In flywheel-mounted clutches, you'll find the pilot bearing is actually a bushing housed in the flywheel. Restoration involves pulling and replacing this bearing. These are cheap, reasonably easy to replace, and replacement now is great insurance against a premature engine pulling two years down the road. Place a dab of grease in the bushing after installation.

For drive shaft alignment, some tractors use a carrier bearing (usually a needle bearing) that is mounted rearward of the clutch or in the flywheel. Be sure to inspect, clean, and lubricate these bearings. To inspect, install the drive shaft and look for excessive play. These bearings should have very little movement perpendicular to the drive shaft's orientation. They usually have some type of access for exterior lubrication, and lubrication of these bearings can wait until the tractor is assembled. Inaccessible carrier or pilot bearings require a dab of grease or a drop of engine oil now. Belt pulley or other drive line bearings will have to be inspected, cleaned, and lubricated at this time too. When the belt pulley is installed, shimmed, and adjusted according to your service manual's suggestions, you should feel no wobble, no grinding, and no looseness when turning the belt pulley. Replace any bearings that will not shim and adjust properly or exhibit any sign of rough operation after installation.

Clutch Adjustments

Most belt pulley–mounted clutches can wait until final tractor assembly for final adjustment, but flywheel-mounted clutches must be adjusted now. Here is where the measurement we took earlier comes into play. Your manual may or may not contain any specifications for the clutch finger height and friction disc thickness; they commonly don't. If the specifications exist, mount your pressure plate and friction disc according to the manual and make adjustments to return the finger height to specification. Adjustment is achieved through bolts or nuts that will raise or lower the pressure plate fingers.

If the clutch is being assembled without reconditioning the pressure plate, you can safely mount the clutch with

The thrust bearing seen here presses against the clutch fingers to disengage the clutch. Bearing operation should feel smooth, with no noticeable side-play, when the bearing is pressed firmly against a hard surface and rotated by hand.

no further adjustments (unless you had clutch problems before). If you reconditioned the pressure plate, or if you are using a pressure plate of unknown origin, you will need to verify adjustment. To do this, mount the pressure plate and friction disc and adjust the fingers (using the bolts or nuts provided for the purpose) to replicate the height you found at disassembly, being sure to use the same exact measurement procedures. Remove the clutch so the flywheel can be mounted, and then remount the clutch.

Next, the clutch and belt pulley should be reassembled. Replace any bearings that exhibit significant play or rough operation when rotated. Seals, studs, keys, and adjusting nuts that do not pass visual inspection should be replaced too. Worn clutch linkage parts need to be repaired or replaced.

Belt pulley clutches and other easily accessed clutches are often adjusted, so you will usually have to loosen the adjusting bolts and nuts before assembly. The primary specification here is the amount of pull required to disengage the clutch. John Deere belt pulley-mounted clutches also require the mechanic to adjust the clutch to obtain a sharp, crisp "snap" when the clutch engages. As usual, service manuals will help when setting up and making your final adjustments. Whenever you are installing clutches with new friction plates, remember that the current adjustments may be too tight for the new disc, and you may need to adjust the clutch. This is especially true with easily accessed clutches, on which the previous owners may have done quite a bit of their own adjusting.

On John Deere horizontal two-cylinder engines, install the flywheel first. Simply slip it onto the crankshaft, then tighten the mounting flanges. Be sure the end of the crankshaft is flush with the outside face of the flywheel. Also be sure to retorque the flange bolts after 15 minutes and after 1 hour of running time after the rebuild. Loose flywheels ruin themselves and the crankshaft they are attached to.

One of the recurring themes in this book is that you should take nothing for granted. Every part should be looked at and every assembly should be cleaned, adjusted and tested for smooth, problem-free operation. The clutch, belt pulley, and flywheel assemblies of the tractor are no different, and paying attention to detail will reward you with an engine that only has to be installed once. There is nothing more frustrating than finding you must pull a freshly installed engine because you did not pay close attention to a 20-cent pilot bushing. (I've done it—take my word for it.)

REMOVING AUXILIARY SYSTEMS

On most vertical tractor engines, the front timing gear cover (the cover that houses the crankshaft and camshaft gears) is where you'll first access the inside of the engine. On horizontal-engine John Deere tractors, the initial access is made by removing the crankcase cover and governor assembly. While governor assembly removal isn't necessary for light engine refurbishing, most thorough rebuilds will remove the governor and restore it as well. Regardless of engine design, most of the auxiliary systems (hydraulic pumps, distributors, etc.) of a tractor engine are driven off of, or mounted to, these governor assemblies and timing gear covers. Removing these auxiliary systems comes first.

Though water pumps do not mount to the front cover on most vertical engines, now is also the time to remove the water pump. On a John Deere horizontal-engine trac-

tor, the water pump is near the radiator and out of the way for engine overhaul. Removing it is not necessary for engine access, but a thorough engine rebuild includes rebuilding the water pump. After removal, all of these auxiliary systems need to be inspected and restored as well, as we'll discuss in a later chapter.

To remove the auxiliary systems, loosen and remove the fasteners that hold them on, being sure to carefully save any studs or bolts. These studs and bolts are often of odd lengths, and they should be marked as to their original location and saved for reinstallation or replacement. When removing auxiliary systems, be aware that the distributor or magneto, and the governor that drives it, must be accurately timed to the engine, so marks between gears and between housings should be punched to ease installation worries. Also refer to your tractor's service manual to be sure that any other timing considerations, such as punch marking the actual drive gears, are addressed as well. For example, most magnetos and distributors have a flat drive flange with a groove to make synchronization during assembly

While the engine's top end is open, there is still work to do on the engine front cover and auxiliary systems. Here we can see the water pump and fan assembly, the front cover, the governor, and the distributor.

While removing auxiliary items, close open ports and holes to prevent dirt and grime from entering them. In this case, a piece of tape is used on the governor.

As you can see from this photo, the front cover has a front half and a backing plate. Usually the camshaft timing gear or some other assembly prevents the removal of the front cover if the backing plate is still attached. Here all the backing plate bolts, save two, have been removed so the backing plate can be removed.

The lye soaking solution I recommend in the next chapter for cleaning dirty parts will destroy or damage nonferrous parts. An example is this aluminum front timing cover from a Ford 8N. If the part is so dirty identification of the metal is difficult, a magnet test will work just fine. If the part attracts a magnet, it's safe to soak in a lye solution. If a magnet is not attracted to the metal, clean the part with a commercial degreaser safe for nonferrous metals.

Here is the inside of a typical (Allis-Chalmers WC) front cover. In the center of the inside surface is a bronze rubbing block that maintains the free play of the camshaft. Often this rubbing block is spring loaded, and you must be careful not to lose the spring during removal.

ket, between the block or crankcase and the gasket, so the gasket comes off with the cover. After the gasket's loosened, the cover lifts right off.

When removing timing gear covers, there are a couple of things to be aware of. The camshaft end play may be controlled by a spring and rubbing block made of brass or bronze. These parts (at least the spring) may fall out when the cover is removed. In addition, a part that resembles a large saucer-shaped washer, called an oil slinger, can be found. Be careful not to damage it when you remove the cover. Remove the oil slinger, being sure to note the orientation of the slinger before removal. Typically, the concave side of the slinger faces outward. Its orientation is important so oil is distributed evenly and completely to the timing gears.

Removing John Deere Governor Assemblies

Removing the governor assembly starts with removing the oil lines to the tappet cover, then the governor and engine crankcase cover. If you haven't removed the starter shield and flywheel covers mentioned earlier, do so now. On some tractors, you must now remove an oil line that runs from the crankcase to the governor housing. Loosen and remove the bearing collar that supports the fan shaft, and the fan shaft. Remove the distributor also. At this point, remove the governor assembly's mounting screws and lift it off.

REASSEMBLY

Assembling and mounting the engine access covers and auxiliary-driven components takes place after the rest of the engine is refurbished. You must be finished with any crankshaft, camshaft, bore and sleeve, and reciprocating parts restoration before continuing with the rest of this

easy. However, some do not, and the drive mechanisms are simply straight-cut gears. This makes correct installation nearly impossible without some type of reference.

When removing engine-driven hydraulic pumps, be sure to drain hydraulic fluid reservoirs first. Other items to remove now include diesel fuel injection systems, spark plugs and associated wiring, oil filter brackets and housings, breathers, and steering pedestals that may still be mounted to the timing cover.

Removing Covers, Slingers, and Such

To remove the engine covers, gently loosen the grip the gasket has on the engine block/crankcase and the cover. To preserve the gasket, you will need a small, thin putty knife to wedge between the gasket and the engine block. Do this all the way around, trying your best to get up under the gas-

THREAD COATINGS: LUBRICANTS, SEALERS, AND LOCKERS.

Assembling parts is more than just tightening a few bolts and moving on. Every time you bring out the wrench, you have to consider:

(1) How much should I tighten the fasteners?

(2) Are the fasteners the correct hardness grade?

(3) Should I use a lubricant, sealant, or locking compound? The first two questions we answered elsewhere, but here we will discuss thread lubricants, sealants, and locking products used to enhance a fastener's ability to do its job.

Thread lubricants lubricate a fastener's threads to aid in the fastening process, and they act as an anti-seizing agent to make removal easier. In addition, most lubricants protect against rusting, galling, and other corrosion. You will want to use lubricants whenever the service manual mentions that the fastener should be fastened with a lubricant applied, or you believe galling or corrosion may create problems for future removal.

You don't want to use a lubricant when a thread sealant or thread locking compound is called for. These products are not interchangeable. Another note of caution: Thread lubricants can cause you to break fasteners much more easily during tightening if proper torque values are not followed. For instance, if your manual says 40 lb-ft of torque, and doesn't mention whether the fastener should be installed dry or lubricated, assume they mean dry. Then slowly apply force, watching for signs of bolt stretch well before 40 lb-ft. Forty lb-ft. of torque applied to a fastener with lubricant would break a bolt designed to be installed with 40 lb-ft dry. To save a little money, engine oil makes a great lubricant in many circumstances. Commercial products do a better job of protecting against corrosion, but as a lubricant, they aren't better than engine oil.

Thread sealants can act as a lubricant, but more important, they seal the threads, preventing fluids or gases from leaking past them. The most common application for these products is to seal cylinder head fasteners. Any fastener, however, that extends into a cavity with fluid or gases under pressure is a candidate for a thread sealant. Most thread sealants are not rated for fuel, so be sure to check your product for use around fuel line compression fittings. Sealants that are rated for fuel should be used when fitting up fuel lines, since many fuel fittings in antique tractors are prone to leak. A little ingenuity will reveal other uses for thread sealants. For instance, you might apply a little around the edges of freeze plugs to prevent minor leaks. In some circumstances, Teflon plumber's tape can be used in place of thread sealants. Tape should be limited to fasteners external to the engine—don't use it on cylinder head fasteners, water pump studs, etc.

Thread locking compounds are just glues that hold the fasteners into place. All manufacturers sell their locking compounds in various strengths. The two main categories are "power removal required" or "permanent." "Power removal" (my term, as various compound manufacturers use different descriptions for this type of strength) means the thread locking compound will require an air wrench, and possibly mild heat to remove the fastener. Permanent strength supposedly means just that—the fasteners are in there for good. I say supposedly because some manufacturers claim that fasteners installed with the permanent-strength product can still be removed in some circumstances. Sometimes, the right combination of parts, fasteners, heat, and power removal can indeed remove the fastener without destroying the fastener or parts.

Permanent thread locking compounds have no real use in antique tractor restoration, and the "power removal" grades have limited use. Most fasteners in antique tractors critical enough to require thread locking compounds already have mechanical locking systems—cotter pins or mechanic's wire. There are a few fasteners on antique tractors where mechanical fasteners aren't used, other than maybe a lock washer, and application of a thread locking compound would make sense. An example would be structural bolts that mate the engine or frame to the rear half of the tractor. These typically need to be upgraded to modern Grade 8 bolts and fastened with thread locking compounds in addition to a lock washer. If you do use a thread locking compound, be sure not to use the permanent grade.

As you can tell, fastening parts is not just a mindless endeavor. Every bolt, save the most inconsequential fasteners, requires a few seconds of thought and study before installation. This thought process should include the question, "Do I need any type of thread coating?" With the information provided here, the answer should come quickly.

chapter. Mounting of these components and covers requires diligence in two areas: gasket making and alignment. The gaskets for many driven components and covers are critical for proper alignment or are critical to eliminate the possibility for leaks. For example, front covers are notorious for leaking, so use great care in the gasket making, dressing (applying sealant), and installation.

Assembling the engine access covers and auxiliary systems is mostly the reverse of disassembly. After the engine has been rebuilt, and you are closing up the engine access covers and mounting the auxiliary systems, first make sure you have studied your manual's techniques for synchronizing the distributor or magneto. Somewhere in those instructions is a procedure for positioning the crankshaft and reciprocating parts to a certain point in the firing cycle of the engine. For vertical engines, this usually means positioning the first cylinder at the top of the compression stroke (both valves closed and the piston at the top of its travel), also known as top dead center, or TDC. On John Deere horizontal-engine tractors, orient the flywheel so the timing mark on the flywheel lines up with a register mark on the crankcase or crankcase cover.

Precise engine timing will still be needed, but this synchronization will get the timing in the ballpark, so final timing adjustments can be made with the magneto and distributor.

Installation of the covers is straightforward. Be sure your gaskets are new, and that you use proper gasket sealant. Front cover and water pump gaskets require sealants designed for high temperature, while gaskets that aren't exposed to extremely high temperatures can use a standard gasket sealant. As I mentioned earlier, be certain your new gaskets are identical in material and thickness to the original—especially any gaskets you have made. The original gasket is probably compressed from use, so the new gasket material may be slightly thicker.

Other items to watch during installation: It's easy to damage crankshaft seals when installing the crankshaft pulley, so do this carefully. Use new woodruff keys for the crankshaft pulley, and remember to put the dust seal on the pulley before it is mounted. When tightening the pulley fastener, use a thread sealant on the threads and manually tighten it. An air impact wrench can be used initially if you are careful and the wrench has been set on the lowest setting. These fasteners do not have to tightened excessively, so stop using the wrench as soon as the nut stops turning. Use a torque wrench, not an impact wrench, to arrive at the final torque value. A helper can hold the flywheel or pulley (with a V-belt) long enough for a reading on the torque wrench.

A WORD ON GASKETS

When removing the auxiliary systems, crankcase covers, or timing gear covers, you will run across several gaskets that should be carefully removed to preserve as much of the gasket as possible. There are two reasons. First, some or all of the gaskets may not available. Second, if they are available, they may be expensive or of inferior quality. For these reasons, you may need to make your own gaskets. Preserving the old gaskets will help you find the right gasket material, and they give you a pattern.

Be aware that the gasket between auxiliary systems also act as a spacer or shim between driven parts. An example is a hydraulic pump mounted to the front cover. Usually these engage the camshaft gear, and fiber paper gaskets are used. If you were to use thick cork-style gasket material instead, the gear mesh pattern would be offset, resulting in abnormal gear wear. If the gasket was thick enough, you would damage the gears. (True cork gaskets are no longer used, but the newer synthetic material looks and feels like cork.)

This chapter stepped through one of the easier parts of engine disassembly and assembly. I hope that including some manufacturer specific information did not make it overly difficult or tedious. In the future, when you own a different antique tractor and begin to rebuild the engine, you'll appreciate the great variety of flywheel, clutch, and engine access designs. I also hope that when you rebuild that next engine, you will be able to pick up this book, reread this chapter, and realize that it is still helpful, applicable, and complete in its coverage.

THE CYLINDER HEAD

CYLINDER HEAD REMOVAL

Before you remove the cylinder head, double-check to make sure you have drained all coolant from the engine. While draining the coolant through the radiator petcock is usually sufficient, some engine blocks have a separate drain petcock. If your cylinder head has a top-mounted distributor or any brackets or mounted supports for other parts, such as an oil filter housing, remove them now. Don't forget the temperature sending unit and associated wiring, if your antique tractor has them. Also be sure to remove any radiator hose elbows or bolt-on thermostat housings. The cylinder head should be free and clear of any part attached to it.

The cylinder head fastens to the block with a large number of cylinder head studs or bolts. Depending on the size of your cylinder head, you will have 8 to 20 fasteners or

TIP

If the fasteners of your cylinder head extend into the block's coolant cavity, be sure to treat the ends with a thread sealant to minimize the risk of coolant leaks.

more. Using a stout, long-handled breaker bar and socket, start loosening the head fasteners. It may help to use a die to chase the threads above the nut if they need it. Some studs may loosen from the block—instead of the nut loosening from the stud—when you turn the wrench. This isn't a big problem, and you can completely remove the stud and bolt and proceed if this happens.

To remove the head, first remove the spark plugs. If the spark plugs are rusted into position, however, you can wait until after the head is removed. Then you can take the head to a workbench and soak the spark plug threads with penetrating fluid from the bottom side of the head.

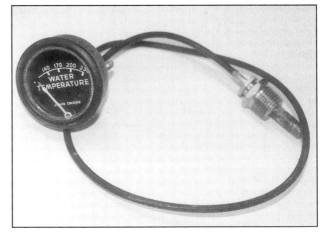

In preparation for head removal, be sure to remove all brackets and connections from the head. Now is the time to remove the temperature sending unit if your tractor has one. This John Deere coolant temperature gauge, capillary tube, and temperature sending unit is carefully removed and stored.

MAKE YOUR OWN ENGINE CLEANING SOLUTION

One of the most important parts of a rebuild is to make sure the engine is as clean as possible before you start making your inspections, assessments, and assembly. By far, the best way to clean engine components is to dip them in a warm lye-based caustic solution. This stuff will strip any trace of grease and old paint, leaving the part looking like new. While large items such as engine blocks are best left to professionals, you can make your own professional-grade cleaner to soak and clean smaller parts such as cylinder heads, valve train components, etc. To make your own cleaner, simply mix 12 ounces of granular lye to 4 gallons of water. Place the solution in a large steel drum that can be securely closed when not in use, and gently warm. Do not boil! Here are some very important safety tips for making this solution:

- Lye and water are highly reactive. Always add the lye slowly to the water. Never add water to the lye. Adding water to the lye, especially if you do it slowly, will create a very strong chemical reaction that may cause the solution to bubble and fume, leaving you covered in a very dangerous liquid that causes serious chemical burns.
- Always wear caustic-resistant gloves, splatter-proof eye protection, and clothing that covers all your skin any time you are around lye.
- The lye solution will dissolve some types of metals, especially aluminum and bearing materials. Make sure you don't put anything in the solution that isn't exclusively steel or iron.
- If you're cleaning parts with odd shapes, you should be able to design and build odd-shaped soaking tanks, out of thick, heavy plastic lining and wood.
- Lye is sold in grocery stores, and it is inexpensive.
- Large plastic tubs with lids make great inexpensive tanks, but can't be warmed.
- This lye-based cleaner is simple, inexpensive and more effective at cleaning than virtually anything else.

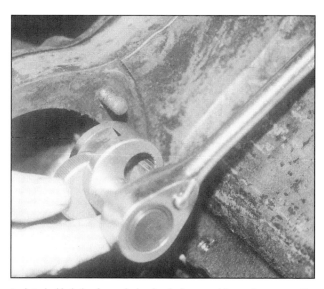

Studs in the block that fasten the head and other assemblies are best removed by a tool called, appropriately enough, a stud extractor. The concentric knurled disc, seen here in the hand of the mechanic, pinches the stud between it and the inside edge of the holes found in the upper and lower plates of the tool. This device tightens studs too.

While replacement is usually called for, head studs and head bolts can be reused in a pinch. If so, you should "chase" the threads of the fastener first to ensure proper tightening. While this should be done with the fasteners off the engine, or at the very least with the head off, sometimes a second pass is needed after the head is installed. Here some last-minute thread conditioning is performed with a die.

After completely removing all the nuts and bolts, double-check and make sure you removed everything from the head. A little coaxing may be needed to separate the head from the block. If the head doesn't pull free, break the seal

Milestone Number 1 in a rebuild: Your first look inside your antique tractor's engine. In your eagerness to peek inside, remember that lifting the head from the engine requires care. The head may be slightly difficult to remove, and many a head has been dropped and cracked after it slips from the mechanic's hands after the head breaks free. Here a firm grip on the coolant neck and a rear stud helps the mechanic keep a sure grip on the head.

Thorough cleaning of your cylinder head will require submerging it in a caustic heavy-duty cleaner. You should remove all plugs, such as this drain plug, before you begin cleaning.

between the head gasket and block by prying with a paint scraper under the head gasket. This should break the head away from the gasket. Lift the head up and away, being sure to clear any studs left in the block. Many a head has been dropped by snagging a combustion chamber on the end of a head stud. Take the head to a sturdy work surface, and return to the tractor.

Now, look at the pistons and rings and make sure you see no surprises in terms of unexpected rust or damage. Return to the head, and clean the surface of the head that mates to the engine block. Remove any residue, remnants

TIP

You can find high-quality stainless-steel engineer's rulers used for the cylinder head trueness test at most arts and drafting supply businesses.

of the head gasket, any sealant, and carbon buildup. If the valve train is in the head (overhead valve engine), now is the time to remove all the valve train components. Skip ahead to the valve chapter for specific instructions on removal.

You are now ready to thoroughly clean the cylinder head. This calls for a dip in a caustic cleaning solution after you have removed the worst of the grease and carbon buildup by hand. The "recipe" for this solution in found in this chapter's sidebar. Dip the head in the solution, leaving it in overnight if possible. Before doing so, inspect the head for any bushings, serial number tags, or other items that are made of aluminum or galvanized, as the cleaning solution will ruin them. When it's done, rinse and thoroughly dry the head. (After a caustic dip, the head is left without any protective coating, such as paint or grease buildup, and it will rust immediately if you don't dry it.) Pay close attention to the valve guides and valve seats, and make sure they are dried quickly. Do not put any type of protective film of oil on the head yet; we have to wait until after the next step.

INSPECTING THE CYLINDER HEAD

To assess the condition of your head, there are three important things you need to check for: "trueness," cracks, and the condition of the coolant cavity. If it's an overhead valve engine, you have other inspections to make as well, but they are covered in the valve train chapter.

Initial visual inspection of the head should be performed right way. Scrape away as much paint, grime, and carbon as you can. This will allow you to find any serious or obvious problems with the head.

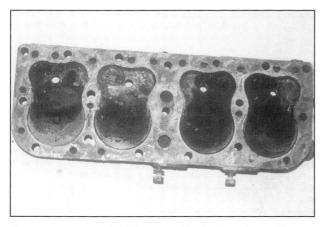

This antique tractor engine head shows signs of head gasket sealant used by a previous mechanic. This created quite a mess and some problems during removal. The heavy carbon buildup in the combustion chambers seems significant, but since all flathead engines tend to have lots of carbon buildup, this particular head is normal.

TIP

While inspecting for cracks is important in all types of cylinder heads, those from overhead valve engines are more susceptible to cracking, and their cracks can be tough to spot.

To avoid problems with oil and coolant leakage at the head gasket, and to minimize the risk of a blown head or manifold gasket, all mating surfaces must be flat, clean, and square. The trueness of the head refers to just that: how flat, square, and true these surfaces are. Measuring the head's trueness is simple. You first find a perfect straightedge, and lay it on edge along several different positions and orientations along the mating surface of the cylinder head. I place the straightedge at two or three positions along the length of the surfaces and diagonally. This will give you plenty of readings to make an accurate check of the cylinder head's "trueness."

For the straightedge test, I use an engineer's 2-foot steel ruler, which is handy in two ways. First, it is a very accurate and true straightedge. Second, how far the surface can be out of true is occasionally specified as a ratio. First example, Continental (a popular engine used by many tractor manufacturers) specifies that the trueness of the bottom of the cylinder head must be less than .00075 inch per inch of test length. This means that if the block mating surface of your cylinder head is 16 inches long and 8 inches wide, then no gap anywhere along the length of that surface should be greater than .012 inch deep (16x.00075 inch). No gap anywhere along the width of the surface should be greater than .006 inch deep (8x.00075 inch). Therefore,

you need to measure each test (which makes using a ruler as straightedge handy) and multiply it by the ratio. The engineer's ruler makes measuring precise and handy.

Here are couple of other notes about trueness:
- All dips and humps should be gradual and uniform. Steep localized dips are a problem and should not exceed 3 to 5 thousandths of an inch (.003 to .005 inch)
- I have heard many times to use a business card to check the gap. However, a business card is much too thick for most specifications. I think this piece of misguided advice originated from checking the trueness of a manifold mating surface, where one-eighth inch is an acceptable gap. If you can slip a business card under the straightedge when checking the head, it definitely needs milling by a machinist.
- Be sure to measure several orientations.
- All manufacturers seem to have their own standard, and you should check your engine's documentation. In the absence of those recommendations, those given above will serve any engine well.

If your head is out of true, then you must have the head milled. Any local automotive machine shop can help you, and the procedure isn't overly expensive or time-consuming. Before you rush out and have this done, let's take a look at a couple of other things. We may find other machine work that needs to be done at the same time.

Next, check for cracks in the cylinder head. Visual inspection is usually sufficient, but I also use a dye penetration product. When applied to cracked metals, dyes will penetrate the cracks. There are two groups of dye penetration products on the market, and the only difference is in how the cracks are located after penetration. Both are similar in that they require the part be incredibly clean before a liberal application of dye. The dye is allowed to sit, then the excess is removed. Here's where the products differ. The first type now requires that a fixing agent be applied. The fixing agent wicks the dye from cracks, making it visible under normal light to the naked eye. The second type requires no fixing agent, but the dye fluoresces under ultraviolet light. When you shine a "black light" bulb on the parts in a darkened shop, the dye glows and highlights any cracks.

Another crack detection method is called magnetic flux anomaly detection. Don't let the name fool you—the process is simple, though it does have to be done in a

TIP

Dropping a cylinder head is one sure way to crack it. Handle heads carefully.

TIP

When tightening an overhead valve cylinder head to the block, be sure the valve train is not installed.

professional shop. The iron or steel part (usually a head or block) is hooked up to a high-amperage electric current, which essentially turns the part into a huge magnet. Cracks in the part create anomalies in the magnetic field. Iron filings are sprinkled onto the part, and they orient themselves to the magnetic field, allowing the anomalies to be spotted. While I am simplifying the process to an almost criminal degree, this is the basic idea of Magna-Fluxing. Magna-Flux is the trade name of a test machine.

Last, the coolant cavity should be inspected for excessive scaling and rusting. Excessive scale and rust inhibits heat transfer. This can cause overheating, which leads to cracking or warping of the head. Rust and corrosion will be obvious in the coolant cavities that you can see into. If you need to remove rust, fill the head with a rust and corrosion fighter, such as radiator flush and scale remover. In severe cases, ask the local parts store about heavy-duty acid-based products that are safe to use in this situation. I have used a phosphoric acid product and liked it.

Start rust and scale removal by turning the head upside down and making sure it is level. Place a stopper or duct tape over any lower opening in the head, such as the coolant exit at the top or side of the head. Make sure drain plugs are in place and temperature sending unit holes are plugged. Then pour the descaling solution into the head though the coolant holes in the bottom. Leave this to sit overnight, agitating it as often as you can. In the morning, drain and very thoroughly rinse the coolant cavity. This will require a good deal of rinsing to remove all the rust and cleaner. Again, dry the head as quickly as you can to minimize new rust formation.

The only way to remove significant rust from a cylinder head is to have the head "electrolytically" dip-stripped. Electrolytic dipping involves more chemistry lessons than we want to go into here, but several sources on the Internet can provide you with the details, including how to set up your own home apparatus.

In a nutshell, the parts are placed in a nonmetal container full of washing soda (not the same thing as soap!), and a negative charge is placed on the part. A positive charge is placed on another steel electrode in the tank. A low-voltage direct current is then run through the solution; this causes an electrolytic reaction that breaks the bonds between the iron and oxygen molecules in the rust. When finished, all the rust is changed chemically to a black iron compound that is easily rinsed off, and the original unrusted iron is unharmed.

Just remember that the part will flash-rust if it's not dried immediately. Also, any grease, oil, or paint must be removed first, or it will protect the rust from the process. Some nonferrous metals, such as aluminum or bronze, will be ruined in this process, so be sure to remove serial number plates, etc. The rust removal is complete, and frankly, quite amazing. Professional engine restoration shops or automotive restoration shops may be able to provide this service. Or, with care, more information from qualified sources, and a tremendous safety consciousness, it can be done in your home shop.

MACHINING

If your inspections revealed problems with trueness or cracks, a trip to the automotive machine shop is in order. They can mill these surfaces back to true, and many types of cylinder head cracks can be successfully repaired. Before you make this trip, you should continue with the next several chapters, as other parts may need machine work as well.

If you are rebuilding this tractor to compete in antique tractor pulls, then you should consider porting and polishing the intake and exhaust ports (in a valve-in-head engine; porting and polishing in flathead engines is done to the block). These procedures enlarge and smooth the passages in the head for improved air flow. If you don't want to port and polish the head, I recommend at least using a small die grinder to remove the roughest spots in these passages.

Cylinder Head Installation

Installing the cylinder head is the reverse of disassembly, but you need to follow several precautions to ensure a

Here a head is set up on a milling machine, ready to be surfaced. The machinist will, in multiple passes, mill metal away from the bottom of the head, returning the surface to "true."

The surfacing operation leaves razor edges on the outside edges of the head and on the edges of each combustion chamber. Here, the machinist removes the razor edges with a die grinder. This step is very important to prevent serious cuts to hands and damage to the engine and head gasket during head installation. In addition, these edges may break away during engine operation and drop into the bores, damaging the engine.

leak-free head. First, replace head studs and bolts if at all possible. Install the studs and bolts with a high-temperature thread sealant at the ends to prevent coolant from leaking past the threads.

After the studs are in place, lay a new head gasket (never reuse gaskets) on the block. Correct gasket orientation is very important; coolant or oil leaks will be your reward if you don't orient it correctly. Every head gasket has a smooth side, and a side where the "lips," or edges of the metal covering, are obvious and exposed. The smooth, "lipless" mates against the engine block, and, the "lip" side of the gasket faces the cylinder head.

I recommend installing the head gasket dry, but I have used a flat black paint as a gasket sealant on the advice of a mechanic at NASCAR driver Jimmy Spencer's speed shop. This worked well enough, and there were no ill effects or leaks. John Deere used to recommend soaking the gasket in engine oil before assembly. This probably can't hurt either. There is one consensus among rebuilders though: Do not ever use any type of heavy-bodied gasket sealant, even if the product specifically mentions it can be used on head gaskets. It isn't needed and may make remov-

ing the head gasket a real nightmare. If for some reason you are dead set on using a commercially prepared gasket sealant, use one of the light-bodied copper-based sealants. These typically do not create big problems in the future.

After dressing the gasket, lay it in place and put the cylinder head on the block. Verify that all the cylinder head bolts line up and the gasket is oriented correctly. (Remember, lip side up.)

Tightening the cylinder head requires special attention. First, if your engine has overhead valves, do not install or tighten the rocker arm assembly until after you

TIP

To obtain proper, true torque values while tightening the cylinder head, be sure the fasteners are thoroughly clean and lubed. If you reuse fasteners, chase the studs or bolts with a die to restore the threads.

have tightened the cylinder head completely (the valves must be installed first, though). The head, though it looks solid and immovable, will move and deform under the clamping forces of the rocker arm assembly. This could cause problems when you torque the head fasteners.

Likewise, tightening the head fasteners in the wrong sequence will deform the head. To illustrate, let me make an analogy. Let's say you are folding a piece of paper in half. When you begin the crease, you always start in the middle and work your way outward, right? The paper will buckle and move if you try to work the crease from the outside edges toward the middle. Working from the ends, it's also difficult to keep the crease smooth and tight, and difficult to keep the paper lined up.

The same is true of the cylinder head. To make sure all clamping forces exerted by the fasteners on the cylinder head are consistent, you must start in the middle and work your way outward. In addition, it is best to first tighten them in sequence, to approximately two-thirds of the final torque values (as specified by your manual). Then repeat the process, tightening the fasteners to the final torque values. While this may seem tedious, it is universally accepted as the only way to minimize the risk of coolant, oil, and compression leaks.

When you install the bolts or nuts, use fresh copper or lead crush washers between the top of the cylinder head and the fasteners. This will contain any minor coolant and

TIP

If the head fasteners do not extend into the coolant cavity of the engine block, then thread sealant isn't necessary. However, to obtain proper torque, the fasteners need to be dipped in oil, then wiped thoroughly.

compression leaks that find their way from the block along the threads of the stud or bolt.

To wrap things up, install the rocker arm assembly according to the instructions in the valve chapter, then install the thermostat and upper radiator hose outlet if your cylinder head has them. Now is the time to make sure the temperature sending unit works by connecting it to the gauge and immersing it in water near that is almost boiling hot. Replace the temperature sending unit or the gauge, or both, if it doesn't register anything on the gauge as soon as you immerse it.

The important things to remember about this chapter are the importance of thorough inspection and assessment, and making sure your head is flat, true, and square. After that, make sure you install the head properly, tightening the fasteners in sequence according the manual, and paying particular attention to the torque values.

THE VALVE TRAIN

W hile there are no unimportant systems in an engine, some systems will have a greater impact on the restoration than other systems. Valve trains, in particular, have a tremendous effect on the rebuild and the engine's running characteristics. For example, if you rebuild the engine, but ignore the valve train, the engine may still smoke, sound like a washing machine, and run poorly under load or high rpm. Fortunately, valve train restoration is not difficult or expensive, and most parts are easy to obtain.

VALVE TRAIN DESIGNS

Most antique tractor engines have one of two primary valve train designs: overhead valve and "flathead"(otherwise known as "L-head," or valve-in-block). Overhead valve engines have performance advantages that have virtually eliminated the flathead design, although it was popular during the heyday of antique tractors.

Old valves often carry logos and other impressions. This makes lapping the valves difficult with a suction cup lapping tool. The suction cup may have to be trimmed to size to completely cover the logo without extending past the edges of the valves.

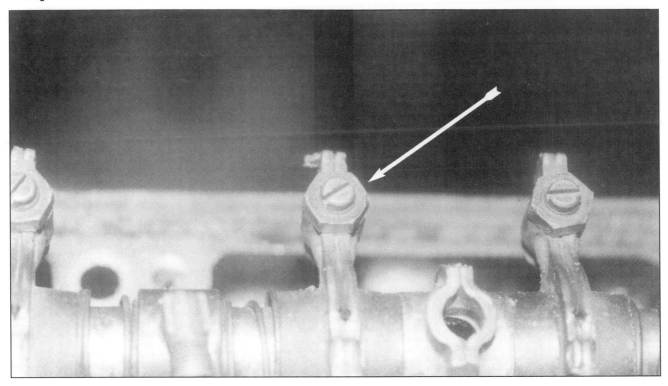

Valve lash (the amount of play in each valve linkage) is adjusted on an overhead valve engine via these small adjusting screws, which are locked in place by a locking nut also seen here.

In flathead engines, the valve lash adjusting screws are found on the tappets, which are accessed by removing the side covers on the engine block.

In overhead valve engines, the valves are in the cylinder head, and they are operated from one side of a set of levers, called rocker arms (sometimes tappet levers) that rotate on a shaft bolted to the top of the head. The other end of each rocker arm is operated by a push rod. The push rod is in turn operated by a camshaft follower that rides on the lobes of the camshaft. These eccentric lobes lift and lower the followers in time with the firing cycle of each cylinder.

The flathead engine operates on the same principle, but does away with push rods and rocker arms. The valves are located in the block, and are opened and closed directly by adjustable followers, called tappets. Very little distinguishes the two systems during restoration except the extra linkage of the overhead valve system. Valve and valve seat restoration does not change, nor does camshaft restoration. Tappet and follower restoration procedures are identical, and adjustment procedures are similar. The only difference is the location of the valves.

VALVE TRAIN DISASSEMBLY
Valve-in-Head Engines

Disassembling a valve-in-head engine's valve train begins with removing the rocker arm assembly. It is much easier to reach cylinder head bolts after you remove the rocker arm assembly, so do this first. Typically the rocker arm is secured with two to four bolts, although studs are sometimes used.

Once the valve train area of an overhead valve engine is exposed, remove the mounting bolts for the rocker arm shaft. Often you will find oil troughs and wicks, seen here on a Farmall F-20, above the rocker arm shafts, attached to the rocker arm shaft mounting bolts or bases. John Davis uses an air impact wrench to remove the troughs.

During removal, look for oil passage lines passing from the head to the rocker arm assembly that may be easily damaged. The rocker arm assembly is usually in two halves, separated with a coupling, a spring, or both. It is easy to lose these parts, so be careful. Lift the rocker arm assembly straight up while holding the two halves together, and set the assembly aside in a box. Next, remove the push rods. Pushrods should be returned to their original locations on reassembly, so it helps to number them, usually from the front of the engine back. I recommend marking the push rods, or making a small wooden hanger with slots or holes to hold them in order.

When disassembling a valve train, remember that all reused components must return to their original position in the engine. During storage, make a cardboard or wooden keeper that will keep the parts organized by position.

Once you remove the valve cover of a John Deere B, this is what you will find. Obviously, as it is a two-cylinder engine, you'll find just four valves instead of eight or more as with other engines.

To access the valve train on a flathead engine, valve cover plates will have to be removed from the side of a block. Here the second of two plates is being removed from a Ford 8N engine.

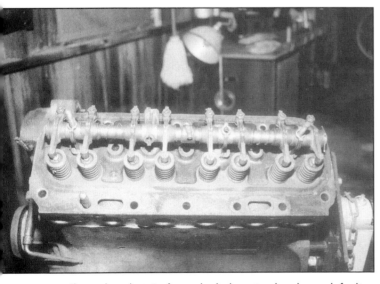

The complete valve train of an overhead valve engine, shown here ready for disassembly. Note the four mounting bases (the second base from left is slightly turned) that have a hole for the valve cover studs. Also note the L-shaped oil fitting in the center of the rocker arm shaft. Any oil line from the block connected to the shaft must be disconnected from the rocker arm prior to removal. After loosening the mounting bolts, the rocker arm shaft lifts off.

Next remove the head, following the advice in the previous chapter. After removing the head, take it to a suitable work space where you can remove the valves and valve springs. Valve and valve spring removal is covered a little later on in this chapter.

Flathead Engines

Disassembling the valve train of a flathead engine is a bit simpler, as there is little work to do before you remove the valves. First, you need to gain access to the valves. The valves in a flathead engine are covered by an access plate in the side of the engine block. Remove this plate, being careful to save the gasket in case you need to copy it. Once this plate is off, valve and valve spring disassembly can begin.

VALVE SPRING REMOVAL

Regardless of the valve train design your engine has, valve and valve spring removal procedures are identical. The valves are held closed by valve springs, which are held in place by backing plates and keepers. To release the keepers, the valve springs must be compressed. Valve springs are strong and can require 100 psi or more to compress them far enough to remove the backing plate and keeper. You'll

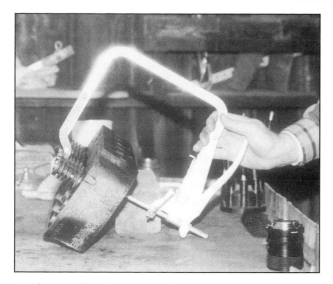

1 Valve removal begins by compressing the valve spring, using a spring compressor, shown here. If you have an overhead valve engine, this must be done with the head removed.

2 Here a valve spring compressor compresses the spring, exposing the small cone-shaped locking device, known as a "keeper."

3 The keepers are usually in two halves, though some models have snap rings or small pins for keepers. Be warned, the keepers love to fall inside block cavities, just out of reach!

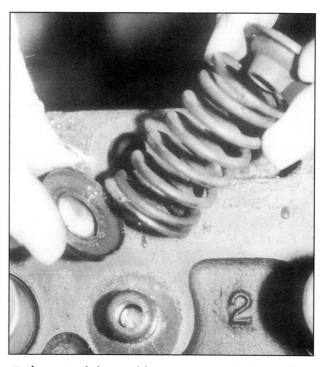

4 After removing the keeper and the spring compressor, the valve assembly will come apart and the valve slides out.

need a set of impact-rated safety glasses to do this job. Valve springs, keepers, and backing plates can fly apart dangerously if spring tension is released abruptly. Never work on valve springs without impact-rated safety glasses.

To compress the springs, you use a valve spring compressor. There are two designs in popular use. The first is the C-shaped valve spring compressor, which will work with any type of valve train design. When using the C-style compressor on valve springs in overhead valve engines, the head must be removed. The C-shaped tools are simple: The bottom of the "C" sits against the bottom of the valve whose spring you are compressing, while the other half of the "C" (the half with the "fork") compresses the spring.

1 Removing valve springs from a flathead engine requires similar effort and procedures, though there is some variation. As with the overhead valve engines, the valve spring is compressed using a spring compressor.

2 With the spring compressed, the keepers are removed from the bottom of the valve stem, and the valve assemblies come apart.

3 Some flatheads, such as this Ford 8N motor, have a different valve removal procedure, though. This procedure is typically used on all valves in engines whose exhaust valves have a special rotator cap at the end of the valve stem. Because of the cap, normal keepers cannot be used, nor is there enough clearance between the end of the valve stem and the tappet adjusting screw to remove the cap.

4 To remove these valve assemblies, you must first use a hook tool to remove a locking clip that immobilizes the valve guide in its bore.

The second type of compressor is for overhead valve engines. It has two forks that compress a spring from the top and the bottom at the same time. It is smaller and easier to operate, but it doesn't work on flathead engines.

After you compress the spring, remove the keeper. Some keepers are small pins that go through small holes in the valve stems. They are long enough to overhang the valve stems, and the overhanging ends sit in grooves in the backing plate. A "cone" keeper is analogous to a metal cone split vertically into two halves. On the inside of each half

is a small ridge that fits into a small groove cut into the valve stem. The spring forces the backing plate to compress and seat the cone-shaped keeper ever tighter onto the valve. This ensures that the keeper sits firmly against the valve stem, retaining the backing plate and spring.

After removing the spring and keeper, you can slide the valve out of the head or block. Valves, if reused, should be returned to their original position, so again I would recommend making a wooden hanger. Mark the holes in the wood to correspond to positions in the head or block. As

5 Here's what the clip looks like removed, still hooked to the removal tool.

6 With the clip removed, use a jack-type lift, or as shown here, a valve-spring compressor installed so the compressor's top anvil is not on top of the valve.

7 As the lift (or compressor) is tightened, the entire valve assembly, including the valve guide, is lifted from the engine block.

you remove each valve, place it into its proper hole in the wooden hanger. Note that in the vast majority of engines, the intake and exhaust valves are different and cannot be interchanged.

TIP

A thorough soak in parts cleaner is a must for valve train components.

8 The valve assembly removed. To disassemble the valve assembly, lift off the rotor cap, compress the spring, and disassemble as outlined earlier. This procedure can be a little tedious and time consuming, but some patience and care will get the job done.

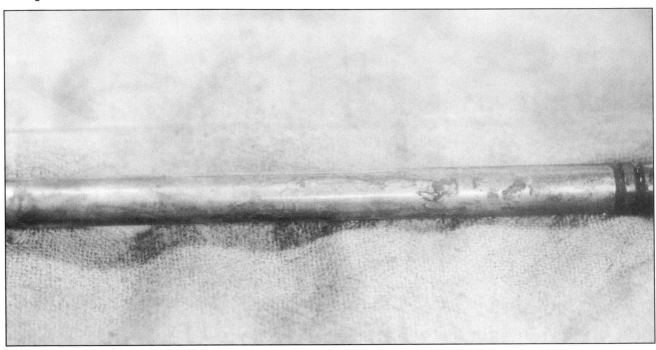

After removing the valves, inspect them closely. This picture shows rust stains on the stem of the valve. This valve from a John Deere B was rusted into place and required penetrating fluid to press out. Remember, valves are brittle; don't use hammer blows to remove them. Penetrating fluid and slow steady pressure are needed to safely remove stubborn valves.

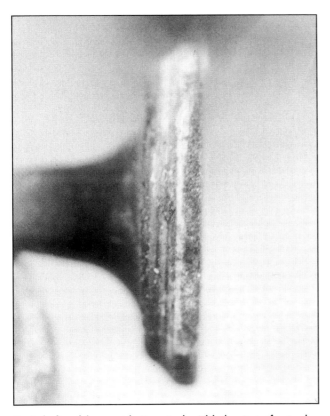

Here's the face of the same John Deere B valve. While there is significant carbon buildup, the valve face and seat were in good shape and needed only some light valve lapping to bring the valves up to operating standards.

INSPECTING VALVE TRAIN COMPONENTS

After removing and disassembling the valve train, inspection comes next. Inspection consists of looking for obvious signs of wear, making a few measurements, and comparing them against specs. I find the majority of antique tractor service manuals don't provide adequate specifications for valve and valve seat parameters. If that is the case, your local machinist can help you assess your valves and valve seats. Before doing so, read through this chapter and accompanying photos. You may be able to glean enough information to accurately ascertain the health of your valve train.

First, inspect the valve train components for obvious damage. Push rods, tappets/followers, and valve faces and seats seem to be the most frequent components that show damage and wear. Push rods are occasionally bent; tappet or follower faces (the side that rides the camshaft lobes) are often chipped, show abnormal coloration, or have surface blemishes; and valve seats and faces are often eroded or pitted. Unless the engine had lubrication problems in the valve train, the rocker arm assembly is typically in good

TIP

Valve springs are under tremendous tension during disassembly and assembly. Wear eye protection whenever springs are under tension.

Never soak any valve spring that has any kind of coating or paint. This coating is there to prevent rust and most cleaning agents will remove the coating!

During the valve train restoration, if you find that the valve seats need grinding, consider replacing the valve seats with hardened valve seats instead.

shape. Valve springs, while occasionally weak or rusted, are usually OK too.

You'll need some specifications to assess valve wear. Your service manual should at least provide specs for valve stem thickness and spring tension. Valve seat and face angles and width, as well as valve stem-to-guide clearances are often provided, but not always. Measuring the valve stem thickness helps determine whether the valve stem is worn so far that the valve guide can't control oil leakage past the valve stem. Since valves and guides should be replaced in pairs, any worn valve that is replaced should also have its guide replaced.

If the valve guides need to be removed, use a valve guide driver (a specialty tool) or a shop hydraulic press combined with a suitably sized arbor. The valve guide may have a shoulder, forcing you to drive the guide out from one direction, so look before pressing it out. Pressing them can easily damage the guides, so if there is any chance you may need to reuse them, be very careful.

VALVE TRAIN MEASUREMENTS

First, measure the valve stem diameter midway up the stem. The valve is either within specification or it is not, and replacement is the only answer for out-of-specification valves.

Measure the valve seats next. The seat width is simply the width of the area on both the valve and the valve seat where they contact each other. This area, after thorough cleaning, should be discernible and should measure within specification. If there is pitting, if the seat areas are not discernible, or if there is any other damage, then your valves should be reground. Here is a short list of other valvetrain dimensions and their explanations:

Valve seat angle: You won't need to measure the valve seat angle; it's a reference for the machinist when he or she grinds the valves or valve seats.

Margin: This is the thickness of valve material between the seating area of the valve and the face of the valve. After a valve regrinding or two, the margin may be thin enough to prohibit further grinding.

Valve guide bore diameter: This is a difficult measurement for the part-time mechanic to make, as it requires a special set of "plug" gauges or an expansion (also known as a telescoping) gauge in conjunction with a micrometer. Since guides should be replaced with the valves, this mea-

surement isn't even taken unless all the valves check out and can be reused. Even then, buying a set of new guides can be cheaper than finding the right tools or paying someone to take this measurement.

Spring tension: This is the amount of weight (or pressure) required to compress the spring a certain distance. Both the weight and the distances will be specified by your service manual. The specification is usually expressed twice, once as a "valve closed length" (the length of the spring when the valve is closed), and "valve open length" (the length of the valve spring when the valve is open). Also expressed is the weight required to compress the spring to these two lengths. Valve spring testers can be rented, but a little ingenuity and accurate scales can suffice for your own home-grown tension readings. However, some larger engines will have strong springs that will be difficult to test without the proper tool.

Hardened valve seats also need to be mentioned here. It was common in most older tractors to machine the valves seats directly into the block or head. Due to excessive pitting and erosion due to the heat, these seats are occasionally beyond repair. If your valve seats are in very bad shape, a machinist can machine recesses in the block or head that will accept special hardened valve seats.

These new seats will last much longer. In fact, many people believe that today's unleaded gas causes valve seat erosion and deterioration to happen at a much faster rate. The reasoning is that lead not only boosted octane, it also helped cool and lubricate the valve seats. These same people argue that adding hardened seats makes good sense anytime you are rebuilding an engine, even if your engine doesn't need valve seat work. This is one of those debates that includes a lot of opinions without a lot of cold hard data, and the truth is difficult to find. My recommendation is this: If you plan on using the tractor for long-term productive use, add hardened seats. Otherwise, a valve grinding job should be sufficient.

After inspection and measurement, you should be able to make an accurate assessment of your engine's valves and what needs to be done. If there is no damage or excessive wear and the valve train meets the specifications, you can feel free to reuse everything. If not, a trip to your local machinist should be next. He can tell you if the valves and seats can be rescued through a regrind, advise you on the wisdom of hardened seats, and install the seats and guides.

Your valve train may need professional machining to bring it back to life. This valve is getting a new face ground on a valve grinding machine.

Here a flathead block is getting new valve seats cut. Any valve face or seat that's damaged, significantly pitted, or eroded should be professionally machined.

In antique tractor engines, many valves train parts, such as springs, keepers, guides and valves, were actually common sizes and designs that were used in other types of engines. Because of that, your machinist may be able to find replacement parts through other channels.

TAPPETS AND FOLLOWERS

After valve and valve spring (flathead) or after push rod removal (overhead valve), the cam followers or tappets can be removed. In flathead engines, this is simple. Through the access hole in the side of the engine, pull each tappet clear of its bore and mark it with its position. Like valves, tappets and followers should be returned to their original position if reused.

In overhead valve engines, the followers are removed through the pushrod cavities and up through the top of the block. Cam followers usually look like chess pawns, and the top is easily grasped by hooked parts retrievers or a magnet on a stick. In some engines, long fingers are all that is needed. Followers should also be marked for position.

The follower face (the part that rides on the camshaft), and the lead (the follower tip that pushes the push rod) or striker (the part on a tappet that contacts the valve) should

On overhead valve engines, the followers (seen here from a distance) can be removed after the push rods. As with all components that are to be reused, they should be returned to their original position, so be sure to number push rods, follower, tappets, valves, and the like with their position.

be solid and free from any visible damage or wear. Tappet diameter is important and must be measured. This is a "go or no go" type of measurement. Tappets can't be restored or repaired if their diameter is worn beyond specification, they must be replaced.

CAMSHAFT-DRIVEN SYSTEMS

Before camshaft removal, you need to remove some auxiliary systems such as the oil pump, distributor, hydraulic pump, and governor. Your tractor may not have all these but nearly all have an oil pump that's driven from the camshaft and needs to be removed.

Disconnect any oil lines, then dismount the pump, loosening the bolts that attach the oil pump housing to the engine block. You may need to rotate the pump shaft or camshaft as the pump is removed in order to clear the camshaft gear. On many engines, the governor and the hydraulic pump are also driven from the camshaft gear, or from a helically cut gear in the middle of the camshaft. All

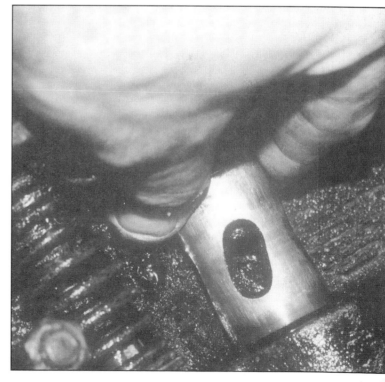

In flathead engines, remove the tappets from their bores with a steady upward pressure.

of these systems should be removed and stored for restoration covered later in the book.

CAMSHAFT AND CAMSHAFT BEARINGS

Now you can remove the camshaft—but only after you make sure the index marks that time the camshaft to the crankshaft exist and are visible! Timing a camshaft to a crankshaft without index marks is an exercise in frustration. If you can't find any marks, make your own with a hardened steel drift, but be careful not to break the gears!

There are two main designs used to mount and control the placement of the camshaft in most antique tractor engines. The first is simply a free-floating camshaft where fore and aft movement (end play) is controlled by a spacer and spring between the camshaft gear and the front cover of the engine or a plate mounted to the crankcase. More commonly, you will find the camshaft mounted with a thrust plate (or plates—one at each end of the camshaft), or with a mounting plate that controls end play with shims, spacers, and occasionally springs. The idea is to ensure that the camshaft gear is aligned with the crankshaft gear. Since the camshaft gear is mounted solid to the camshaft, meshing it properly with the crankshaft gear ensures that the camshaft lobes are properly positioned under the valve train.

Before removing the camshaft, measure the bearing clearances between the camshaft journals and the bearings (or cam bores, if your engine doesn't use bearings). This distance is critical to maintain proper oil

Ouch! Not one of the things you want to see when you open up your engine. This camshaft timing gear has been dealt a fatal blow; probably from a piece of metal working its way between the crankshaft and camshaft timing gear teeth. Replacement is necessary; here the locking nut of the camshaft has been removed and the gear is ready to be driven from the shaft.

This camshaft gear is in better shape, and the camshaft is ready for removal. Notice the mechanic's wire locking the camshaft timing gear mounting bolts into place. After removing these bolts, the camshaft gear will come right off. Removing the gear isn't necessary if it's in good condition.

pressure and camshaft bearing life. This measurement can be made from the bottom of the engine, using thin, narrow (approximately 1/4-inch-wide) strips of feeler stock (small pieces of metal of specified thickness). If the clearance is too large, remove the camshaft and measure the diameter of the journal (the part that rides in the bearing or bushing). Journal diameter only applies to those camshafts that ride in bores or pressed in bearings. If your camshaft rides in manufactured ball or tapered roller bearings, this measurement doesn't apply.

If your camshaft journals are worn, then, you can have the journals turned to a standard undersize and use oversized bearings. If your engine did not use camshaft bearings, you may have to insert special bearings or get a new camshaft. If oversized bearings are not available,

you must replace the camshaft. If the camshaft journals measure within specification, but the clearance is still too large, new camshaft bearings are needed.

It helps to double-check the camshaft bearings inside diameter measurements against the specifications in your manual. If the inside diameter is out of specification, then the need for new bearings is confirmed. If not, then a mixture of camshaft wear and bushing wear has created the clearance. In this case, new bearings will restore the bore diameter, but not the original factory clearances.

If both the camshaft bearing's inside diameter and the camshaft journals are out of specification, consider oversize bearings and turning the camshaft to a standard undersized diameter. Otherwise, new bearings may just barely bring the clearance back to specification. The

Removing the camshaft requires tremendous care to ensure that the camshaft bearings (if your engine has them), also called camshaft bushings, are not ruined in the process. Slowly ease out the camshaft, with one hand on the camshaft gear and one hand in the engine, guiding the camshaft journals through the bushings.

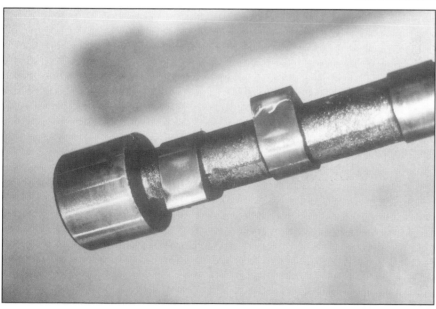

Here is a photo of camshaft lobes in good condition: no striations, no grooves, and a nice sharp profile at the tips. Rounded tips or any damage call for camshaft replacement.

MORE POWER!

BETTER BREATHING FOR BETTER PERFORMANCE

When making performance modifications to your engine, don't neglect the engine's breathing system. For the engine bore to fill completely with the fuel-air mixture, every part of the engine involved with delivering the fuel-air mixture must be leak-free and smooth, and it must remain open during every available moment of the intake stroke. Nothing in the intake system is excepted here. From the carburetor and manifold all the way to the camshaft and the valves, everything must operate perfectly.

Because of the low rpm range in antique tractor engines, some of the common retrofits made to cars, such as camshafts that overlap valve timing, actually make very little difference in antique tractor engines. However, many common enhancements made to cars do make sense for tractors. For example, porting and polishing is a good idea. Porting and polishing all intake passages and exhaust passages is a big help in reducing horsepower-robbing turbulence in air and exhaust passageways. Strong valve springs and good clean valve seats and faces are another important item. Camshafts with worn lobes are common in antique tractor engines, so be sure to replace your camshaft. Flathead engines often accumulate carbon in the combustion chamber. According to the Nebraska Test Labs, removing the head and brushing out the carbon every so often will add 10 to 15 percent more horsepower in an engine that has just a minor carbon buildup.

Rebuild or replace your carburetor and don't forget the exhaust! Stock carburetors for antique tractors, because of their simple updraft design, do not create air flow restriction problems. However, they are notoriously poor at delivering accurately metered fuel to the air mixture at all rpm in all weather conditions. A performance carburetor shop can help you here. Modern mufflers are designed to reduce noise, even if it means robbing a few horsepower. Use straight pipes in competitive situations, but your hearing is too important to use straight pipes in the field for any length of time.

An engine that breathes will run longer and harder than one that doesn't. Be sure your valve and air intake system is in top shape for added horsepower and torque.

clearance may fall out of specification after just a few hundred hours of operation.

To remove the camshaft, you must access and remove the plates and housings that mount and position it. You will usually find these plates and housings directly behind the camshaft gear. You may also need to remove a second plate on the other side of the block. To remove the front plate, access the plate bolts through a hole in the camshaft gear. Leave the camshaft gear installed on the shaft for now. The camshaft gear is usually press-fit onto the camshaft and requires a hydraulic press to remove.

After loosening the mounting plate, if required, the camshaft can be very carefully pulled from the engine. Wear often creates sharp or rough edges on the camshaft lobes and journals, so you must be careful not to scratch or damage the camshaft bearings as you pull the camshaft.

After removal, inspect and assess the camshaft. If the camshaft gear has missing or damaged teeth, replace it. Likewise, the camshaft must be replaced if there's any damage to the helical gearing used to drive auxiliary sys-

When installing the camshaft, coat each journal liberally with assembly lube. Coat each journal right before it passes through a bushing. Then right before final placement, leave a thick ring of the lube all the way around the leading edge of the journal. Then slide the camshaft in the rest of the way; this smears the lube across the entire journal. Finally, carefully spin the camshaft to distribute the lube.

To lap valves, coat the valve face with lapping compound, which contains fine abrasives. Then, attach the suction cup of a valve-lapping tool to the head of the valve.

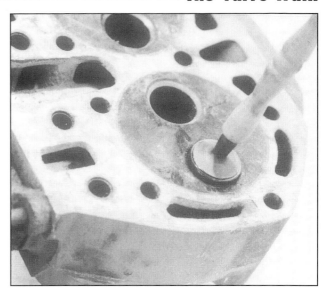

Place the valve in the valve guide (without any of the springs, etc., installed). Use the valve lapping tool to spin the valve rapidly back and forth. This is much like the movement you would use to warm your hands on a cold day. The valve is properly lapped when the face and seat show matched polished areas that are smooth and clean. This step is not a substitute for valve grinding and surfacing, and can only be used to clean up and polish valve faces and seats that are otherwise in good shape. Make sure all the valve lapping compound is removed before the head or engine is reassembled.

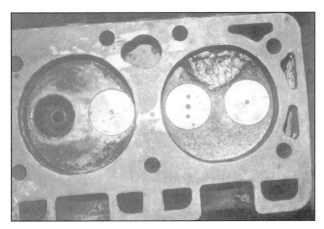

Second from left is an old valve that has two holes. Old-style valve-lapping tools used two prongs instead of a suction cup to engage the valve.

tems. Camshaft lobes should have a bright finish and be free of damage, excessive scratches, striations, or noticeable wear.

VALVE LAPPING

Lapping a valve is a great way to hone up rough, dirty valve faces and seats that need some cleanup, but not a regrind. If the valves are in bad shape, they need to be reground by a machinist and lapping them will not be necessary. To lap valves, you must have the head off the engine. If it's an overhead valve engine, lapping is best done with the head on a bench. In all engines, the valve guides must be in place.

As I mentioned before, each reused valve must be returned to its original position, so be sure you lap each valve into its proper seat. Start by placing a 3/16-inch bead of medium-grit valve lapping or valve grinding compound

along the face of the valve, right where the valve face mates to the valve seat. Then install the valve into its seat.

You lap the valve by rotating it back and forth using a valve lapping tool, which is nothing more than a suction cup on a stick. Older valves will often have marks or slots in them to accommodate older-style valve lapping tools, but these older tools will not be necessary—the newer suction cup style works fine. In rare circumstances, the embossing and lapping grooves on the valve head prevent the suction cup from gripping the valve. In this case, manufacture your own tool that fits the valve's groove or marks, or find a vintage tool that will work.

Continue lapping, constantly alternating between clockwise and counterclockwise. Stop occasionally to inspect your work and to replace old valve lapping compound with new compound. You are done when there is a smooth, clean, bright stripe ringing the valve face and the valve seat. If I must lap for more than five minutes and

TIP

For an accurate valve-spring testing tool, place a very accurate scale on the table of a shop press. Then, compress the spring with the arbor of the press while measuring the spring height with a small steel rule.

■■TIP C

When lapping valves, water-based valve grinding compound is best and should be used liberally. A wet rag is all that is needed to remove all traces of grit.

more than three applications of valve lapping compound, I usually back up and reexamine the valves to see if regrinding is necessary. Lapping is finishing work that is meant to remove surface blemishes, very light pitting, and carbon deposits. It's not a substitute for valve grinding.

Clean up very thoroughly after lapping, and make sure you remove all traces of grit, especially from the guides. Make one last inspection of every valve and valve seat and make sure the faces and seats are finished to your satisfaction.

CAMSHAFT INSTALLATION

If you removed the camshaft gear, now is the time to reinstall it. Be sure to line the gear up with the indexing marks provided or with the marks you were directed to make at the beginning of the chapter. Press the gear onto the shaft, all the way against the shoulder. Don't use the retaining nut to drive the gear onto the shaft, since this may strip or damage the threads at the end of the camshaft. After the gear is in place, tighten the nut and set the locking tab, pin, or wire if one was used originally.

Camshaft and Bearings

The next step in valve train assembly is to install the camshaft bushings or bearings. Bushings can be pressed into place with a gentle, even force from a shop press, or with gentle blows from a well-mated shop-made driver and light mallet. *Be sure to line up any oil holes in the bushings with the oil holes in the block!* Install the camshaft the reverse of removal, being very careful to slip the camshaft through any bushings without damaging them. If your tractor's engine uses ball or roller bearings instead of bushings, place the camshaft in the crankcase, then mount the rear camshaft bearing to the bearing housing and install the housing. The front bearing and bearing housing may control the gear lash between the crankshaft gear and the camshaft gear, so installing the front bearing can wait until assembly of the crankshaft and crankshaft gear.

If the camshaft front bearing housing or thrust plate does not control the gear lash, then continue installing the camshaft. If your camshaft's end play is controlled through springs and spacers, no additional work is required at this point. If bearing housings or thrust plates control the end play, then you will need to check and adjust end play next. As you install the camshaft, remember to line up the index marks on the camshaft and crankshaft gears.

Adjusting Camshaft End Play

If the camshaft end play is adjusted with shims and gaskets, assemble the housings or plates using the same shims that came from disassembly and new gaskets if needed. (New gaskets must be of the same thickness as the original, as the gasket was probably acting as a shim.) After assembly, push the camshaft in as far as it will go, mount a dial caliper to the engine block, and position the caliper over the front tip of the camshaft. Without forcing it, use a small lever between the crankcase and the camshaft gear to move the camshaft out as far as it will go. The caliper will now read the end play, which should be within specification. If the measurement is too large or too small, add or delete shims or switch to a thicker or thinner gasket. You should find a combination that brings everything within specification.

Gear Lash

After adjusting the end play, you may need to adjust the gear lash between the camshaft gear and the crankshaft gear, or between the camshaft and driven components, such as governor gears. This is unusual, and it shouldn't worry you if your service manual doesn't cover this adjustment. In fact, bushings and thrust plates are not adjustable. Only camshafts with tapered or ball bearings are normally adjustable in this way. To make this adjustment, rotate or slide a bearing housing. This moves the camshaft to bring gear lash within specification.

Unfortunately, specifications are hardly ever provided, and you will have to do this by sight. A properly meshed set of gears will be as close as possible while maintaining enough distance for the gear teeth to clear each other properly. To mesh gears without specifications, look at the gears closely. Pick one gear tooth and follow its mating against the opposite gear. If the gears are too close, the tooth you are following will touch a tooth on the opposite gear, and the following tooth on the opposite gear will touch the back side of the tooth you are following. This binds the tooth you are following, and the gear lash is too close. If the gears are helically cut, the same holds true, but the job requires a little more concentration and mental gymnastics to visualize. After adjustment, there should be little space or "slop" between the gear teeth, but the gears should still turn each other freely without any "chatter" or abnormal background noise.

■■TIP C

When removing and installing the camshaft, be extra careful not to damage bushings.

VALVE TRAIN INSTALLATION

After the camshaft has been installed and adjusted, the rest of the valve train can be installed. The installation is the reverse of removal, with no special procedures except lapping, which we covered previously. Install the tappets, then place the valves in the head or block. Next, install the spring, backing plates, and keepers. On overhead valve engines, the push rods and rocker arm assembly can be installed next, but only after you have tightened and properly torqued the cylinder head.

INITIAL VALVE TRAIN ADJUSTMENTS

Next, you need to make the initial valve lash adjustment. Valve lash is the distance between the valve stem and the rocker arm (in overhead valve engines) or the tappet (in flathead engines). If your service manual specifies adjusting valve lash when the engine is cold, you are in luck. While the engine is being rebuilt, it is as cold as it is going to get. Simply take the measurement, set the lash, and you are done. If your manual specifies adjusting valve lash when the engine is hot, then you need to add 10 to 20 percent to that dimension to account for expansion, since we will be setting the initial valve lash while the engine is cold. Either way, hot or cold, the initial valve lash has to be set during assembly.

Start with your Number 1 cylinder set at top dead center in its compression stroke. This will leave both valves for that cylinder closed, and the gap between the valve stem and tappet or rocker at its largest. Loosen the locking nut at the striker of the tappet or rocker, then turn the adjusting screw or bolt in or out to bring the lash to the correct dimension. When the correct lash is obtained, hold the adjusting screw or bolt still while you turn the locking nut, or the adjuster will turn. Of course, it helps to have a third hand while doing it, but the concept is simple.

OIL DISTRIBUTION

While assembling the valve train, inspect all the oil passages and holes, drain holes, push rod passages, and oil galleys in the rocker arms assembly to make sure they are not plugged or excessively dirty. Of particular importance are the oil passages to the valve cavity in flathead engines, and the main oil passage to the rocker arm assembly in overhead valve engines. In particular, there is often a sleeve or oil line between the cylinder head and the rocker arm. On some engines this sleeve or line may be easy to pinch or obstruct when installing the rocker arm assembly. While most engines let oil from the overhead valve area drain down the push rod cavities, some engine designs have a separate sump and drain that need to be properly oriented during assembly. For example, the F-20 engine photographed for this book has a separate drain and a small metal chute that diverts oil return. This chute just lies in place and is easy to dislodge from the block or forget about during rebuilding.

PUSH ROD SLEEVES

Most push rods pass through cavities in the head and block that are separate from the coolant cavities. However, some engines, such as John Deere horizontal engines, have push rods that pass through sleeves, much like cylinder sleeves, which pass through the coolant cavity. Removal of these sleeves is sometimes required, especially if the sleeves leaked or if the head or block needed machine work. Removed sleeves can be pressed back into place by a shop press or by driving them in carefully with a mallet and brass drift or wood block. Remember to coat the outside ends of the sleeves with thread sealant or high-temperature gasket sealant before installation. This will help prevent coolant leaks.

One of the most enjoyable things about working with older tractors is seeing the wide variety of designs and technologies used to gain a competitive advantage in the marketplace. Valve trains were no different; designs evolved and changed as manufacturers struggled to make their engine more reliable and efficient. While there are many differences between valve train designs, the differences are superficial, and none were fundamentally different from the others. All required valve faces and seats that were in good condition, guides and stems that didn't leak oil, springs and tappets and rockers arms to open and close the valves, and a camshaft to keep the valves in time with the engine. Like all mechanical designs, valve trains have their share of bearings and bushings, adjustments and assessments. Restoring a valve train is not difficult, but it requires careful and thorough work. Take your time, stay organized, and don't try to use parts that are questionable in specification or quality, and you will have great success restoring your valve train.

TIP

> Due to the cost and scarcity of replacement camshafts, most restorers ignore cam lobe wear as a reason for replacement, as long as the wear is minimal enough to be compensated for by valve lash adjustments. Using worn camshafts does slightly alter engine aspiration, but performance degradation would only occur in extremely worn camshafts. If a replacement camshaft is available for a reasonable price, that is still the best alternative.

ENGINE BORES

When most people think of rebuilding an engine, they think of new pistons and refurbished bores. Either the engine was "stuck"(pistons and rings rusted to the cylinder walls), or the bores and rings were so worn that the engine lacked power and burned oil excessively. Whatever your reason for rebuilding, do the job thoroughly and completely.

By now you have a bare engine block, but it still has an unworn ridge at the top of the cylinder walls. If your engine's pistons have to be removed from the top, you can't remove the pistons or connecting rod yet, since the ridge will prevent this. If your engine's pistons can be removed from the bottom, remove the pistons and connecting rods now.

If you are just refurbishing the engine, or have torn into the engine to address a specific problem with the bore and piston (poor oil control, engine knock, etc.), the engine is probably still mounted to the tractor, with the crankshaft in place. If you are completely restoring the engine, you probably have removed the block from the tractor and removed most of the other components, such as the crankshaft. If you are going to leave the crankshaft in place, you should completely cover the crankshaft journal bearing areas under each bore before beginning any bore refurbishing. Likewise, make sure the crankshaft main bearings are waterproofed as well. These precautions will ensure that solvents, tailings, and metal fragments don't find their way onto these critical areas or oil galleys. I have had luck

Restoration of the engine bores is what people think of when they hear engine "restoration." Lined up on a worktable are three of the four sleeves from a Farmall F-20.

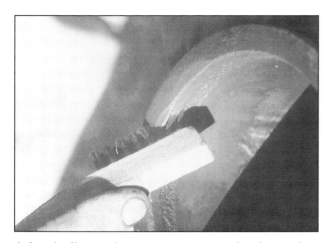

The first order of business is bore inspection. Your engine may have sleeves, as shown here, directly cut bores, or dry sleeves. The first question is whether they are in good enough shape to hone and reuse, or if they need replacement or reboring. This sleeve is showing serious rust markings that at first glance would indicate sleeve replacement. Further study shows that the rust markings are above the uppermost limit of piston ring travel. This means the sleeve, if no other problems are found, could be reused if money is tight. New sleeves, however, would be better.

wrapping things up tightly and completely with a long strip of plastic that is then wrapped in duct tape. Depending on the block, the main bearings seem to be a little tougher to guard, but they can be protected with a little tape and some plastic.

BORE INSPECTION

Whatever level of rebuild you're doing, you should do a thorough assessment of the engine bores. Whether your engine is sleeved or bored (bores cut directly into the block), you first need to clean and measure the bores so you can decide how to proceed. First, assess the condition of the bores. Are the bores heavily rusted? Was the engine stuck, leaving marks or rings of rust on the bore walls? Are there any gouges or other surface defects on the wall? When looking at the underside of the engine, is there any evidence of coolant leaks? If you see any of these things, then you will need to do some additional work to the bores before they are ready to accept pistons.

Here are some typical defects and problems a visual inspection will reveal, and their consequences:

Rings and piston stuck to cylinder wall: This may only be a slight problem that can be overcome by refurbishing the bores. While galling and rust cause the engine to stick, this corrosive material may be slight, and boring or sleeve replacement may not be necessary.

Rust in the bores: If the cylinder walls are significantly rusted or pitted, then you should overbore or sleeve the engine.

Surface defects: Any gouges, heavy scratches, cracks, bowing, or other structural problems are cause for overboring or sleeve replacement. Here is a simple test: Scratch

the defects with your fingernail. Any defect you cannot catch with a fingernail is OK, but anything that catches a fingernail will need to be removed through machine work or new sleeves.

Coolant leaks: If there's evidence of coolant leaks from around the outside of the bottom of the sleeves, the sleeve O-rings are bad and need to be replaced. The sleeve can be reused if it is in good condition.

CYLINDER MEASUREMENTS

Before doing any other work to the cylinders, you need to measure them. You'll need one of two tools; the first is a bore gauge and the second is a set of inside micrometers. Bore gauges are my favorite and I recommend them. The gauge I use is a small sled-like device that has a movable extension on one end and a base on the other end. These actuate a small dial caliper that records a distance, and it records variations in the cylinder's diameter. It is this ability to easily record variations that makes the bore gauge preferable.

Inside micrometers measure the bore much like the more common outside micrometers. They have a small thimble that turns, and on the thimble axle there is a vernier scale from which you take your reading. Unfortunately, both inside micrometers and bore gauges are expensive. The least expensive set that is acceptable in quality and accuracy will run nearly $200 (1999 U.S.). Therefore most restorers ask a friend with a gauge or micrometer to come and take readings, or they take the block down to a machine shop and for a reasonable fee have measurements taken there.

At the top of every cylinder is a small unworn area known as a "ridge." You must measure this ridge *before* you ream the ridge of the cylinders or sleeves. The ridge is the only spot in the cylinder that will give you an accurate prewear diameter measurement. To measure this ridge, first clean it very thoroughly, using a wire brush to remove stubborn carbon. Then measure the inside diameter of the ridge. Using a standard hand caliper, take several measurements about 45 degrees from each other. Repeat this for all cylinders, being sure to take notes. These ridge measurements should be nearly identical, but will vary about .001 or .002 inch around true bore diameter.

When averaged, this large sample of measurements (eight times the number of sleeves or bores) should tell you

TIP

Accurate measurements are important during cylinder restoration. Having an experienced friend help assess the bores is a good idea if you are unsure of your abilities.

1 Measuring cylinder bores is critical for determining if sleeves or bores are useable. Before ridge reaming, the unworn portion of the bore (the unworn ridge found at the top) must be measured. Measure the diameter using a standard dial caliper, then lock the caliper, using the caliper's locking nut; you'll need this dimension soon. Now skip ahead, ream the ridge, and remove the pistons.

2 To measure the bore, you must first "zero" the bore gauge. To do this, set up the bore gauge and its extensions so the bore gauge, at rest, is slightly longer than the distance between the caliper arms. Push the bore gauge extension arm in a little way, place the bore gauge between the caliper arms, and set the gauge's dial to zero. The bore gauge and its dial are now set so the bore gauge, when placed in the bore, will read zero if the cylinder diameter is exactly identical to the unworn diameter measured at the ridge. Since the bore is worn, the bore gauge will read slightly more than zero when the bore gauge is in the cylinder.

Next, set up the bore gauge using the photos here as a guide. The process involves installing extensions on the gauge until the gauge very closely approximates the measurement found at the ridge. Then adjust a set of calipers to the exact dimension found at the cylinder ridge. In our example, we would set the caliper to 5.020 inches. Then compress the bore gauge extension and place the bore gauge between the arms of the caliper. Turn the bore gauge dial face so it reads zero. Now the bore gauge dial face is set to the true unworn diameter of the cylinder. Then place the bore gauge at various depths of the cylinder and spin it in the cylinder. At the very least, you should take the measurement of the bore approximately a quarter-inch below the ridge, and then about halfway down the cylinder wall. The bore gauge will read exactly how much the cylinder is worn, and will also give you a reading as to the variation of diameter (engines cylinders don't wear evenly; they wear in an elliptical pattern). The diameter of the worn areas and the variation are the two specifications we are looking for. Be sure to record your notes from this procedure. Compare your measurements against the specifications in the manual, remembering that the specification that limits the variation in diameter is as important as over-

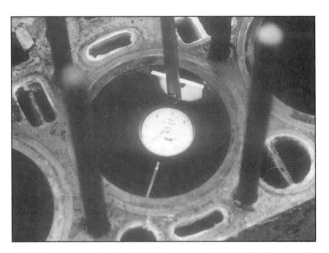

3 The bore gauge, when placed in the bore, now reads .015 inch. That means the bore is worn to a diameter that is .015 inch larger than original. Most antique tractor engine service manuals require sleeve replacement or reboring if the bore is worn more than .006 to .010 inch. This sleeve is a candidate for replacement.

what the bore cylinder was at the factory or at the last rebuild. For example, let's say your diameter readings all hover around 5.020 inches. Let's also assume that when the tractor was new, the bores were 5.000 inches. That means that in the past the engine was rebuilt, and the sleeves or bores were "overbored" by .020 inch. This is common, and you might see overbore diameters of up to .120 inch (for a total of 5.120 inches for our example).

Original factory sleeves may be safely overbored up to .020 inch, so you may see overbore diameters with your sleeved engine. Replacement "power-sleeves" may have larger-bore diameters than the original sleeves. With some models of tractors, such as the Farmall A, finding these thinner-walled, larger-diameter sleeves is common.

TIP

If you are not restoring the crankshaft, and don't intend to remove it during restoration, make sure it is completely sealed against the cleaners, lubricates, solvents, and metal particles generated during cylinder restoration.

1 Use a ridge reamer to remove the unworn ridge at the top of the bore. This device centers itself in the bore, and uses a knife to scrape away the unworn portion, leaving the top of the bore flush with the rest of the bore. Here the ridge reamer is properly positioned in a sleeve.

2 To prevent the reamer from chattering, and to help make your job easier, keep the ridge coated with oil during reaming.

3 The reamer is turned in the bore with a wrench; the knife can be adjusted during the process.

4 After the ridge is cut away, you will be rewarded with a gleaming, smooth band where the ridge used to be.

all wear. If your engine cylinders are under the acceptable limits of wear, but the variation in diameters is excessive, then you must still refurbish the bores by replacing the sleeves or boring the cylinders or sleeves.

RIDGE REAMING

Even if the cylinders must be bored or the sleeves replaced, ridge reaming is still necessary. This is a mandatory first step before honing, and is done with a ridge reamer. Ridge reamers are not horribly expensive and you should find a nice unit for affordable money. However, this is one case where a buying a used tool is not recommended, as the knives dull pretty quickly, and a used unit may have dull

knives that do a poor and frustrating job. There are several designs, but the primary idea behind all of them is to center the tool exactly inline with the cylinder so hardened knives on the side of the tool can scrape the ridge away as you turn it. Apply lots of oil to the cutting knife. If the tool turns in the cylinder along with the knife, then oil the cylinder walls too.

BORE RESTORATION
Pulling Sleeves

Pulling the sleeves out of your engine isn't hard—if you have the right tool. Turning your block upside down and beating the sleeves out with a sledge and a block of wood

1 To pull wet sleeves you will need a sleeve puller, shown here installed on a block. Dry sleeves cannot typically be removed with a sleeve puller. If your dry sleeves are thin and made of steel, then they can be collapsed and crushed using punches and drifts, and removed. If they aren't the thin steel-type sleeves, the sleeve will require professional removal.

3 Since a tremendous quantity of rust and scale can usually be found on the sleeve, pulling these sleeves can require tremendous force. Penetrating oil, patience, and periodic tightening will eventually break stubborn sleeves loose and begin their journey upward.

2 The wrench is in place and sleeve pulling started. By turning the nut, the distance between the top of the anchor bar and the bottom plate at the bottom of the sleeve is shortened, drawing the sleeve upward.

4 This shows the extensive coating of rust and scale found on the outside of the sleeves. These sleeves will have to be sandblasted to be cleaned up properly.

just isn't an option unless you enjoy frustrating procedures. Fortunately, sleeve pullers aren't hard to make, nor are they terribly expensive. In addition, you can rent one or borrow one from a friend with a well-stocked tool cabinet.

A sleeve puller consists of three primary parts: a bridge, a threaded rod, and a bottom plate. The bottom plate is a thick, stout piece of steel that sits squarely on the bottom of the sleeve. The tool usually comes with a selection of steel plates that match the outside diameters of various sleeves. These plates are held onto the bottom of the threaded rod by a nut and a large washer. The bridge is nothing more than a U-shaped or pyramid-shaped piece of cast steel or cast iron that sits directly on the top of the cylinder block. The rod and bottom plate are then installed from the bottom of the sleeve and up through a hole in the bridge. A nut at the top of the rod is threaded on, holding everything in place. The bridge has a thick bearing washer to accept the stress load from the top nut.

The procedure from there is straightforward. First, you double-check the tool installation, making sure the bottom plate centers perfectly on the bottom of the cylinder and the bridge sits squarely and safely on the cylinder block. Then you simply tighten the top nut. This shortens the distance between the bottom plate and the bridge, pulling the sleeve upward. I recommend tightening slowly, allowing the cylinder time to move in response to the pulling action. Remember, there is 50-plus years of scale and rust on the outside surfaces of the sleeves, and this material is being scraped off by the top of the block as you pull the sleeve upward. For that reason alone, the sleeve seldom pulls easily until most of it is free from the block.

The force exerted on the sleeve and the tool are tremendous. Wear eye protection in case the tool shatters (not likely unless your tool is of poor quality and includes cast parts). Never buy or make sleeve pullers that don't have hardened nuts and a threaded rod. You will strip the threads on both if they are not hardened. Last but not least, be patient. Take your time. The sleeve will break loose if you continue to apply pressure. The hardest part is getting the sleeve to start moving. Simply apply lots of penetrating oil to the bottom and top of the sleeve, and tighten half a turn every five minutes or so. Eventually the sleeve will begin to move, and from there finishing the job is easy.

Crushing Sleeves

Some engines, such as those in early Ford N series tractors, use dry sleeves that are not pulled in the traditional manner. If inspection indicates replacement, then the sleeve is simply split using a special tool called a sleeve crusher. This tool wedges between the block and the sleeve, deforming and splitting the sleeve inward away from the cylinder wall. Once split, the sleeves can be easily removed. I have never seen this tool for sale, but a metal fabricator can easily reproduce one for you. Be sure to have the fabricator harden the tool after shaping. Fireball Heat Treating, mentioned in the appendices of this book, can harden the tool if the local fabricator is unable to.

Boring Cylinders

If your engine has nonsleeved cylinder bores, and if your inspections indicate that they need to be bored, you have

Sleeve pullers are no place to cut corners on quality. Be sure to buy a nice-quality puller, and you will not be disappointed.

MORE POWER!

BORE IT OUT

There is no substitute for displacement when greater power is needed. To achieve greater displacement, one of the things you can do is increase the bore of the engine. This increased bore will increase the compression ratio, another desirable attribute for your engine.

When increasing the bore of antique tractor engines, there are two things you can do. If your engine has wet sleeves, you can use thinner wall sleeves. Typically, bore can only be increased on the order of .060 inch with sleeves. The sleeves will fail if the wall thickness becomes too thin. A common way to increase the bore of some of these wet sleeve engines is to use replacement sleeves for either a newer, more powerful version of the engine, such as using Farmall Super A sleeves in a Farmall A. Another approach is to use the block, sleeves, and pistons from a similar, but slightly larger, engine.

Much of the same applies for dry sleeve engines. You can bore dry sleeves thinner than you can wet sleeves, or you can do away with the sleeves and try to find pistons that will ride directly in the bore the sleeves used. This typically requires custom-made pistons.

If your engine uses a bored block, the sky is the limit. The only limit to bore size is the structural integrity of the side walls and available pistons. The machinist doing the boring can advise you. Replacement pistons are often available up to .120 inch oversize. Past that, you often must find pistons from another application or have a set of pistons custom made.

---

to take the block to a qualified machinist. There are no home-remedy tools for this step. *Before* you bore your engine though, you must first determine if pistons are available. There is no sense boring your engine .040 inch over diameter if there are no .040-inch pistons available. Now is the time to buy pistons and rings. Then, after you have bought them, you know exactly how wide to bore the cylinders. You should send the block to the machinist along with the pistons, and he'll bore the block to fit the pistons. You'll still need to hone the bores, though, and you'll need to do a few other things such as checking the fit of the pistons. We'll discuss that later in the book.

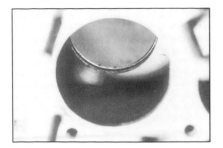

1 If your engine has wet sleeves, remove the old O-ring from the O-ring groove found at the bottom of the block. (This photograph is taken through the top of the block.) Clean the groove thoroughly, then turn your attention to the sleeve.

2 Any nicks or surface irregularities where the sleeve seats against the O-ring should be lightly filed smooth.

3 Finally, sandblast all the rust and scale from the outside of the sleeve. This will improve heat transfer between the sleeve and the coolant that surrounds it.

Custom Dry Sleeving

What do you do if the bore condition is so poor that even the largest possible overbore won't remove the imperfections? The answer is simple, but a little on the costly side: Have a machinist fit custom dry sleeves to your bores. This solution works well and will save your engine block from the scrap heap.

First the machinist machines the bores to a diameter that will accept these custom sleeves. This diameter will be a little snug, and the tight fit helps the sleeves stay in place after they're pressed in place. The machinist will leave a small ridge at the bottom of the bore to keep the sleeves from moving downward, while the head and head gasket will keep them from moving upward. While custom sleeving may be more expensive than finding a replacement block, it will keep the tractor original. It is often the only alternative, since good used blocks for certain tractor models are difficult to find.

Installing Wet Sleeves

Installing sleeves is much easier than removing them. The first step is to replace the O-rings at the bottom of the crankcase. Even if you end up reusing the same sleeves, new O-rings are a must. The O-rings are usually in surprisingly good shape, but occasionally they are cemented in place by crud, and fragile with old age. Taking the time to remove at least one ring intact is very helpful when finding replacements. Often the parts or salvage yard dealer that provided your new sleeve set will provide the O-rings too. Fortunately, the O-rings of yesteryear are no different than the O-rings of today, so any gasket and seal supplier or plumbing contractor can help you obtain the proper set.

To install new O-rings, you first need to clean out the machined grooves at the bottom of the block where the O-ring resides. A wire brush, a little soap and water, and you should be good to go. Stubborn rust and scale can be

TIP

Dish soap, sparingly but completely applied, makes the perfect and safe lubricant for installing sleeve O-rings.

1 A leak-free sleeve requires careful installation. This view is from the bottom of the block, showing the rubber O-ring in place near the groove it seats in.

2 Coat the O-ring with a small quantity of dish soap and begin working it into the groove. Don't use oil or Vaseline, as these petroleum lubricants may break down and soften some types of O-rings, especially NOS O-rings.

3 Carefully slip the O-ring into the groove. Remember, the groove may have sharp edges, so be careful not to damage the O-ring.

4 Next, apply a small bead of dish soap on the outside of the sleeve, right below where the O-ring seats against the sleeve.

5 Push the sleeves into the bores. The sleeves should press in most of the way by hand, but the last few inches may require some persuasion. Here, a sledge hammer and block of wood do the job.

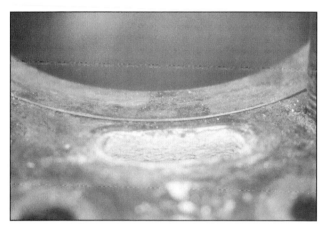

6 Wet sleeves are installed so the sleeve is left a few thousandths of an inch above the deck of the block. Your service manual should give the exact measurement.

7 Use a feeler gauge laid on the block deck next to the sleeve to measure how far the sleeve protrudes from the block.

removed with standard rust and scale removers and some more scrubbing with a wire brush. After you have gotten the O-ring grooves as clean as possible, install the rings with a small amount of ordinary household dish soap. The soap will help the rings slide completely into place. Some folks use Vaseline for this job, but Vaseline is petroleum-based and contains solvents that will soften and weaken the rings over time. While this probably isn't much of a risk with newer O-rings, I'd rather not take the chance. Be sure

While dry sleeves require professional removal, they can be installed with a normal affordable shop press. Dry sleeves usually seat against a recess in the top of the block. Before installing the sleeve, coat the engine bore with light oil, such as WD-40, wipe dry, and then clean the recess. Here a cheap screwdriver ground down to a handy profile works great.

Then, using a shop press and blocks of wood to protect the sleeve, press the sleeve down into the engine bore. If the sleeve and piston came as a set, mark each piston with its sleeve number, as each piston must remain with the sleeve it came with.

Dry sleeves are installed so the top of the sleeve is flush with the top of the block. If the block was decked and a significant amount of material was removed, dry sleeves may protrude from the top of the block. If that is the case, you must hand file the tops of the sleeves back down until they are flush with the top of the block.

TIP

Even if you are not replacing your sleeves, pulling the sleeves and replacing the O-rings is a good idea. Old O-rings are usually in poor shape.

to double-check your work and be sure the O-rings are completely in place, or they may be damaged when the sleeve is installed.

Now that you have the O-rings in place, you can install the sleeves. Again, a little liquid soap on the sleeves (just around the lower quarter) will help minimize the chance of O-ring damage. The sleeves will slide in with hand pressure, except for the last two or three inches. After you have driven them in by hand as far as you can, make sure the O-rings are still undamaged and the sleeves haven't pinched or moved any of them. Now you simply drive the sleeve in the rest of the way with a maul and a block of wood. How far is ". . . the rest of the way," you ask? The top of the sleeve must protrude above the top surface of the block by a few thousandths of an inch. Your service manual may specify, but in the absence of any guidance there, I would use .002 inch.

Congratulations! You have now removed and installed a set of sleeves. Not too hard, and fully satisfying in my opinion. We still have some more work to do to the bores before we are finished though, so read on. But first, just look over your sleeve installation and make sure all of the sleeves stand above the block the prescribed amount, and make sure the O-rings are all sitting properly, snug against the sleeve. Properly installed O-rings will be hard to see in the very slight gap between the sleeve and the block. A bright light will illuminate any problems; you should be able to tell if the sleeves took out a chunk of the O-ring, or if any part of the O-ring has been pinched and partially pushed out of its groove.

Honing the Bores

At this point, you either have your sleeves replaced, your sleeves bored, your cylinders bored, or even a set of custom sleeves installed into your engine's cylinders. In any case, you have clean, smooth, blemish-free surfaces for your pistons to ride in. Now is the time to hone those bores and make them ready for pistons and rings. In a nutshell, honing intentionally and purposefully damages those nice pretty surfaces you just paid a lot of money for! Why would we do that? Simply put, a slightly etched surface does a better job of holding oil and provides a more uniform surface for the compression rings to seal against. A perfectly smooth cylinder wall will not retain oil as well and will not let the compression rings seat properly.

The tools of the trade include a cylinder hone (medium grit), a portable drill, and copious amounts of a honing solu-

tion made from one part diesel fuel mixed with one part kerosene. This solution provides lubrication and flushes the metal particles away from the bore. To hone the bores, you move the cylinder hone up and down in the cylinder while the drill turns the hone. A honing job that removes elliptical wear, creates the necessary honing pattern, and limits the amount of artificial wear created during honing requires a nice tool. Don't cut corners by buying a bargain-basement honing tool.

The less-expensive tools require no setup before honing, but the better-quality honing tools do. These tools have an adjustable collar that allows you to adjust the amount of spring tension, which dictates how much pressure the honing stones apply to the cylinder walls. In essence, you want to set spring tension so the stones cut into the metal quickly (you don't want to be doing this all day), but you don't want so much tension that the stones load up with metal particles before the honing solution (that diesel fuel/kerosene mix) can flush them away.

To test your spring tension setup, insert the cylinder hone into the bore and spin it at very low speed for just a few revolutions. Your wrist and hand should not feel an undue amount of torque from the drill, nor should the etching left behind be excessively deep from just a few revolutions. By the same token, spring tension should be enough to make a distinct, discernible pattern in those few revolutions. If in doubt, set the tension up a little on the high side and use liberal quantities of the honing solution to prevent the stones from loading up with metal particles.

Honing a cylinder wall is a bit of an art, and it takes practice to become proficient. Ideally, the drill's rpm and the speed at which you move the hone up and down should be matched so the resulting spiral patterns are oriented at about 30 degrees to each other. In other words, the spirals you creating going upward will be 30 degrees "out of phase" with the spirals you create going downward. Of course the exact angle isn't important (32 degrees isn't going to hurt anything) and I certainly hope you don't try to measure this. But a 30-degree angle is the reference to strive for.

This is hard to describe in words, so look over the honing pictures included here to get an idea. If you move the hone up and down too quickly while running the drill too slowly, the spirals will be too steep, resulting in too large an angle between the upward and downward spirals (maybe 60 or 75 degrees). If you run the drill too fast, or move the

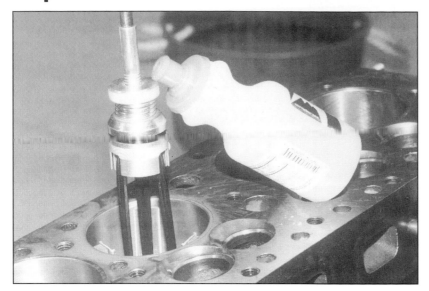

A few words on the art and science of honing. First, make a 50/50 mixture of diesel fuel and kerosene. This is a lubricant and coolant for the honing stones. I like to use a sports drink bottle as an applicator of this mixture. Never store your solution in this bottle permanently for obvious safety reasons.

A wet sleeve can be honed before installation, by using a piece of wood with a properly sized hole to hold the sleeve. Move the hone up and down in the bore as you go, and keep the hone lubricated with the diesel/kerosene mix. This also flushes metal particles away from the hone.

After honing, you will have a nice hatchmark pattern in the sleeve or bore that looks like this. The honing spirals should be offset approximately 30 degrees. The vertical marks you see here are not scratches in the bore, but are bits of residue left in the honing fluid during cylinder hone removal.

TIP

Honing is an art as well as a science, and it requires a little practice. Scrap engines found at junkyards and small engine shops make for great practice engines while you learn.

hone too slowly up and down, then the angle between the spirals will be too small, about 20 degrees or less. The latter is the most common mistake. I prefer to run the drill slowly and move accordingly. It takes longer, but I don't feel like the pump man at an old-fashioned fire-fighting crew either, and my shoulders and upper arms thank me. I recommend practicing with a junk engine block from a lawnmower shop to get the feel for it before you tackle one of your own bores.

Now, to bring the degree of difficulty up a notch or two, you must also apply a lot of honing solution to lubricate the hone and to keep it from loading up with metal particles by flushing the particles from the bore. Even lightweight oils are too thick for this job. Penetrating fluids work, but are expensive for the amount needed, and some are flammable enough to rule out. Once started, you have to hone while applying the lubricant. This is where a second set of hands really helps out. Professionals can maintain a good cutting pattern with one hand while applying oil with the other, but most of us weekend mechanics won't be able to do that. While you certainly can alternate honing and lubing, I find it easier to maintain a consistent cutting pattern while a helper applies the lubricant.

THE ENGINE BLOCK

Your tractor's engine block is a static hunk of metal with no moving parts. (From here on out, we'll use the term "engine block," though I refer to both the block and the crankcase if your engine has both.) At first glance, it doesn't look like it would need much in the way of restoration. While the amount and difficulty of the work doesn't hold a candle to, say, crankshaft restoration, there are several things that need to be done. The engine block is the foundation for the entire engine, so it has to be carefully inspected and cleaned. In addition to block cleaning, we need to cover several other procedures. These include machining (such as the mating surfaces between the block and the cylinder head), inspecting for cracks and structural defects, replacing freeze plugs, and restoring oil pressure relief valves. We'll cover these steps one by one, and at the end, you'll have the foundation that your engine needs.

Where should you be at this juncture? The disassembly procedures of the first section of the book should have left you left with a nearly bare engine block. Most important, you should have inspected and measured your bores or sleeves and have a pretty good idea of what needs to be done there. Since a thorough cleaning requires removing all parts from the block, you should now pull the sleeves if you haven't done so already. Another reason for pulling the sleeves is that the caustic cleaning solution can weaken or ruin sleeve O-rings. In addition, sleeves must be removed before any machining of the block mating surfaces.

Most common engine blocks seem to have more than their fair share of studs: cylinder head studs, water pump studs, front cover studs, and more. One of the challenges of block reconditioning is removing these studs. It is especially difficult to remove studs near sources of heat and water, such as those for water pumps and exhaust manifolds.

If you decide to remove the studs, use a stud extractor. This tool is typically more successful in removing studs without damaging or ruining them. Not all studs have to

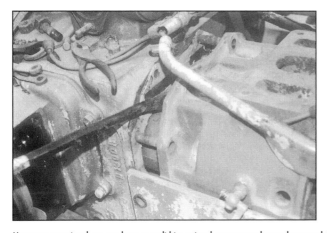 

Most tractor engines have one large monolithic casting that serves as the crankcase and the engine block. Properly, the block is the casting that houses the cylinders, and the crankcase is the casting the crankshaft rotates within. There are many models of antique tractors that have separate crankcase and block castings. John Deere horizontal two-cylinder tractors are a famous example, but many others, such as Minneapolis-Moline, employed separate castings. Here the engine block of a John Deere B is being separated from the crankcase.

be removed, though. For example, there is no reason to remove any small, unobtrusive studs associated with brackets or the front cover. Others, such as exhaust manifold studs, are often so difficult to remove, and the likelihood of stud damage is so high, that you should have a really good reason to remove them if they will not be in the way of machining or cleaning. Cylinder head studs should be removed and replaced. These studs have usually been tightened and retightened to the point where they can no longer provide the clamping force needed for adequate head gasket sealing.

BLOCK INSPECTION AND MEASUREMENT

Before anything else, you must inspect the block for any damage or structural problems that may cause problems down the road. A common problem that many encounter is a block that has cracks. Some of these cracks may seem earth shattering, but are actually not a problem. Others are a real problem and will require finding a replacement block. How do you tell which cracks present problems and which ones don't? It's difficult to summarize all the blocks, their common crack severity, and make a judgment from an author's chair. I will outline typical cracked block scenarios and the probable decision you will need to make about them. When in doubt, talk with a local machine shop or mechanic whose opinion you trust.

Cracks Between Cylinders—Sleeved Engines

If these cracks are small, hairline cracks in the top of the block running directly between cylinders, you are probably OK. Allis WC engines typically show this type of crack. They are notorious for cracking between the cylinders, but these cracks seldom cause a problem.

Cracks Between Cylinders—Nonsleeved Engines

These are almost always a problem, and require a new block. Small engine blocks seem prone to this, such as the Farmall Cub and Continental N62 engine used on Massey Harris Ponies and Allis Chalmers G.

Oil or Coolant Leaks

If an engine exhibits these symptoms before you begin rebuild, you need to inspect it very closely for cracks.

While earlier in the book I included a recipe for making your own caustic cleaning solution, engine blocks are grimy enough, large enough, and difficult enough to handle that professional caustic cleaning is recommended.

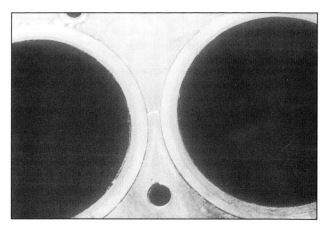

Searching for cracks or other casting defects and problems is the first order of business when restoring the block. Some cracks are serious problems, others are not. Here is a small crack between two cylinders in an Allis Chalmers WC engine. This crack is minimal; it did not leak before restoration, and it's well sealed by the head gasket. This block was reused without problems.

While there are other numerous possible causes for these symptoms, such as cracked cylinder heads, bad head gaskets, or leaky push rod tubes on John Deere horizontal engines, you should also suspect a cracked block.

Freeze Cracks

Early in these tractors' lives, it was common for owners to use plain water as a coolant, then water was drained each winter before cold weather set in. Occasionally this seasonal draining was forgotten, and blocks were broken by expanding ice as a result. This expanding ice usually created a crack on the outside of the engine, and it may also have created a separation crack, usually parallel to the crankshaft, in the top of the block.

If the crack is limited to the outside water jacket, some skilled welding can typically fix the block. If the crack radiated to the top of the block, then block replacement is always called for. When you see exterior freeze cracks, look closely for internal cracks that would represent mechanical problems.

Now is the time you would also very closely inspect other areas of the block. Every block is different, and where you look for additional structural defects will depend entirely on the model of the block and the individual block itself. Anywhere you see a casting defect, such as a bubble or "inclusion" (where slag or some other foreign material is included with the metal) is a good place to look. In addition, the pouring and casting of an engine block is a difficult procedure involving many variables, such as time, temperature, mold condition, and foundry operator. Therefore, individual blocks have their own characteristics and weaknesses that are not representative of the entire model of engine. There is no substitute for closely looking over each block. Some likely places to check are mounting

Making sure the surface of the block is flat and true requires laying a perfectly flat straightedge across the block and measuring any gaps between the straightedge and block. Lightly filing the block with a large flat file will clean up the surface in preparation for measurement, and it also helps reveal areas that may be a problem. The file will miss low places, creating a contrast between bright clean metal of high spots and the dull, dirty surface of low spots.

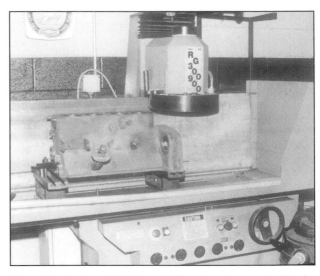

Using a mill to "true" up the block is required if your inspections reveal anything but a flat surface. Machining the head mating surface of the block is called "decking," and any automotive machine shop can perform this job.

flanges, bases and bosses for distributors and governors, and anyplace the block has suffered an impact, even if the impact didn't leave any discernible severe marks.

One of the handiest ways to find and detect cracks is a procedure using a dye-penetrant product. This and other crack-detection methods were covered in the cylinder head chapter.

If your block looks like a good candidate for a rebuild, then the next step is to make sure that it is square, true, and smooth on all the mating surfaces. The top of the block must be very flat to avoid coolant, oil, and even compression leaks. Compression leaks usually result in blown head gaskets, and the oil and coolant leaks create their set of problems, especially if the oil and coolant intermix. Testing the block for trueness is necessary.

Fortunately, this is very simple. To test the block's "flatness," or trueness, you simply find a perfect straightedge and lay it on several different spots and several different orientations on the top of the block. Ideally, there should be no dips or humps in the block that create gaps under the ruler. In reality, you will see a slight gap or two. The details for performing this test can be found in the cylinder head chapter, and the same procedures apply for the block. If your block has sleeves, the top of the sleeves will protrude ever so slightly above the top of the block. This will affect your readings if you don't make sure your straightedge misses them. Also, the area immediately around the head studs or bolts may be slightly deformed, and you should not let the straightedge cross a stud hole for that reason.

If the block is out of true, then you must have the top of the block machined. Any local automotive machine shop can help you, and the procedure isn't overly expensive or time consuming. Before you rush out and have this done, let's take a look at a couple of other things. We may find other machine work that needs to be done that the machinist can do all at once.

MANIFOLD MATING SURFACE

We're discussing the manifold mating surface here because flathead engines mount the manifold to the engine block. If you have an overhead valve engine, you can apply these same techniques to the manifold mating surface on the cylinder head.

The manifold mating surface of the engine block must be flat and true, and you test for trueness the same way you did in the last section. With this surface, precision isn't quite as important, and specific measurements and distances are not crucial. This is because manifold gaskets are more supple and conform to surface variations better than head gaskets. Simply using a business card for checking gaps is sufficient. Again, you are looking for gradual variations and no surface defects. If the surface doesn't pass the business card test, or if you see significant localized warps or "steps" in the surface, then the manifold mating surface must be machined back to true.

TIP

Some cracks found in the engine block may be harmless. Do not discard your block solely on the presence of cracks. An automotive machinist can help you determine if the cracks in your engine block are a problem.

This machine is nothing but a big dishwasher for engine parts. This is called a jet washer—one of two primary types of washers used by machine shops to clean blocks and heads.

BLOCK CLEANING

Cleaning the block is important, and these old engines usually have a tremendous buildup of sludge and grime from years of hard work and nondetergent oil. You can clean the block two different ways. Your first option is to clean the block by soaking it in a warm caustic solution. This is known as "hot-tanking" or "hot-dipping." This is the most thorough and complete way to clean your engine block. The second method, and the most common with antique tractor engine restorers, is to manually clean the block.

Hot-tanking is usually done by a professional service, usually an engine machine shop, and is often free (or possibly for a small fee) if you have that same machine shop do the machine work. I highly recommend that if you are going to have machine work done that you think seriously about having your engine hot-tanked.

There are some disadvantages to hot-tanking, however, and you need to think through these before you make up your mind. The first disadvantage is that the cleaning solution will eat through some bearing materials. Therefore you cannot hot-tank an engine with any bearings installed. Removal of some types of bearings, such as poured-in-place main or camshaft bearings, is not advisable. Some other alloys, while not likely to completely disintegrate,

The second type of block cleaner is a hot tank. This tank holds a caustic cleaning solution that is warmed to 120–135 degrees to increase its effectiveness. Cleaning a block in this type of cleaner is called "hot tanking."

will have their surfaces so etched that they become unusable. The machine shop you use to hot-tank your engine should point these out to you.

Some oil passageways, as seen here in this Farmall F-20, are not galleys in the block, but are plumbed separately. Note the nozzle (arrow) and the small oil line leading upward. The nozzle lubricates the journal bearings and the oil line leads up to, and lubricates, the main bearings.

Manually cleaning the block is your only option if you do not plan to remove the block from the tractor, or if you plan to save some or all of the bearing materials. While manually cleaning the block can yield excellent results, it is tedious work that requires great care. A sloppy cleaning job on an oil galley (an oil delivery passage) can plug the galley, starving the components it was meant to serve with oil. If your only motivation for manually cleaning the block is to save a little money, then you may want to reconsider. As you can imagine, manually cleaning a block leaves behind a large amount of waste. The job requires safe and adequate disposal of the resulting mixture of grime, grease, dirt, sludge, and cleaning solution that runs from the block as you are cleaning it. Safe disposal of this hazardous waste is the law (not to mention just good common sense) in most parts of the country, and often isn't cheap. Professional hot-tanking services handle all of the disposal problems for you.

If you are going to manually clean your block, you need to keep a couple of things in mind. To adequately clean the oil galleys, you must remove the galley access plugs in the block. Even more important, you must remember to replace these plugs with thread sealant afterward. A forgotten plug will result in an engine with no oil pressure. To install a forgotten plug, the engine needs to be mostly disassembled and reassembled.

A good cleaning solution to use for most parts of the engine is a lye-based cleaner sold under various trade names in gallon jugs. A local auto parts store can help decide among locally available brands. To clean small passages and difficult-to-reach areas, you have no choice but to flush the area with a cleaner in a pressurized can. Carburetor cleaners, brake cleaners, and other high-strength, solvent-based cleaners work well here. With all cleaners, you must wear splash-proof safety goggles, adequate rubber gloves, and clothing that covers all skin. Cleaning tools, such as a gasket scraper and a polyester-based scrubbing pad, will help loosen the worst of the grime. Galley swabs work well for long passages. I make my own using a lint-free light cotton cloth wrapped and glued around a wooden dowel. Someone once told me that I reinvented the wheel, and that similar swabs are available at auto parts stores. I haven't seen them but maybe you can find them in your area.

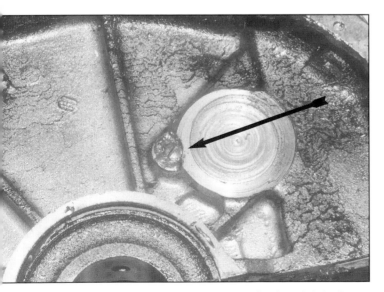

When cleaning a block, don't forget to remove the galley plugs, which plug the main oil passageways. Even more important, don't forget to reinstall them. The galley plug here is a small screw that has remnants of thread sealant around the head (arrow).

1 Freeze plug removal and installation is a task every restorer will have to do eventually. Remove the old freeze plug by punching a hole in the middle and then prying it out. Try to avoid shoving the plug inside the block.

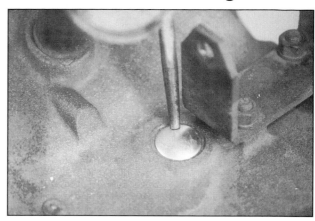

2 Installing the new plug entails cleaning the landings, placing the new plug in place, and then tapping around the edges to make sure the plug is well seated. A little high-temperature sealant around the edges of the landing will prevent leaks.

3 Then expand the plug by driving a flat metal rod sharply down onto the middle. Here the peening end of a ball-peen hammer is used as the anvil and a sledge is used as the driver.

4 The end result—a new freeze plug that has been expanded and locked into place.

REMOVING FREEZE PLUGS

Replacing freeze plugs makes good sense, and it is less difficult than it seems. Hot-tanking your block helps, since the cleaning solution will flush out any accumulated debris and grime. To remove a freeze plug, simply punch a hole in the center of the plug. Thread a short, stout lag screw in the hole, deep enough to give the screw a good solid footing. Then, using a crowbar seated against a block of wood, pry the plug out. (Do not ever seat the crowbar against the block, or you may crack the casting!) You can also use a slide hammer to pop out freeze plugs. This method works equally well with the "cup"-style or the saucer-style freeze plugs. Instead of punching a hole, you could drill a hole, but I don't like the idea of metal shavings being dropped into the water jacket.

To install freeze plugs, first make sure the circumference of the opening, and shoulder if there is one, is clean

and free of burrs and nicks. Then carefully apply a light coat of high-temperature sealant on these surfaces. I use the same gasket sealant I use for water pump gaskets. Again, a knowledgeable auto parts store can steer you toward a product available in your area. Saucer-style freeze plugs are installed with the "hump" pointing toward you. Place the plug in the opening; the circumference of the plug should rest against the shoulder of the hole with hand pressure or some gentle persuasion. When it's in place, take a wooden rod whose diameter is nearly as large as the freeze plug, and place it on the freeze plug. Then sharply rap the rod with a mallet, forcing the plug to flatten. In the process of flattening the plug expands and seals against the edge of the hole.

The holes for cup-shaped freeze plugs are prepared the same way, but these plugs have to be driven into place. The plugs are installed with the hollow of the cup facing toward you. Place the cup on top of the hole, making sure it is square

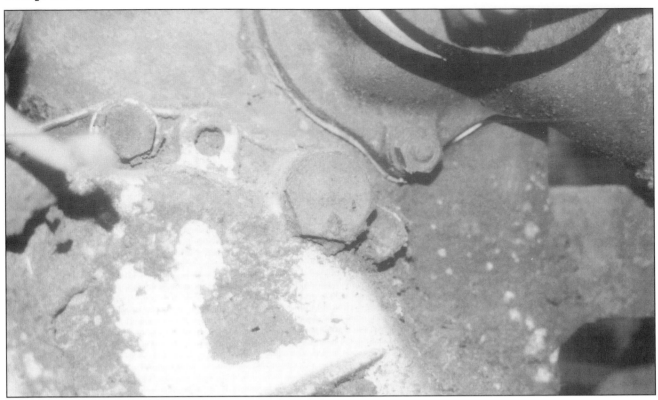

Oil relief valves are usually housed directly in the block, and they need be removed before block conditioning. Usually the valve assembly is a large bolt that either backs or houses a spring-loaded ball or needle valve.

This shows a typical ball-and-spring oil relief valve. Remember, the engine's running oil pressure cannot be adjusted with this device. It is simply a safety valve that dumps oil back into the oil pan, should pressure become too high.

TIP

Contrary to conventional wisdom, freeze plugs are easy to remove and install yourself. Check out the text for simple-to-follow instructions.

against the hole and not cocked in any direction. Once again, a wooden rod is placed in the plug, and the freeze plug is simply driven in. There are a few hints to make this a little easier. It is imperative that the plug be square in the hole as it starts its way in. With these plugs, you want to rap gently against the wooden rod to get the plug moving into the hole. Then, when the plug is far enough in that there is no danger of it canting to one side or the other, you can drive it in with harder blows to the rod. Often, these plug holes don't have shoulders, and you'll have to judge for yourself when the plug is in far enough.

OIL PRESSURE RELIEF VALVES AND POP-UP GAUGES

Every antique tractor engine with positive-pressure lubrication (the vast majority of them), will have some type of oil pressure relief valve. Some older antique tractors, in addition, had pop-up, or "red-head" oil pressure gauges (an example is an early John Deere Model D). Both oil pressure relief valves and pop-up gauges work on the same principles and use similar parts, so their restoration is covered together here.

Restoration of pop-up gauges and relief valves involves cleaning and inspecting the parts for damage, rust, or wear. Most of these devices are simply spring-loaded plungers that activate when oil pressure reaches a certain point. As oil pressure climbs, the plunger starts moving. In the case of the pop-up gauge, a visible marker "pops up" from its housing and becomes visible. These plunger heads were often painted red, hence the name "red-head" oil gauge.

In the case of oil pressure relief valves, the plunger isn't visible. When the pressure becomes too high, the plunger retracts far enough to divert oil flow back to the oil pan. To adjust the pressure at which this happens, the designers used shims or spacers in addition to spring tension to set the initial starting position of the plunger.

Common problem areas are springs that are worn or rusted, or spacers and shims that were removed by previous owners to increase oil pressure. (This was a mistake, because the relief valves have little or no effect on running pressure.) In the case of pop-up gauges, rust, grime, and corrosion may cause the gauge head to stick. If the spring is bad, replacing the entire assembly is usually advised; it's difficult to find replacement springs that exactly match the characteristics of the original. In addition, the plunger is usually unique and difficult to find as an individual part on the parts market. Spacers and shims can be made and replaced, but again, testing for proper operation of the unit afterward is difficult and time consuming. New relief valves and oil pressure gauges are typically available, inexpensive, and easy to install.

PISTONS AND RECIPROCATING PARTS

The reciprocating parts of the engine take the brunt of the punishment of field work, and because of the constant rapid movement, these are the parts most likely to wear. They operate under tremendous temperatures and are asked to do this in all kinds of conditions, the vast majority of which are nowhere near ideal. Therefore, I think I can safely say that there is something here in this chapter you will have to pay close attention to.

Before starting, you need to gather up a few tools and manuals. The work in this chapter is exact and precise, and you will need a service manual for your engine in addition to high-quality measuring tools. Piston ring expanders and compressors, a torque wrench, and a clean work area are necessities as well.

Before diving right in, I hope you looked over the cylinder restoration chapter. One of the problems of presenting these topics in a chapter format is that it may give the reader the impression that each system on the tractor can be evaluated on its own merit, without considering other areas. This just isn't so, and this chapter is a perfect example. How you refurbish the reciprocating parts of your engine will be determined largely by the condition of your engine's cylinders.

If your engine cylinders are highly worn, you learned in chapter 6 that the cylinders must be bored or sleeved. This bore work will necessitate a new set of pistons, but you have to get those pistons before deciding on the size of the cylinder or whether the sleeves can be replaced. Likewise, if your pistons are badly worn, or if you have a broken piston, then the size of available replacement pistons will determine whether you need to bore or sleeve the engine. This is sort of a modified chicken and the egg dilemma. You can't make a decision on pistons or cylinders in a vacuum. They must be evaluated in relation to each other.

One other issue: Many manufacturers recommend using sets of pistons matched to sleeves, or if the engine

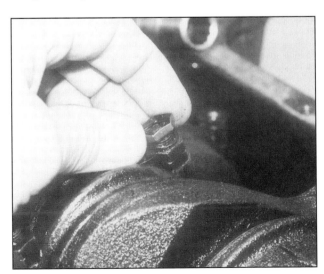

Removing the reciprocating parts of the engine starts, after reaming the ridge at the top of the cylinder, with removing the locking devices on the rod journal fasteners. Here are the two most common locking devices: a cotter pin and locking nut.

Removing the journal bearing cap sometimes requires a little persuasion. One method is to drive the piston and connecting rod away from the rod journal cap with a soft-faced mallet, as shown.

If that doesn't work, you can drive the cap up by tapping it with the same soft mallet, being sure to alternate sides after every tap or two.

has bored cylinders, they recommend replacing the pistons as a matched set, even if just one needs replacement. Antique tractor restorers currently disagree as to how firm this requirement is. The consensus seems to be that using matched sets is important for tractors that will be used for production. Collectors and other folks who use the tractors lightly may not need matched piston and sleeve sets.

PISTONS

Besides the obvious damage and cracks, there are three important areas of wear you must assess when checking the condition of your pistons: Piston wear, wrist pin hole wear, and wear in the piston ring "lands" (the groove the rings reside in). Most engine service manuals have wear tolerances for these three areas. Piston fit (general piston wear)

<table>
<tr><td>MORE POWER!</td></tr>
</table>

IT'S IN THE PISTONS

You can make a few performance modifications to your engine when you refurbish the reciprocating assemblies. The most common is using pistons designed for high-altitude farming in low-altitude tractors. The pistons have a different crown profile that will increase the compression ratio of your engine.

Machining the piston crowns to improve combustion properties is another trick some folks use. Other performance improvements include better piston rings, balancing the reciprocating assemblies, and adding another compression ring to tractors with only two compression rings. Probably the greatest performance enhancement you can make to reciprocating assemblies, though, is to pay particular attention to their restoration. High-precision fit and finish of the rings, wrist pin, journal bearings, and piston make a great difference in how well the engine runs. Be sure to pay attention to the basics as well as possible performance modifications when rebuilding your engine.

Remove the piston and connecting rod as one piece. Most can be removed from the top of the engine, but this engine from a Farmall F-20 allows removal from the bottom. Some antique tractors have "hand holes" in the crankcase; this photo is taken through a left-side handhole.

is usually expressed in terms of the force required to pull a certain-size feeler from between the piston and bore. For example, your manual may say that a feeler of a certain size, when installed between the piston and bore at a point 90 degrees from the piston pin, requires a 10- to 15-pound

Honing cylinders is not just for creating the perfect surface for oil control, it is also done to fit the piston to the cylinder bore. If you are reusing pistons, or if your engine is a wet sleeve engine and you are using new sleeves and matching pistons, fit is not usually an issue. If your engine is a dry sleeve engine, or if you are using new pistons in a bored engine, then you must hone the cylinder until the pistons fit perfectly. Piston fit is usually specified in terms of the amount of pull required to pull a certain-size feeler gauge from between the piston and bore. Usually the piston is inverted for the test and the feeler gauge is installed away from the piston pin hole. Here the feeler gauge and the piston are ready for the test to begin.

After removal, do a quick visual inspection to look for problems. Here an immediate problem stands out: The oil control ring is missing. Other than that, this piston appears to be in good shape.

pull to remove the feeler. Wrist pin hole wear will be a measurement, and land wear will most likely be an inspection, but may be a measurement.

If your manual doesn't include these wear tolerances, you have to make some observations and then judge if the piston is suitable for further use. The pistons should exhibit no significant wear along the skirt area. Glazed, striated areas along the skirt are your biggest clue that the piston has worn appreciably. If your piston has a very uniform skirt all the way around the bottom, then measuring the piston skirt thickness at several places along the skirt may help you get an idea of any problems related to skirt wear. Skirt wear will be minimal directly below the wrist pin holes, and will be greatest at right angles to the wrist pin holes.

The wrist pin should feel snug but smooth in the piston wrist pin holes. The piston ring lands should be very square, without any rounding of land edges or any signs of

Assembly starts after all cleaning, inspection, replacement, or repair. Reused parts must be returned to the bore they came from. It is paramount that you take notes and organize the parts if you expect to be able to do this. Notice along the wood at the bottom of the first photograph: The cylinder number the pistons and connecting rods came from is noted on the wood.

If your organizational skills leave a little to be desired, you may be in luck anyway. Often the cylinder number is stamped on the rod and/or rod journal bearing cap. This photo shows, faintly, the cylinder number stamped on a connecting rod.

This picture shows another orientation issue. Connecting rods and their caps must be oriented within the cylinder correctly. Usually service manuals call for the markings on the rods and rod caps, shown here, to be oriented toward the camshaft.

After removing the rings, some other problems crop up. The second piston ring groove is showing breakage at the top edge. This problem is localized and very small. If need be, the piston could be reused after cleaning up the edge with a small grinder or file. Of course, piston replacement would be ideal.

damage. The rings should rotate around the piston freely in their lands, but should not have enough room to move up or down significantly.

If you are going to reuse your pistons, they need to be refurbished and brought back to working order. Refurbishing pistons may require machine work, but even highly worn pistons can be made like new with these procedures. The two common restoration procedures done on pistons are piston land regrinds and adding bushings to the piston's wrist pin holes. These procedures can be expensive, and are only typically done if they save you from reboring or resleeving your engine bores, or if replacement pistons are unavailable.

Piston ring lands often develop a bevel near the outer edges of the lands. This bevel prohibits the rings from seating squarely and completely against the land and the cylinder wall, creating unusual wear and incomplete compression. In the worst case, it can lead to broken piston rings. Repairing the lands is fairly easy for an accom-

plished machinist. The lands are simply cut wider, then a spacer is installed beside the rings to take up the extra space. This is a common and acceptable repair if your piston ring lands are worn.

Wrist pin hole diameter specifications are occasionally available through service manuals, and you should take this measurement if you have a specification to work from. Be sure to measure each hole two or three times; these measurements should not vary by more than .001–.002 inch. If no specifications are available, then assessing the fit of the pins, as outlined later in the wrist pin section, is all you can do.

Worn wrist pin holes can be dealt with in one of two ways. The first is to drill the wrist pin hole out, then install a bushing in the hole. The bushing is then drilled to specification. The other common approach to this problem is to drill the wrist pin hole out to an acceptable oversize—usually .005 to .010 inch—then use an oversize wrist pin. The wrist pin holes of your connecting rods may also have to be drilled wide to accept the oversize pin, even if your

Another problem became apparent, but two mechanics handled the piston dozens of times before they noticed it. Compare the piston pin holes in the two photographs: The flared edge at the top and bottom of the piston pin hole in the second photo is the result of a broken oil control ring, the same one noted as missing earlier. Our theory is the oil control ring failed and broke, which then broke the small amount of metal between the piston pin hole and the oil control ring groove. A loose edge of the ring trailed downward into the piston pin hole area. The movement of the broken end of the ring, as the piston traveled up and down, caused the flared edges.

connecting rods use a locking wrist pin. Some connecting rods have their own bushing that allows the wrist pin to rotate within the connecting rod; these will definitely need to have the connecting rod bushing drilled and reamed to accept the oversized wrist pin.

There are other piston repair procedures as well, such as crack repair, or piston crown (the top of the piston) rework. The first is self-explanatory, while the latter is done to either repair crown damage caused by burning, or to enhance performance. I do not recommend crack repair unless your engine sports incredibly rare pistons that necessitate such a step. There are problems with balance, excessive wear to the cylinder walls, and the likelihood of cracks reoccurring. That makes this procedure a bad gamble for all but the most difficult-to-find pistons.

Crown work is uncommon and usually unnecessary. If you are doing it for performance reasons, the machine shop that will do the work will be a better source of advice than I can be. Whenever any kind of crown work is done, everything will most likely have to be balanced afterward to make sure the mass of the piston is symmetrical. In addition, the other pistons may need to be balanced against the newly repaired piston, making sure all pistons weigh the same and are balanced onto themselves and each other.

PISTON RINGS

Inspecting your piston rings is pretty simple, and there is only one measurement you can take that will help you decide whether they are still suitable for service. First, they should look straight and feel springy when compressed. Any ring that feels "dead" or shows a lack of elasticity should be replaced. Look very closely under a hand lens to find cracks or any signs of damage.

The next assessment you can make is to measure the ring gap. This is the gap seen when you place the ring (by itself, without a piston) squarely in the cylinder. The ring will not be quite long enough for the ends to touch each other, resulting in a gap. As the rings and cylinders wear, this gap increases. If the gap becomes too large, you will begin to see problems related to insufficient ring "seating" (the seal between the ring and cylinder wall). These problems include diminished compression and glazing of cylinder walls.

Ring end gap is measured with a feeler gauge. If the gap is too large, then a set of oversized rings will have to be purchased. Excessive ring gap is especially common if

the cylinders or sleeves are not rebored, but are worn .005–.010 inch above nominal cylinder diameter. In this case, you will buy oversized rings and then file the ends of the rings until the proper ring gap is reached. If you adjust ring gaps, make sure the gaps are within specification. If the gap is too small, the ends of the ring will meet when the ring expands with heat; this can cause broken rings. If the gap is too large, the engine will have many of the same problems as an engine with old, worn rings, namely poor oil control and compression loss.

Of course, if you overbore, or use overbored sleeves, then new rings are necessary. My recommendation is that piston rings should always be replaced. Rings lose elasticity over time with fatigue and wear, and this elastic property is important in helping an engine quickly develop pressure during the compression and power strokes. Last, but not least, rings—even custom-made rings—are typically inexpensive. Reusing rings is a false economy in most circumstances.

WRIST PINS

There are two types of wrist pins: locking and floating. Locking wrist pins have a machined surface in the pin, and a bolt in the connecting rod locks the pin to the connecting rod. A locking wrist pin still floats and rides in the piston's wrist pin holes, but the pin doesn't rotate within the connecting rod, nor does it move from side to side.

The floating wrist pin is free to rotate in the connecting rod. Its side-to-side movement is controlled by clips installed in grooves at the piston's wrist pin holes.

Inspection and visual assessment of the wrist pin is important. There is typically only one specification here that is of much use, and that is the wrist pin diameter.

Piston ring gap is the measurement between the ends of a piston ring when it is installed in the cylinder. The ring is set near the top in this photograph to make the photograph clearer, but you should install the ring about one-third to one-half of the way down the cylinder wall to make this measurement. To install the ring, compress it by hand and place the ring in the top of the cylinder. Then use a piston to push the ring down; this ensures the ring is square in the cylinder. Use a feeler gauge to measure the gap. Too much gap and the ring must be replaced. Too little, and the ends of the ring must be filed to meet specifications.

There are two types of connecting rod-to-piston pin fastening designs in use in antique tractors. The first, shown here, is the "locking" type of connecting rod. A bolt at the top must be loosened and removed before the piston pin can be removed.

Here's the rod and pin disassembled. As you can see, the pin has a small land in it that the locking bolt seats against.

This piston assembly uses a floating-type piston pin. The pin's side-to-side movement is controlled with clips placed in the ends of the piston's wrist pin holes.

Above and right: Cleaning piston ring grooves is easy with this groove cleaning tool. The bottom of the tool maintains alignment, while the top of the tool has a series of cutters (in various sizes to fit almost all pistons). The piston is rotated within this tool to scrape the grooves clean. Be careful with aluminum pistons, as the knives are steel and will cut into the piston if too much pressure is used.

TIP

Pistons and sleeves are often surprisingly inexpensive, especially for the more common tractors. Before reusing borderline components, check into the cost. It may be affordable enough to justify replacement.

Using a micrometer, take several diameter measurements around the circumference of the wrist pins at the ends, and in the middle if the wrist pin floats. This will determine how much wear the piston and connecting rod caused. This wear is often elliptical, and the elliptical wear can even be visible in the worst cases. If the diameter of the pistons' wrist pin holes is specified in your manuals, take those measurements using the advice in the piston section.

To assess the fit of the wrist pin, apply oil to the wrist pin, and place it in the piston and connecting rod wrist pin holes. The wrist pin should feel snug with no extra play, but should slide and rotate smoothly in the wrist pin holes. Be sure to check fit at the connecting rod if your pin is of the floating type; also be sure to check the condition of the wrist pin snap rings and replace them if necessary. There isn't much you can do to save wrist pins if they are worn beyond use. Wrist pins should be considered a replacement item. They can be reconditioned by a machine and plating shop if necessary, though replacement will almost always be cheaper and easier.

CONNECTING RODS
Connecting rods accept a tremendous amount of stress during operation and therefore require attention and close inspection during a major rebuild. The three areas of concern are journal bearing seat, straightness, and wrist pin hole wear or deformation. The journal bearing seat should be inspected for damage and should be free of cracks. If

Refurbishing connecting rods means replacing the wrist pin bushings. To drive out the bushing, I use a hydraulic press and a carriage bolt whose head has been ground to match the inside diameter of the connecting rod bushing hole.

a specification for the connecting rod's wrist pin hole is available, the wrist pin holes should be measured several times and the readings compared. None of the readings should be more than .001–.002 inch in disagreement. If the measurement is out of spec, the connecting rods need to be replaced, or rebushed if the wrist pin holes have bushings. If replacing the rods isn't an option due to cost or scarcity, even connecting rods without wrist pin bushings can have custom bushings made and installed to take up the wear.

The structural integrity should be checked too, and this involves close inspection and a test for straightness. Often a simple straightedge can be used to test for any twist or bend in the rod, or you can hire an automotive machine shop to more thoroughly check them for you. They will have a shop fixture that will mount the connecting rod (with the

Install the new bushings with your press; the next step is to size the bushing to the piston pin. Use a very small hone (I use the smallest-size brake cylinder hone available) and hone the bushing until the piston pin is a "slip fit" in the bushing. What is a "slip fit"? Slip fit means that a part will slide into place with no binding or difficulty, but at the same time, the part will exhibit no play or looseness.

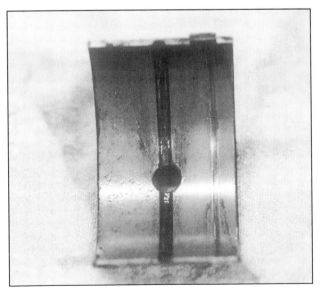

This rod bearing is heavily scored, requiring replacement. Connecting rod journal bearings are more likely to be in rough shape than main crankshaft bearings.

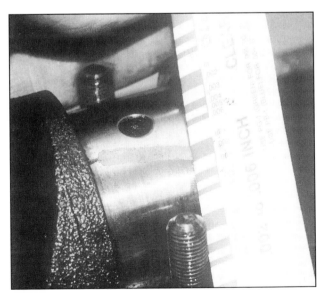

Before removing the pistons and connecting rod, be sure to get your rod journal bearing running clearances, using a product called Plastigage. There are some additional photographs of this product and its use in the crankshaft chapter.

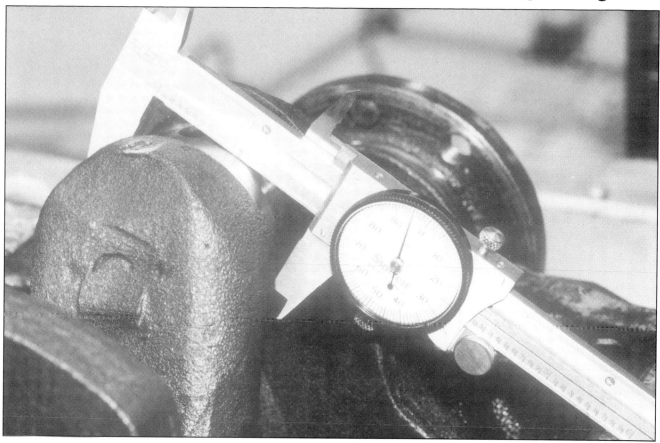

With the cap off, measure the rod journal of the crankshaft, using a dial caliper. Be sure to rotate the tool and take measurements every 45 degrees. Since rod and main journals often wear elliptically, multiple measurements are necessary to find nonconcentric wear.

While we covered shimmed bearings in the crankshaft chapter, rod journal bearings are occasionally shimmed as well. The shims used for bearing adjustment on this John Deere B connecting rod are seen between the connecting rod and the journal bearing cap.

journal bearing cap installed) and check the connecting rod for acceptable geometry between the journal bearing seat and the wrist pin hole.

JOURNAL BEARINGS

Journal bearings are often worn beyond use, even in engines that are otherwise only slightly worn. Bearing inspection involves looking for excessive striations, grooves, "spalling" (small areas of bearing surface missing) or any corrosion or galling. Bearing clearance is an important measurement; this measures the amount of space between the bearing and the crankshaft journal.

To measure the journal bearing clearance, use a product called Plastigage, which is simply a soft piece of plastic that deforms in a predictable way. First, place a piece of Plastigage across the crankshaft journal. Then, you install the connecting rod with the bearings and cap. After tightening the cap and rod into place using the torque specifications found in your service manual, you remove the rod and cap. The Plastigage is left behind, and will be crushed in direct relation to the clearance between the bearings and

This rod journal looks to be in good shape with no marks, grooves, or other damage.

crankshaft. Using the special rule provided with the Plastigage, you can then measure the deformation, which gives you the bearing clearance. Compare this clearance with the clearance specification found in the service manual.

Any clearance measurement that is out of specification calls for bearing replacement. Before you order new bearings, you also need to measure the crankshaft journal diameter, and compare it against specification too. This measurement will identify any machine work (called grinding) done to the crankshaft in the past. Your manual will specify what the diameter should be. If the crankshaft rod journal diameter is less than .010 inch smaller than factory specification, the crankshaft journals have not been ground in the past. If they are out of specification though, they will need to be ground. When the crankshaft journals are ground, the journals will then be too small for your current bearings, or even new bearings, so new bearings that are "oversized" to fit the new journal diameter will have to be purchased.

One problem during journal bearing inspection is identifying crankshafts that have been ground in the past. If your journal measurements are .010 inch or more smaller than the specification in the manual, odds are the crankshaft has been ground at least once in the past. To help identify this, look for numbers that machinists will often stamp on the rough casting of the crankshaft near each journal. Unfortunately, this isn't always done, so a lack of a turning stamp isn't conclusive. You may also find that oversized journal bearings are marked on the back of the bearing (i.e., they may have ".010" written on them). Crankshaft journals

are commonly ground .010 inch below factory, occasionally to .020 inch below factory, but seldom more than .020 inch for reasons of structural integrity.

Determining how to correct running clearances that are out of specification involves several factors. You must take into account past grinding, current condition, availability of bearings, and intended use of the tractor. To help illustrate this, let's use an example: Suppose your manual says the crankshaft journal should be 1.249 to 1.251 inches in diameter, and that the journal bearing running clearance should be .002–.006. inch Then, after measuring your crankshaft journals, let's say the journal diameters are only 1.228 inches but are otherwise in good shape, and your bearing running clearances are within specs, let's say .004 inch. You can then safely suppose the crankshaft journals have been ground in the past to .020 inch undersize (1.230 inches) and .020-inch oversize bearings were used. In this

TIP

Never buy new pistons or journal bearings until final dimensions for boring or crankshaft grinding are determined. Likewise, never commit to a certain-size boring or crankshaft grinding until bearing and piston availability have been determined.

scenario, the whole shooting match, if it meets your visual inspection, is acceptable for reuse.

Since it isn't likely that you know the entire history of the tractor, no one measurement will be a "watershed" that dictates your decision. For example, the diameter measurement isn't that important if the clearances are OK. But if your clearances are bad, *and* the journal diameters are out of spec, then new bearings may not do the trick. In this case, even new standard-sized bearings will not generate clearance measurements that are within specification if the crankshaft journals are worn. Here is a list of ideas to help guide you through the forest of possibilities for connect rod bearing and journal restoration:

- Damaged crankshaft journals always require grinding, regardless of how worn they are.
- Connecting rod crankshaft journals that have only slight damage, such as very minor scratches or striations, may not need grinding and can instead be "polished" out. The machinist will let you know how he has to correct the problem and how you should proceed in terms of new bearings.
- If the connecting rod crankshaft journals are only slightly worn (and aren't otherwise damaged) somewhere in the neighborhood of .003 to .005 inch smaller than specification, then you can use .002-inch oversized bearings, if they're available.
- If the crankshaft journals measure significantly smaller than specification, such as .013–.015 inch or .023.–.025 inch, then your crankshaft journals have probably been reground. If the running clearances are out of specification, then availability of new bearings will determine how to proceed. Occasionally, .012 and .022 bearings that will help you avoid grinding the crankshaft are available, but this is not universally true. Bearings generally only come in .010 and .020 inch oversize.
- If the connecting rod journals are worn more than .005, have a machinist grind the crankshaft. He will recommend what work should be done and advise you as to which size bearings you should try to locate.

ASSEMBLING AND INSTALLING PISTON ASSEMBLIES

The order and orientation of the reciprocating parts during installation is important; you cannot just install them any way you choose. The pistons and connecting rods must be returned to the cylinders they came from. New pistons, if they come with a matched set of sleeves, usually have a specific cylinder they should be used in. Often pistons, when bought individually, do not have any kind of position stamped on them, so in this case you have no choice but to install the pistons in whatever cylinder you choose.

Connecting rods, in addition to ordinal position, also have an orientation in relation to the engine. This orientation is usually expressed in relation to the camshaft. Often

TIP

> When in doubt as to the acceptable condition of sleeve or bore, piston, or crankshaft journal, have a local automotive machinist take a look at it. He or she can guide you in the right direction.

the connecting rods have a part number or other identifying marks or features, and the manual will call for the rods to be installed so these marks or features face the camshaft. It can be different for each engine, so read your service manual carefully.

Once pistons and rods are matched to the cylinders, and the orientation is determined, assemble the pistons, wrist pins, and connecting rods. Coat the outsides of the pistons with liberal doses of oil. Liberally oil the wrist pin, the connecting rod's wrist pin bushing/hole, and the piston's wrist pin holes. If your wrist pin is retained with keeper clips that reside in grooves in the ends of the piston's wrist pin holes, insert one of those clips now. Insert the wrist pin through the other side of the piston, then through the hole in the connecting rod and then into the wrist pin hole in the opposite side of the piston. Make sure the pin bottoms out against the retaining clip. If the wrist pin is locked in place via a locking bolt on the connecting rod, make sure the small indentation on the wrist pin is oriented toward the bolt. If the locking bolt won't go in, slowly spin the wrist pin until the bolt drops into place in the groove. Install the other keeper clip or install the lock bolt, being sure to torque the bolt correctly. Double-check your work, making sure the wrist pin locking bolt or wrist pin keeper clips are secure. If you will be doing a thorough crankshaft and main journal bearing restoration, set the piston assemblies aside until you have done the work to the crankshaft and main bearings.

To install new rings, you must first remove the old rings from the pistons. Compare the new and old rings and make sure they're identical in size and shape. Most (but not all) rings need to be oriented in a certain way in relation to the piston; first you must determine the rings' proper orientation. The most accurate information for orientation is usually the instructions the rings are packaged with. Next, check your service manual for orientation information, and as a last resort, use your memory or notes from disassembly. Unfortunately it is common for rings to be installed incorrectly by a previous owner or mechanic, so simply replicating what was in your engine before isn't the wisest path. To help you with orientation in case you have no resource (no notes, packaging, etc.), rings are generally installed so any bevel or dots are facing upward. This rule

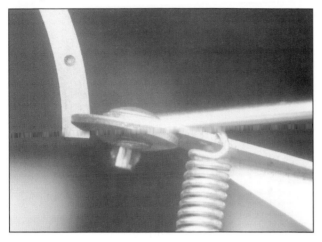

1 Installing rings without damaging or breaking them requires a piston ring expander. To start, first orient the piston ring. Often there are marks and bevels that must be oriented a certain way. The package the rings came in will spell this out. This ring is gripped by the expander; the orientation is marked by the small dot.

2 To install, simply expand the ring and slip it over the head of the piston. Install piston rings from the bottom groove first, and work your way up.

3 Here you can see how the ring expander grips and spreads the ends of the top ring on this piston.

4 Coat the pistons, rings, and ring compressor with oil, then install the piston ring compressor so it squeezes all the rings, but still leaves the piston skirt exposed.

of thumb does have a few exceptions, so be sure to pursue all available documentation first.

Installing rings usually takes two hands, so mount each piston-connecting rod assembly in a vise during ring installation. Put the connecting rod in the vice jaws, not the piston; protect the connecting rod from the metal vise jaws with blocks of wood, and don't overtighten the vise, just enough to keep the parts from moving around. Liberally apply oil to the outside of the piston and the rings. To install the rings, start with the oil control ring (it is often a multipart ring: two thin rings and corrugated spacer). Grab the first thin ring of the oil control ring with a pis-

ton ring expander, spread the ring just enough to fit it over the piston, and place the ring over the piston and down onto the bottom of the oil control ring groove. Next, install the corrugated spacer in the oil control ring groove; this can usually be done by hand. Then follow with the other thin ring of the oil control ring. One-piece oil control rings and the remaining compression rings can be placed exactly as you did the individual thin rings of the oil control ring. Simply bathe them in oil, expand with the tool, and set in place with care. The rings may try to twist and move with the force of the ring expanders; it helps to use your free hand to guide them.

5 Coat the bore with oil, then situate the ring compressor and the piston over the bore. You should probably keep a container of oil handy; you'll use it. Note that ring compressors have small lips or legs at the bottom that will prevent them from entering the bore as you slide the piston down into the bore. Make sure you have installed the compressor so these legs, or lip, are at the bottom.

6 With the piston and compressor in place, simply tap the piston into the bore with a wooden dowel or hammer handle. Install all the pistons before connecting the rods to the crankshaft, and be careful not to mar the crank journals with the rod ends.

To install the piston-wrist pin-connecting rod assemblies, you first need to coat the piston, rings, and cylinders with oil. While you don't need to be excessive, don't be bashful either; oil everything up real good. Then install a piston ring compressor on one of the pistons. One end of the compressor will have a land, ridge, or thick place on the outside of the compressor. The compressor is installed with this edge toward the bottom of the piston. Tighten up the compressor just enough to compress the piston rings smaller than the cylinder's diameter. Do not tighten the compressor until it can tighten no more. This means you may have completely closed the ring gap or you may have the compressor tightened up against the sides of the pistons.

Place the rod down the cylinder from the top, and bottom out the compressor against the top of the block. Using a small wooden rod, such as a mallet handle, tap the piston down out of the compressor and into the cylinder. If the

TIP

Install pistons carefully to avoid damaging the rings.

crankshaft is in the block, you must guide the rod end carefully so it doesn't scratch the crank journal. That's all there is to it!

There are a few problems that may occur, but they are easily rectified. First, the rings may catch on the top of the engine block. If that is the case, tighten the compressor a little further. Second, the compressor may try to enter the cylinder with the piston. This is most common when the compressor has been tightened too far, or the wrong end of the compressor is against the block. Loosen or reverse the compressor and try again. Whatever you do, *never* force a piston into a cylinder.

Chapter 9

THE CRANKSHAFT

The signature of a thorough engine overhaul is a "bottom-end," or crankshaft, rebuild. Many folks avoid doing bottom-end work though, for various reasons. The cost of the rebuild can quickly escalate with significant crankshaft and bearing work, and some folks allow the cost to keep them from doing the work, even when it is warranted. Also, the precision fit of the components is critical enough that doing the job correctly is vitally important. (It's important through all phases of engine rebuilding, but significantly so during crank and bearing work.) Part-time mechanics often don't have the confidence to do this work themselves, and talk themselves out of it, again even if the work is warranted. In addition, many legitimate reasons exist for putting off bottom-end work. For example, if the problems necessitating the rebuild were not related to oil pressure or any other crankshaft and main bearing problems, then there really isn't a pressing reason to rebuild the crankshaft and related components.

However, I always recommend at least checking crankshaft end play and bearing clearances, and inspecting the main bearings before deciding to ignore bottom-end work. There is no better time than now to find potential problems. If you find none, then you can rest easy and skip this chapter. If there are good reasons to rebuild the bottom end, crankshaft work will never get any easier nor any cheaper than right now, so don't hesitate to jump right in.

TIP

Crankshaft restoration should be a "go" or "no-go" decision: Either skip the restoration entirely or completely restore the crankshaft, committing to all the inspections and replacements as necessary.

Of course, there are specific problems and symptoms that require you to remove the crankshaft and main bearings and thoroughly inspect and assess them. The most common problem in these old engines is poor oil pressure. Worn main (and connecting rod journal) bearings are the most likely culprit of oil pressure problems. In addition, reciprocating parts failure (bent connecting rod, broken piston, etc.) can occasionally cause bent crankshafts and mean bearing damage. Any engine that was ever filled with water or antifreeze also requires a full and complete removal of all crank components, and most likely requires crankshaft grinding and bearing replacement.

INITIAL ASSESSMENT

Before removing the crankshaft and bearings, closely inspect the operation of the crankshaft. Rotate it by hand several times. If you find spots that bind or seem "rough," you may have a slightly bent crankshaft. Look for play in the crankshaft at the flywheel end by holding the flywheel hub and giving it a good tug up and down. Oil pressure may be fine, but the outboard main bearing (the bearing at the flywheel) may be highly worn. This is particularly true with the horizontal John Deere two-cylinder engines. In addition, look for excessive crank end play. In other words, push the crankshaft back and forth, looking for any significant play in the thrust bearing. Speaking of thrust bearings, check its condition. The bearing may just be a built-up shoulder of one of the main bearings, or it may be a separate bronze washer between a crankshaft journal shoulder and a main bearing. Your tractor's service manual will outline how crankshaft end play is controlled and describe any associated parts.

PARTS ORIENTATION

Before removal, make sure you make notes or even snap a picture or two. It is amazing how easily forgotten details are, such as the orientation of certain parts, when assem-

Before removing the main bearing caps, be sure to note their orientation. Here this Ford 8N bearing cap reveals an arrow that points to the front of the engine.

Some antique tractor engines use roller bearings instead of babbitt- or insert-type bearings. In this case, restoration is simple. Remove and replace the bearings; there are no adjustments or measurements you can take. The crankshaft grinding section of this chapter may apply if the rod journals need grinding, but the main journals will not need attention unless the roller bearing failed and damaged the crankshaft.

Before removing the crankshaft, be sure to identify timing registration marks on the crankshaft and camshaft gears. Use a small punch and make your own marks if you can't find any. Here, the smaller crank gear has a mark on one tooth; the cam gear has marks on the two teeth flanking that mark.

bling the engine two months later.

Here are a few things to keep in mind when making notes about parts orientation:

- **Oil slinger:** This medium-sized saucer-shaped part on the front timing case has a specific orientation. Usually the "cup" of the saucer faces the crankshaft pulley.
- **Thrust bearing:** Its orientation is often important, and it is sometimes possible to install it next to the wrong crankshaft main journal.
- **Timing marks:** Make sure you can find and identify the timing marks on the crankshaft timing gear.
- **Main bearings and bearing caps:** After you assess the condition of the bearings, you may find that you can reuse them. If that is the case, always return the bearings and caps to their original position. Make sure you take notes on the ordinal positions. I mark the back of the bearings with a felt-tip permanent marker.
- **John Deere tractors:** Like many makes of tractors, the main bearings of most John Deere two-cylinder tractors can be shimmed and adjusted. (The H is an exception.) However, John Deere main bearings can be adjusted while the crankshaft remains on the tractor. There is no need to remove the crankshaft to adjust the bearings. The orientation of the flywheel spacer is important. Simply use a punch tool to create an index mark on the crankshaft and flywheel spacer before you remove it.

THRUST BEARING LOCATION AND MEASUREMENT

Before removal, you should measure the crankshaft end play. Push the crankshaft in as far as it will go, using a soft steel or wood lever to assist you if needed. Then place a dial caliper on a magnetic caliper mounting base, and place the base on the side of the block or crankcase. Orient the

The side-to-side movement, called end play, of the crankshaft can and should be measured. Where to measure varies among models of antique tractor, but the most common is beside one of the main bearings, as shown here. The shoulders of the main bearing that controls end play will be larger and built-up more than the other bearings.

1 Measure the bearings' running clearance with Plastigage. This is how the product comes out of the package: There's a special scale, and a long, thin plastic strip of a specific diameter.

2 This shows how to install the product, with a strip of the plastic across the journal. Note that you only have to use a small piece. Install the bearing cap, tighten to specification, and then remove. The Plastigage crushes in direct relation to the bearing clearance.

3 Using the special rule that comes with the product, measure the deformation of the Plastigage after the bearing cap is removed. In this example, the bearing exhibits approximately .006-inch clearance—too much for most antique tractors. (For comparison, note the uncrushed section in the middle of the journal, where the oil groove in the bearing was.)

caliper so it just touches the end of the crankshaft, and then orient the caliper's scale to zero. Then pull the crankshaft out as far as it will go, again using a lever as an aid. Read the scale; if the end play is excessive, there are usually three strategies to correct it. First, on some tractors, such as horizontal-engine John Deere tractors, flywheel installation can provide the necessary adjustment. Second, on others, end play control is provided through a replaceable thrust washer. Third, on some others, one of the main bearings has large shoulders that control the end play, and for these, bearing replacement is the only cure.

MAIN JOURNAL CLEARANCE

The most important measurement you will take during a lower end rebuild is the main bearing running clearance. This is the measurement of the space between the crankshaft main journal and the crankshaft main journal bearings. If there is too much clearance, then oil pressure within the engine will be hard to maintain and the bearings begin

Some antique tractors control bearing running clearance with shims. Here a Case CO main bearing cap and shims are shown. To decrease the running clearance, remove shims, whose thickness should be marked on the shim. For example, if the running clearance is .003 inch too large, then remove a .001-inch and a .002-inch shim to bring the clearance back into specification. If the thickness is not marked, use a micrometer.

to wear at an accelerated rate. Too little clearance and the bearings may overheat and fail, or spin within their housing, causing expensively repaired damage to the bearing housings. Your main goal during a lower engine rebuild is to create proper main and rod bearing running clearances.

You measure this clearance with Plastigage, which was discussed in chapter 8. First, make sure the crankshaft journals and bearings are clean. Then place the Plastigage thread directly on the crankshaft journal, parallel to the crankshaft's longitudinal axis. Install the bearing cap (with the bearing installed) and tighten the cap to the specifications listed in your service manual. Be careful not to turn the crankshaft while the bearing cap is installed. Then remove the bearing cap. The Plastigage thread will remain on the journal, and it will be flattened. Using the rule provided, compare the width of the crushed Plastigage with the width markings on the rule. The rule will translate the width to an actual clearance measurement.

Compare the running clearances with the clearances listed in your service manual. Out-of-specification clearances are cause for concern, and so are those that are almost out of specification. Before jumping to any conclusions or running out and buying new bearings, we need to take a few other measurements.

MEASURING MAIN JOURNALS

Crankshaft main journals need to be measured for wear as part of a lower engine rebuild. Every service manual should include this specification. The procedure of taking a measurement is straightforward, as all you are doing is mea-

The machinist you use for the engine restoration can help you assess your crankshaft and bearings if you are unsure of how to proceed.

1 To remove the main bearing caps, first remove any locking devices on the cap bolts. This will almost always be mechanic's wire.

2 Then using a stout breaker bar, loosen the cap bolts.

3 Lift the bearing clear, being sure to note orientation and position within the engine. Also be sure not to lose any shims or shim backing plates.

4 In some engines, the oil pump is integral with one of the main bearing caps.

suring the main journals' diameter. Take two or three measurements of each journal as a way of double-checking your work. Simply compare your results with the specifications in the manual.

CRANK REMOVAL

To remove the crank, you have to first remove the main caps and bearings. There are two types of journal bearings: poured babbitt and insert-style. Poured babbitt bearings are not removable without destruction. The insert-style bearings are removable, though. To remove the main bearings, first remove any wires or clips that lock the main bearing cap bolts in place, and remove the bearing caps. Remove the bearings from the caps using your fingernail or a soft thin tool. Carefully lift the crankshaft out of the bearing saddles and place it in a safe, clean place. After removing the crankshaft, the bearings under the crankshaft can be removed the same way.

If you are removing the bearing caps one at a time, and you want to inspect the bearings one at a time, the lower

bearing can be removed with a special clip. This clip is placed in the oil galley hole of the crankshaft journal. The clip then engages the side of the lower bearing when the crankshaft is rotated, and pushes the lower bearing out of the housing. There is no special reason to remove the bearings one at a time, unless you are only replacing a known bad bearing and do not intend to inspect or replace the other bearings. If you plan on inspecting all the bearings and the crankshaft, remove all caps and then remove the crankshaft and lower bearings as directed earlier.

TIP

Make sure you identify all timing marks on the crankshaft timing gear and flywheel before removing them.

Initial inspection starts as soon as you remove the cap. This main bearing journal is in great shape. The dark strip you see here is just a slight buildup of sludge where the bearing's oil groove was. It will wipe right off.

DAMAGE INSPECTION

The first thing to look for is any obvious damage to the crankshaft journals. Striations that you can catch your fingernail on, or any gouges, corrosion, or rust mean the crankshaft must be turned and/or polished by a machinist. (More on that later.) Look also for damaged or worn threads or splines at the ends of the crankshaft. Splines that are worn enough to allow movement of the attached part, such as flywheels or timing gears, should be repaired. This is especially true of horizontal two-cylinder John Deere engines. The splines where the flywheel attaches are occasionally worn, and excessive wear will cause irreparable damage to the crankshaft splines or flywheel.

This is a bearing cap and bearing from a Case CO. Note the dark band at the top of the bearing. This is a series of numerous light striations. The rest of the bearing shell is in fine shape. Because of the generally good condition of all the main bearings, this bearing shell was reused.

On the bearings, damage inspection should include a general visual check to make sure there is no rusting, galling, or corrosion on the running surfaces of the bearing. Any bearing with these defects must be replaced. Other parts related to the crankshaft should be inspected at this time. Some items to look over very carefully are the crankshaft pulley, woodruff keys, woodruff key way, alignment pins, flywheel hubs and splines, oil slingers, and the crankshaft timing gear. None of these should have excessive wear or damage.

After removing the crank and bearings, clean all parts thoroughly. While most parts can be cleaned in the lye-based solution mentioned earlier in the book, *please remember* to clean soft metal parts, such as bearings, bushings, or anything made of bronze, tin, lead, or pot metal in cleaners that are *not* lye-based. Be sure to thoroughly clean all oil passages and galleys in the crankshaft.

At this point, you should have thoroughly and carefully removed, inspected, and cleaned the entire crankshaft system. Now it is time to take some critical measurements.

INSPECTING CRANKSHAFT ALIGNMENT

Crankshaft alignment or "straightness" is critical. A crankshaft must turn precisely around its longitudinal axis. If it doesn't, undue pressure will be exerted against one or more main bearings, creating excessive wear in those bearings. To test this, simply take a measurement of the main bearing thickness at several places along each of the main bearing shells. A bent crankshaft will usually create greater wear in one or more of the bearing shells. To elaborate, let's say you measure the thickness of both halves of a main bearing insert. You take six total thickness measurements, and they all hover around .036 inch. You repeat this for every main bearing and find that the measurements for one of the main bearing sets hover around .032 inch. While there are other causes for an abnormally worn main bearing, these unusual thickness measurements should lead you to suspect a bent crankshaft. At this point, you may want to set up a run-out test.

Either you or a machinist can take these "run-out" measurements. If you take the measurements, realize your measurements are a rough measurement only. Accurate run-out measurements require that the crankshaft be

TIP

If you can catch a fingernail on any significant scratch or striation in a bearing or crankshaft journal, you must either replace the bearing or polish or grind the crankshaft journal.

TIP

When installing bearings, make sure the oil passage holes in the bearings line up with the oil passage holes in the block.

mounted on a device that accurately centers the crankshaft for each test. Having said that, you can take some measurements on your own that will help you get a rough idea of the extent of any problems. You take the measurement by removing one of the main bearing caps, then placing a dial caliper with a sturdy magnetic base on the bottom of the engine block. Turn the crankshaft by hand, and measure the movement of the exposed main bearing journal. The dial caliper will tell you how much the journal moves up and down as you spin the crankshaft. Unfortunately, very few service manuals will give a crankshaft run-out specification. Conventional wisdom says that run-out measurements with a total range exceeding 1 or 2 thousandths of an inch is cause for concern. You would also want to repeat the test two or three times for each journal, leaving various combinations of main bearings caps attached. One particular bearing cap may have a clamping effect, minimizing the run out measurement you see. By taking the measurement with different combinations of bearing caps installed, you will remove the possibility that all your measurements have been influenced by any one bearing cap.

OIL GALLEYS

The oil passages within the crankshaft need to be thoroughly cleaned. If the crankshaft needs to be machined, then delay cleaning until after the crankshaft returns from the machinist. The machinist will probably clean the crankshaft as part of his service, but always check behind him or her by following the cleaning advice here. Cleaning the oil passages in the block that lead to the crankshaft is covered in the engine block chapter.

Fortunately, the oil passages in most crankshafts are not long, and can usually be cleaned with very long pieces of wooden dowels wrapped with lint-free cloth soaked in solvent. Long wire swabs, similar to big pipe cleaners, are available at auto parts stores for this job, too. After cleaning, the passages should be blown clean with compressed air to remove any lint or fuzz that may have been left behind. Be extra careful not to break the dowel off in the passages!

Other final preparation steps include very thoroughly cleaning the threads of the flywheel bolts, the threads at the pulley end of the crankshaft if there are any, and straightening and repairing these threads with a die. At this time, everything about the crankshaft should be like new, and all threads, holes, passages, journals, and splines should be

straight, clean, and ready for use. As a last step, coat the entire crankshaft with a coating of 30-weight oil to ward off rust while the rest of the engine is prepped.

COMMON CRANKSHAFT PROBLEMS

There are several common problem with the crankshaft and crankshaft assemblies. Most of these can be repaired, but a few cannot and necessitate part replacement.

Marks and Gouges

There are two different types of marks and gouges you may find on your crankshaft assembly components. The first are normal striations and scratches that are typical of 50-year-old machines. Second are the more serious, and deeper, gouges and scratches that are the result of part failure. The marks from wear and tear can be significant and may require the attention of a machinist, but are rarely "fatal." These can be turned or polished out by any competent machinist, or

This crankshaft shows grooves and light striations on nearly every journal. This crankshaft is a candidate for turning, which means the crankshaft journals will be ground down to a smaller size to remove the imperfections.

The type of damage you hope not to see when you open up your main bearings. Run, do not walk, to a machinist and have any crankshaft with this type of damage ground down to the next smallest undersize. This crankshaft will probably have to be ground to .020 inch undersize. Before doing so, make sure you can obtain .020-inch oversized bearings!

These light scratches and striations can be polished out by a machinist. If your main bearing caps are shimmed, this polishing works great. If not, polishing usually doesn't accomplish anything because "service"-sized bearings (bearings that are just .002 or .004 inch oversized) are often not available—only rebuild sizes (i.e., .010 or .020 inch) are available. Your machinist may not have any choice but to grind the crankshaft instead of polishing it.

at least the worst of the marks can be turned out so they no longer create a problem. The latter type of surface defects, those caused by part failure, are more likely to require part replacement. Serious marks and gouges are usually caused by connecting rod failure, especially "thrown" rods, and oil contaminated with metal particles.

Rust

Rust usually rears its ugly head when water infiltrates and fills the crankcase. Important surfaces, such as crankshaft journals and bearings, have often rusted and corroded to the point of being unusable. Look closely at rust, but don't dismiss a part out-of-hand because of rust. These parts spent their working lives in oil, and often rust doesn't get much of a stronghold if the water has not been in the crankcase long. Light rust on some surfaces, such as crank journals, can often be turned or polished out.

This crankshaft journal shows some rust marks. It could be buffed with emery cloth to remove the marks.

Poor Previous Turning

Occasionally you'll find that your antique tractor engine has been rebuilt previously, and that the crankshaft has been turned before. Unfortunately, not every machinist is a competent crankshaft machinist, and the previous turning may have been done poorly. If your measurements lead you to suspect that the crankshaft has been turned before, ask your local machinist to take a look. Radii left too large will interfere with proper crankshaft end play adjustments, and may place undue stress on the edge of the bearings. Radii that are too sharp introduce a significant weak spot and increase the possibly of crankshaft breakage.

Spun Bearings

One of the most difficult problems you will ever face is a "spun" bearing. This is a bearing that, instead of remaining stationary, begins rotating with the crankshaft. This is more common with main bearings, but it can happen with connecting rod bearings. When a bearing spins, it usually destroys the bearing cap and the engine block or connecting rod. This usually necessitates block replacement, since repair is expensive.

ASSESSING CRANKSHAFT JOURNALS AND MAIN BEARINGS

While taking all these measurements and making all of these inspections is straightforward, interpreting the results isn't. The difference between your crankshaft's measurements and the factory specifications may or may not be significant. That is because, ultimately, the main bearing journal diameter measurement must be interpreted in conjunction with your main bearings' running clearances. The whole process of interpretation is made easier if you remember that the only measurement that matters is the main bearing's running clearance. It does not matter (assuming the journals and bearings pass visual inspection) what size the journals or bearings are. Clearance is all that matters.

This bearing shows signs of "spalling," a condition in which small flecks of the bearing substrate have separated from the bearing shell. As a result, the bearing needs to be replaced.

If you approach main bearing and crankshaft journal assessment with the idea that running clearance is all that matters, then you can steer your way through all the various combinations of measurements and specifications that will try to confuse you.

What should you do if the running clearance is out of specification? An in-depth discussion is in the reciprocating parts chapter under the connecting rod journal section. You should refer back to that section now to reacquaint yourself with these ideas. A combination of crankshaft machining and oversized bearings will bring running clearances back into specification. In addition, the crankshaft may need slight polishing if slight striations or scratches exist. (a machinist will do this for you.) Here is a short chart to help you make a decision if your running clearances are unacceptable:

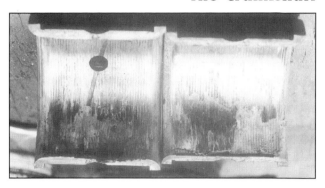

This photo shows total and complete bearing failure. The entire bearing surface has worn away in most places, exposing the backing substrate.

Crankshaft and/or crankshaft journal damage:	Take to a machinist and use his advice.
Crankshaft journal wear: .001–.006-inch	Install .002-inch oversized bearings if available.
Crankshaft journal wear: .006–.010-inch	Have the crankshaft ground or polished to .010-inch and then use .010-inch bearings if available.
Crankshaft journal wear: .010–.016-inch	Probably has not worn this much—it was probably ground to .010-inch once before. Install .012-inch oversized bearings if available. Otherwise, have the crankshaft ground to .020-inch undersized and use .020-inch oversized bearings if available.
Crankshaft journal wear: .016–.020-inch	Probably has not worn this much—it was probably ground to .010-inch once before and worn the rest of the way to this dimension. Grind the crankshaft to .020-inch undersized and use .020-inch oversized bearings if available.
Crankshaft journal wear: Greater than .020-inch	Shop for oversized bearings larger than .020-inch, and if available, consult with a machinist as to the feasibility of grinding the main journals smaller than .020-inch undersized.

IF YOUR CRANKSHAFT NEEDS MACHINING

When even new bearings leave an unacceptably large bearing clearance, then the crankshaft must be "turned." Turning a crankshaft means removing metal from the journals using a specialized grinder. Specifically, the crankshaft journals are turned down to a diameter some even increment smaller than a new crankshaft. Since the crankshaft journals are smaller, oversized, or thicker, bearings are needed to compensate.

There is a close cousin to turning called "polishing." The idea behind polishing is to buff away just enough metal to remove small surface imperfections, such as striations, corrosion, or rust. Polishing removes some metal, but not enough to create the need for oversized bearings. Therefore, if the crankshaft is worn and is already near maximum specification before polishing, polishing may remove enough metal to exceed acceptable limits. Accurate measurements on your part and a consultation with a machine shop afterward will help sort out any problems, possible procedures, and their consequences.

FINDING BEARINGS

Unless your crankshaft checks out completely OK, and a trip to a machinist is definitely not necessary, do *not* purchase any main or rod bearings yet. The reason is simple: Only your machinist can tell you what he can and cannot do, and only a machinist can tell you exactly how much metal he will have to remove. Even then, it is common for a machinist to find that he or she must remove more from the crankshaft than originally anticipated.

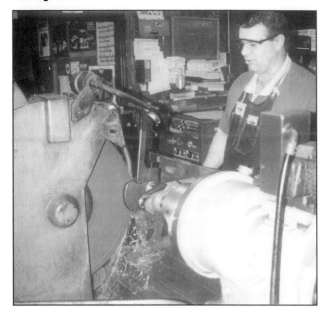

If you have to have your crankshaft ground, here is what your machine shop will do. Mike from Golden Shamrock in Winston-Salem, North Carolina, is grinding a Ford 8N crankshaft. The machine is, in essence, an overgrown, highly accurate bench grinder. The bed of the device rotates the crankshaft, while the grinder removes stock from the crankshaft. The bed offsets to grind the rod journals.

This view shows the marks the machinist draws on the journals. These marks serve as a visual clue to ensure that the journal is being ground back to perfect roundness.

While you shouldn't buy your bearings just yet, you must shop for them now. The supply of main and rod bearings for antique tractor engines is spotty and depends entirely on the make of the engine. For example, the last time I checked, bearings for the Massey Harris engine used in the Massey-Harris 55 have been nearly impossible to find. Yet, bearings for many of the Continental engines that Massey used on other models are quite plentiful. At this juncture, your machinist must know what oversized bearings are available. For example, what good would turning a crankshaft .010 inch undersized do if the only bearings you can find are .020 inch oversized? What if oversized bearings are not available? All of these things must be known and communicated to the machinist before he can make a final recommendation on how to proceed.

What do you do if you cannot find oversized bearings, but your crankshaft needs to be turned? Many surface imperfections, after polishing, may not create any significant problems if the tractor is relegated to light-duty use. If wear and an inability to generate oil pressure are the problem, your machinist may be able to shim your new

standard-size bearings to improve running clearance, although this only works with some types of insert bearings. In extreme cases, engines with insert-type bearings may accept poured babbitt bearings. This only works with some types of rod and main bearing housings and caps, so the advice of a patient machinist is needed.

CONSULTING WITH A MACHINE SHOP
Finding a machine shop that will handle your crankshaft work should not be difficult. While I recommend visiting machine shops that specialize in agricultural and construction equipment, any automotive machine shop should do, since there are no functional or significant metallurgical differences between most antique tractor crankshafts and the crankshaft from your family car. If you are restoring a very large antique tractor, then the sheer size of the crankshaft may be a problem, but otherwise they will be able to help you. When you visit the machine shop, remember that the shop makes its money working on modern equipment. Do not expect them to have available any specifications or understanding of your specific crankshaft. You will have to provide most of the data from your service manual.

GOOD MACHINIST PRACTICES
What will a good machine shop do? Even though the machinists will not have any specific understanding of your model of engine or its crankshaft, they will work closely with you to obtain the information they need, help

When assembling the crankshaft, be sure you remove all traces of Plastigage from the journals.

Shop for bearings and know what bearing sizes are available before consulting with a machinist for crankshaft grinding or polishing.

When installing bearings, coat all the bearings with assembly grease. Be sure to coat both halves!

you measure and assess the crankshaft, and make a recommendation on how to proceed. Specifically, they should explain any problems they notice, how to rectify the problem, and what that will mean for you. They should be open-minded about all possibilities and should understand that compromises might be needed in light of bearing availability problems.

Almost as important, if your crankshaft has been turned in the past, they should identify that, inspect the previous turner's work, and let you know of any sloppy work needs to be fixed. In short, they should listen to you and evaluate the crankshaft in light of your particular circumstance.

BEARING INSTALLATION

Bearings for antique tractors come in three styles. The first style is the removable "insert"-type bearing, used on almost all tractor engines made after the Depression. These bearings are made in two halves and slip into place in the bearing housing and the bearing caps. They are easy to work with and easy to replace, and are still used today in modern equipment.

The second type, and the most common on tractors made before the Depression, are babbitt bearings. This bearing material must be melted and poured into the bearing housings, and a great deal of setup work is involved. Typically, these bearings must be poured by professionals. While pouring these bearings yourself is possible with the right equipment, it is beyond the scope of this book to discuss it.

The third type of main bearings are standard roller-type bearings, and these are not used as rod bearings. In these cases, heavy-duty standard ball bearings are used. This is uncommon in antique tractors, although a notable exception is the Farmall F-20, one of the models outlined in this book.

Insert Bearings

Installation is simple. When installing insert-type bearings, line the notches in the bearing seats with the small tang on the back of the bearing. Typically, it is difficult to reverse a bearing or install it improperly, but with some engines it is possible. Most important, make sure the oil pressure feed holes in the caps and block and rods line up with the holes in the bearings. *Be sure to coat all bearings with special engine-assembly grease!*

Some bearings are pressed into a housing, and may or may not be replaceable without replacing the entire hous-

To finish the job, torque the caps to spec, then install mechanic's wire to lock the cap bolts in place. Install the wire so that the tension of the wire has a tendency to tighten the fastener, and not loosen it. That means wrap the wire so there is tension from the clockwise direction, not the counterclockwise direction.

ing. John Deere H engines have this type of bearing. A one-piece circular bearing is pressed into a receiver in a bearing housing. John Deere manuals always recommend replacing the entire housing, which comes with a new bearing. This design is very similar to camshaft bearings, which are covered in another chapter.

WHAT ARE BEARINGS MADE OF?

Antique tractor main and journal bearings had to be designed to withstand the load imposed on them and to be exceedingly smooth to minimize friction, minimizing wear and heat buildup. Unfortunately, some of the best friction-fighting materials, such as lead, are also very soft. Lead alone, while usable for a short time, is not strong enough as a bearing material and would not last long. To make a usable bearing, lead must be alloyed with other metals. In fact, lead is not strong enough to be used in bearings for high-speed applications, such as automotive engines. (Tractors engines are considered a low- to medium-speed application.)

Poured bearings and insert-type bearings, both covered in this chapter, are made of a material called "babbitt." Insert-style bearings have a strong steel backing to them, but the inside layer of the bearing is indeed babbitt. There are two successful families of babbitt-bearing materials: the lead-based alloys and the tin-based alloys.

All babbitt alloys are assigned an SAE (Society of Automotive Engineers) designation, based on the composition. Within these families, there are two tin-based alloys and three lead-based alloys. As lead has excellent low-load-bearing properties, it is used the most. Lead, however, is a very weak material and tin, antimony, and copper are added for strength. Interestingly, the manufacture and design of the bearings' backing materials can also add significant strength, even though the composition of the babbitt doesn't change. Because of this, Clevite, the best-known bearing manufacturer, developed the microbabbitt, which is a very thin layer of babbitt (.004 to .005 inch) applied to the steel backing substrate.

Tin-based alloys, while better in high-speed applications, are less forgiving of debris or machining abnormalities, and therefore some lead is usually added to improve bearing properties. Tin is also very corrosion resistant, and is usually called on for marine and saltwater applications. Lead is easily corroded, and in the presence of moisture produces an electrolytic action that speeds corrosion.

Today, copper-based alloys show exceptional-strength characteristics, but must be plated with a traditional tin- or lead-based alloy for their surface characteristics. Most of the engine bearings produced today are a copper-based alloy with lead and tin. Aluminum-based alloys are also popular, once again with lead, tin, or cadmium additions. The following table lists the five main tin- and lead-based alloys by their SAE designations, and outlines modern babbitt material and the alloy composition:

SAE 11 Tin base	86% Tin	7% Antimony	6% Copper
SAE 12 Tin base	89% Tin	7.5% Antimony	3.5% Copper
SAE 13 Lead base	84% Lead	10% Antimony	6% Tin
SAE 14 Lead base	74% Lead	15% Antimony	10% Tin*
SAE 15 Lead base	83% Lead	15% Antimony	1% Tin*

* These applications have from 0.5 percent to 1.0 percent arsenic as a strengthening agent.

Many thanks to Larry Dotson, process engineer for Clevite Bearings, for providing the material for this sidebar.

Another issue to consider is that bearings are often "shimmed." That means that between the bearing cap and bearing housing, thin wafers of metal (usually .001 to .005 inch thick) are stacked up between the cap and housing. To adjust worn bearings and crankshafts, it is possible to remove shims and return the running clearances to specification. A problem you may run across is that bearings have been adjusted in the past, and the shims removed by the previous mechanic. If you install new bearings, you may not have enough shims to create enough acceptable running clearance. In these scenarios, you'll have to find

shim stock and cut out your own shims. Again, most machinists can point you to a supplier if they don't have any themselves. If your machinist can't help you, try some of the suppliers mentioned in the back of this book.

Babbitt Bearings

Poured babbitt bearings, common on the oldest of antique tractors, require the assistance of a qualified shop. As I mentioned before, pouring your own babbitt isn't within the scope of this book, but I'll provide some detail here so you know what to expect at the shop. Babbitt bearings are a mixture of tin, copper, and antimony, with varying percentages (from none to approximately 20 percent) of lead added, depending on the grade of babbitt. Babbitt is graded based on the percentage of the various individual ingredients, and the grade used depends on the application. In high-speed applications, Grade 1 is used, while Grades 2–5 are used in less-demanding applications. Originally, antique tractor engines were poured with a lower grade of babbitt that contained lead. These grades are perfectly fine to use, though your machinist may want to use the highest-grade babbitt to protect himself from future claims of babbitt failure. Any grade is perfectly acceptable in the antique tractor, especially if the engine has pressure lubrication. Without pressure lubrication, I would recommend trying to convince the shop to use a grade of babbitt that has some lead.

To pour babbitt, a shop will first build dams behind and around the assembled bearing housings and/or bearing caps, to hold the molten material as it cools. Any oil passages are plugged and a replica of the crankshaft journal (or the crankshaft itself depending on the engine's design) will be placed and shimmed to leave an opening in the babbitt for the crankshaft. After the material cools, the dams and forms are removed, and then the babbitt is bored and/or honed to the proper dimension. Any oil passages are unplugged and the babbitt bearings are ready for use.

CRANKSHAFT INSTALLATION

Installing the crankshaft is basically the reverse of removal, but there are a few extra steps to perform and several things you need to keep in mind. First, this is the last chance to get the entire crankshaft assembly clean. Since the bottom halves of any two-part seals must be installed now, skip ahead to the oil seal installation section later in this chapter. Installing the crankshaft involves careful assembly and a double check of running clearances. Final assembly of all components then takes place. Bearing caps and housings are installed, properly tightened, and then antiloosening devices, such as clips or mechanic's wire, are installed. Afterward, crankshaft end play is checked and adjusted. To wrap things up, a final spin test and a double and triple check is performed for smooth, problem-free rotation of the crankshaft.

I hate to beat a dead horse, but any grit and dust on any part of the crankshaft journals or bearings is a bad thing. Take your time here to make sure all oil passages and journals are as clean as possible. Make sure bearings are clean, and that the bosses and notches that insert bearings fit into are also free of any dirt or grease that may misalign the bearing. Take the time now to double-check the cleanliness of the crankshaft and bearings in particular. Some new bearings may have been coated with a wax or other corrosion-resistant coating, and this will need to be removed now.

MORE POWER!

CRANK IT UP

One of the performance modifications you can make during crankshaft reconditioning is to "stroke" your engine. The premise behind this is to lengthen the stroke of the engine, increasing the displacement. One of the side effects is an increase in the engine's compression ratio. Both the increased displacement and the increased compression ratio add significant horsepower to your engine. Of all the performance modifications, stroking does more to increase the engine's net torque, an attribute that is of particular help on the pulling track or field.

To stroke an engine, the crankshaft's pins (crankshaft rod journals) are moved farther away from the centerline of the crankshaft. Saying they are "moved" is not quite accurate; actually, these pins are "migrated," through welding and turning, away from the centerline. The crankshaft pins are not literally cut out and moved. How much they are moved depends on the engine, your performance needs, the crankshaft, and any obstruction in the crankcase that may interfere with the increased rotational diameter. A qualified machine shop will have to make this modification for you; this isn't something you can do yourself. If increased performance on the track or field is your goal, stroking is probably the most significant performance modification you can make. Keep in mind that stroked crankshafts are more likely to break, so finding a qualified machinist is of particular importance.

After cleaning, you begin installation. It is not possible to give the specific steps to install your crankshaft in a general book, but typically the sequence goes like this:

- First coat any part or surface that rubs or touches another with a coat of assembly grease. This is a special light body grease that will keep bearings and journals from rubbing against each other and causing damage or excessive wear when the engine spins up for the first time.
- Install the main bearing halves (again, with some tractors, main bearings are one piece) that are seated in the crankcase housings or bosses.
- Set the crankshaft in place.
- Place a strip of Plastigage on the crankshaft journal.
- Install the last of the bearing halves and bearing caps, and tighten caps and housings to specs.
- Remove the caps and check the Plastigage for

1 These two pictures show how to remove the rear oil seal. First, rotate the carrier out of the block. Then pull the tar-impregnated seal from the groove in the carrier.

clearance. Add and remove shims as necessary to bring the bearings within clearance. If your bearings can't be shimmed, then you need to ask your machinist and your bearing suppliers why you don't have a proper running clearance. Either the bearings are bad or the machinist goofed.

• If it all checks out, remove all traces of Plastigage and assemble the bearing caps and housing for good, coating the bearings and crankshaft with assembly grease as needed.

• Tighten and torque the bearing caps and housings per specification, being sure to thoroughly clean and oil the bolts or nuts. Lock the bearing cap bolts with cotter pins or mechanic's wire. Use the same type of wire and winding pattern you found upon disassembly.

There are two last steps you need to complete before the crankshaft is assembled. The first is the crankshaft endplay adjustment. This refers to the longitudinal move-ment of the crankshaft, and is controlled by any number of means that defies generalization. On John Deere horizontal two-cylinders, it is controlled by the position of the flywheel. On other engines, it is controlled by a built-up shoulder on a main bearing, usually the centers. Others have a bronze washer that takes up slack. The manual for your engine will specify how end play is controlled, how much end play is acceptable, and how to correct it. Be sure to study that part of your manual and assure yourself that your crankshaft end play is acceptable.

The last step is a spin test. After everything is assembled, double-check your mental list of steps and procedures, and make sure you have covered all the details. Then, simply spin the crankshaft by hand. Make sure you do this before you put the pistons and connecting rods in the engine.

If you reused your bearings, the crankshaft will probably spin very smoothly. If you have new bearings, a well-installed and properly rebuilt crankshaft will feel

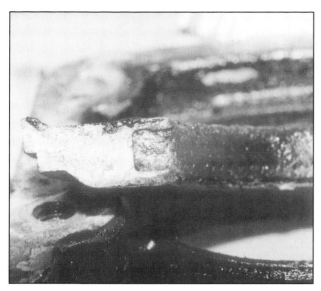

2 To install the new seal, soak it in oil for an hour or two, and then flatten it slightly, so it fits into the groove in the seal carriers. Use a round dowel or socket to slightly flatten the crown of the seal. Rotate the seal back into the block. The lower seal is installed with the oil pan.

TIP

Before installing the crankshaft, make sure the oil passages are clean.

snug as you turn it. In fact, many first-time rebuilders are shocked at how "tight" the crankshaft feels. While there should be no binding or excessive rubbing, it should require a certain amount of effort to turn the crankshaft. How much effort should it require? Actually, the point is moot. If you have installed the bearings and crankshaft so that all bearings have a proper running clearance, the effort to turn it has more to do with the viscosity of the

assembly grease, style of bearings, and your crankshaft's orientation and alignment. As long as there is no specific point in the revolution where the crankshaft binds up tightly, and as long as the crankshaft does not require a Herculean effort to turn it, your crankshaft is properly installed. Oil pressure during operation will build up a bed of oil on the bearings that will eliminate the friction caused by the tight fit of new bearings.

At this point you can install the pistons as described previously, connect the connecting rods to the crankshaft, and begin assembly of the engine after you install the oil lines connecting the main bearing to the oil pump. Double-check the torque on the bolts of the main and connecting rod journal bearing caps or housings. Make sure you have fastened the main and connecting rod bearing cap or housing bolts with mechanic's wire or cotter pins, if the bolts have provisions for these locking devices. Just one last visual inspection for stray parts and tools, and you are done restoring the crankshaft.

CRANKSHAFT OIL SEALS

The oil seals should now be installed. In traditional vertical engines, the bottom halves of the main rear seal should be installed before the crankshaft is laid in place; the top afterward. To install the seal, first flatten the tar-impregnated jute rope that serves as the seal, then insert it into the groove in the seal carriers. After installing the rope, it will stand up in the carrier groove like a ridge.

Trim one of the jute rope seals so it is flush with one of the carriers, but leave the other rope seal a little long at both ends. Which rope seal you leave long and which you trim flush typically isn't important, but your manual may specify which one. In that case, follow your manual's suggestions. One of the rope seals must extend a small fraction of an inch beyond the carrier so the seam between the two rope halves will seal and oil will not leak at this seam. The rope seals are then slightly flattened with a steel or wood rod, and then the seal carriers installed. The front of the engine may not have a seal, though many inline vertical four-cylinder engines have a bolt-on pillow block that looks like the rear seal carrier. Now is the time to install this if you haven't.

THE FUEL SYSTEM

If you want to increase the odds of being able to start your newly rebuilt engine immediately after installation, you should pay particular attention to the next two chapters. An old saw states that an engine only needs three things to work: compression, a timed spark, and fuel. If your engine doesn't start, then one of the three is lacking. Since the engine will be rebuilt when you try to start it, odds are compression won't be the problem. The culprit will be either spark or fuel delivery. Therefore, the next two chapters will have a tremendous bearing on how much fuss and adjustment goes on after the rebuild.

REMOVING LINKAGES AND FUEL LINES

Before we disassemble the fuel system, we need to stop and cover an important safety issue: combustible and flammable fumes in the shop. I have mentioned this threat before, but I want to cover it again. I personally know of nearly a dozen cases of severe shop fires caused by fuel spills. Nearly all were caused by mechanics who broke basic safety rules, did not get adequate training, or failed to react to known problems when they first occurred.

One accident I know of was caused by a weekend mechanic who was blowing out partially clogged fuel lines with compressed air. The fuel bubbled from the gas tank filler neck and splashed a nearby work light. This shattered the light, ignited the entire tank and burned the shop down. Another incident I know of occurred when a mechanic was testing for spark by grounding the spark plug wire near a spark plug hole (with the spark plug removed). Unfortunately, the mechanic ignored a leaking fuel float in the horizontal John Deere engine he was working on. These carburetors will fill the cylinders full of fuel if the floats leak. A helper spun the engine, which in turn blew fuel out of the spark plug hole. The spark at the wire the mechanic was holding ignited the fuel, which burned down the barn they were working in. In both cases the mechanics survived, but they have scars to remind them for the rest of

their lives of the dangers of gasoline. I could go on with more stories, but you get the idea. Gasoline is serious business. Please be careful.

Because fuel spills and their fumes create a significant fire risk, I ask that you do two things before you restore a fuel system: Have a fire extinguisher rated for petrochemical fires handy at all times, and be on the lookout for any signs of leaks. This vigilance is important, but for it to be effective, it's important that you understand flammable fumes and how they move. First, remember that your nose is your best friend. *If you can smell gas, the concentration is high enough for combustion!* Begin ventilation if you smell gas at all. Next, remember that flammable fumes common in shops are heavier than air. That means these fumes accumulate in dangerous concentrations right at the floor level. This, in turn, creates two logical conclusions: (A) If you are standing, you may never smell a serious gas leak, and (B) concrete floors generate sparks nearly every time a metal tool is dropped on them. A dropped wrench may be your last act if you aren't serious about flammable fume awareness. This means positive spark-free ventilation is required any time fuel is spilled or a gas leak is detected. Please, be careful and see your local fire marshal for additional training and fire prevention measures.

The first step in a fuel system rebuild is to remove the throttle linkages and fuel lines. Earlier in the book we covered disassembly of the fuel line and throttle linkage, but now is the time to remove any fuel line or throttle link still attached. Be sure to empty the gas tank with care, making

TIP

Carburetor refurbishing requires care, patience, thoroughness, and a real obsession with cleanliness. The rest is just details.

sure not to spill any fuel. Remove any air breather apparatus, and any glow plug circuitry for diesel engines should be removed now. The glow plug is normally found on the intake manifold.

REBUILDING CARBURETORS

Unless the carburetor was recently rebuilt, there is no good reason for rebuilding an engine without rebuilding the carburetor also. The only question here is whether you will do the job yourself or hire the work out. While most carburetors can be brought back to original operating condition and efficiency with a thorough rebuild, some carburetors are so thoroughly rusty, dirty, or otherwise problematic that you'll want to hire the work out. Unfortunately, deciding if your carburetor needs professional attention is not clear cut. Here are signs that a carburetor needs professional attention:

- Excessive rust
- Damaged parts that are not normally included in a normal rebuild kit
- Significant number of missing parts

Fuel system restoration is mostly common sense, at least until you get to the carburetor rebuild. Removing the carburetor is easy, as usually just two to four mounting bolts or studs hold it on. The fuel line was cut by a previous owner, who had installed an in-line fuel filter. The engine exhibited signs that pointed to a carburetor rebuild—primarily poor idle and overly rich fuel-to-air ratio, which caused sooty black smoke from the exhaust. This Marvel Schebler TSX carb is from a Ford 8N.

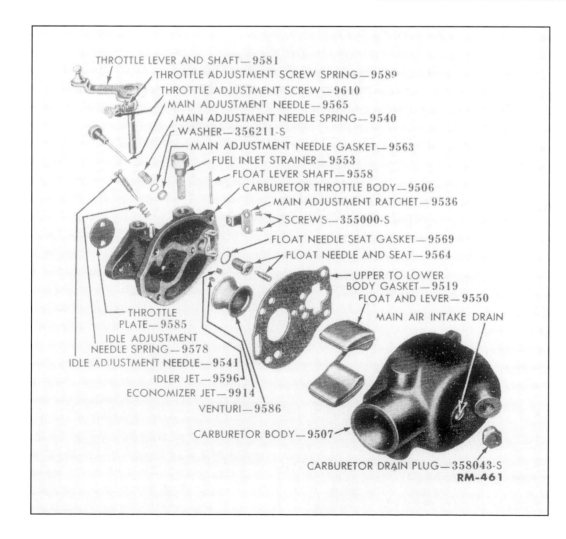

THROTTLE LEVER AND SHAFT—9581
THROTTLE ADJUSTMENT SCREW SPRING—9589
THROTTLE ADJUSTMENT SCREW—9610
MAIN ADJUSTMENT NEEDLE—9565
MAIN ADJUSTMENT NEEDLE SPRING—9540
WASHER—356211-S
MAIN ADJUSTMENT NEEDLE GASKET—9563
FUEL INLET STRAINER—9553
FLOAT LEVER SHAFT—9558
CARBURETOR THROTTLE BODY—9506
MAIN ADJUSTMENT RATCHET—9536
SCREWS—355000-S
FLOAT NEEDLE SEAT GASKET—9569
FLOAT NEEDLE AND SEAT—9564
UPPER TO LOWER BODY GASKET—9519
FLOAT AND LEVER—9550
MAIN AIR INTAKE DRAIN
THROTTLE PLATE—9585
IDLE ADJUSTMENT NEEDLE SPRING—9578
IDLE ADJUSTMENT NEEDLE—9541
IDLER JET—9596
ECONOMIZER JET—9914
VENTURI—9586
CARBURETOR BODY—9507
CARBURETOR DRAIN PLUG—358043-S
RM-461

Most tractor carburetors are fairly simple affairs, as this exploded view of the Marvel Schebler carburetor illustrates. This diagram is from a Ford-New Holland service manual. A service manual for your tractor is an invaluable resource for all phases of restoration. *Courtesy Ford Motor Company Publications*

Excessive rust usually requires some aggressive cleaning, such as removing brass jets and using small manual drills to clear fuel passageways. Removing the jets (small threaded brass plugs found in the fuel passages with precisely sized openings in them), is tedious and difficult, and replacement jets are often not commonly available. Manually drilling fuel passages is an easy way to damage the carburetor, and not recommended for the untrained. Damaged parts, such as cracked bodies, require professional repair, if they can be repaired at all. Missing parts also pose a problem, as you will not have access to replacement parts the way a professional carburetor shop will. In both cases, the carburetor shop may be able to buy your carburetor from you (usually called a "core credit") and sell you a completely rebuilt replacement.

In the absence of these severe problems, you can rebuild the carburetor yourself. Like any part of engine work, it just requires care, patience, and thoroughness.

Carburetor Removal

To remove the carburetor, first drain all the fuel from it. On most carbs, this is done by removing a small drain plug found on the bottom. Unfortunately, these plugs tend to be difficult or impossible to remove without damaging them; your only option then is to carefully remove the carburetor without spilling fuel. To remove the carburetor, loosen the two or three mounting bolts that attach the carburetor to the manifold. Since all linkages and fuel lines have been removed, these bolts are easy to access. As you remove the carburetor, remember to hold it level until you can open it and pour the remaining gas into a safe container.

Note the make and model of the carburetor. Then, before going any further, you should hunt down a carburetor rebuild kit. These are available from any farm supply

store or through mail order from the vendors in the appendices in this book. Many full-service auto parts stores can help with rebuild kits for older carburetors, too.

Disassembly

While a complete and thorough carburetor rebuild is beyond the scope of this book, you can do some cleaning, adjustments, and parts installation yourself that will bring a borderline carburetor back to life. Most antique tractor carburetors are of the updraft design, and their similarities are amazing. The procedures followed here will work on virtually all of them.

Remove all idle mixture and main jet adjusting needles. Before removal, gently tighten them until they seat against the bottom of their seats, noting how many turns it took to do this in the process. Make a note of the turns for later adjustment. Knowing how many turns to tighten the needle will serve as a reference during installation if your service manual or carburetor rebuild kit does not contain adjustment information.

First, remove the fuel strainer from the carburetor fuel inlet elbow. This strainer was in good shape and had a minimum of trash in the strainer screen. Usually these strainers are broken, rusted, and filled to the brim with sediment and chaff.

Next, split the carburetor in half by removing the fasteners that hold the halves together. Usually this is just four small bolts.

Before removal, tighten the needles, noting how many turns it takes to close them. Most needles should close in one to four turns. Record the number of turns for each so that during assembly, you can return the needles back to their original positions. Do not overtighten the needle, or you will damage the seat that the needle bottoms out against.

The first part of disassembly is to split the carburetor in half. It helps to first set the carburetor in a wood-face vise, being careful to apply very gentle pressure to the bowl. From there your hands are free to loosen the three to six bolts that hold the top half of the carburetor to the bottom half. Between the two halves is a gasket that must be replaced, but before you remove it, notice its orientation. If you flip

the new gasket during installation, you may cover an internal passage and render the carburetor useless. After the carburetor is split in half, lift out the venturi tube. This is the brass piece that shapes the throat of the carburetor.

Next, remove the float and needle valve and seat from the top half of the carburetor. The pin that acts as a hinge for the float falls out easily, so be careful. Next, remove the two or three needles used to adjust carburetor performance.

The throttle shaft and choke shaft need to be removed now, but you must first remove the baffles mounted to the shafts. The brass baffle found on each shaft should be secured with two screws that require care during loosening, as the screwdriver slot can be easily stripped. After the screws are out, the baffles may fall right out. If they don't,

1 Removing the carburetor's float assembly starts with pulling the pin that acts as the float hinge.

2 Removing the float assembly exposes the needle valve, which the screwdriver is pointing to. The valve should drop out of the seat.

3 Next, remove the needle valve seat. The seat will have a slot for a screwdriver, but these slots are bigger than any screwdriver I own. I use a small mason's chisel, ground down to the right profile, to remove the seat.

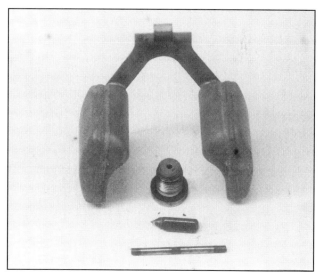

4 This group shot shows the float, the needle, and the seat. Every one of these items, save the float, will be replaced by new ones from the rebuild kit.

After splitting the carburetor in half, work on the top half. Here the throttle baffle is removed from the throttle shaft by taking off two small screws.

rotate the shaft to a position that will allow you to pull the baffle from the slot in the shaft. Use pliers covered with tape to minimize damage.

Once the baffles are out, the shafts will pull right out. The choke shaft is often not sealed, or bushed, and is usually placed under tension with a spring. Be careful with this

Slide the throttle shaft out from the top half of the carburetor. There is a small seal behind a brass retainer, seen here, that must be removed. Pry the retainer out with a properly sized screwdriver, or thread a screw into it if the retainer is really stubborn.

This shows the retainer and the felt seal that it held into the throttle shaft bore.

Any jets that are easy to access and easy to remove should be removed from the top. Care and patience must be used as these jets are very easy to damage. The best way to remove jets is to soak them thoroughly in penetrating fluid. Then a cheap screwdriver can be ground to a profile that fits the slot in the jet perfectly. If they are impossible to remove without damaging them, leave them in. Most of the time the passageways will still get clean during the soak anyway.

spring, as it is easily damaged and occasionally is not included in rebuild kits. The shafts or shaft bores usually don't need attention. The choke shaft is usually not in rebuild kits, and should be cleaned and placed aside until reassembly.

There are one or two seals located in the throttle shaft bores in the carburetor body. They make the shaft airtight so air can't leak through the gaps around the shaft and lean the gas-air mixture. The seals are occasionally kept in place and protected from dirt and crud by small brass retainers that press into the bore in front of the seal. To

TIP

During disassembly of the carburetor, keep all old parts so you can match them up with the parts in the rebuild kit, which is often packaged with parts for more than one carburetor.

remove the seals and retainers, first see if the rebuild kit has new retainers. If it does, then you don't have to be terribly careful with the retainers. Just pry them out with a screwdriver. If the retainers are missing from the kit, be careful not to damage the originals. Usually a screw tightened slightly into the hole in the retainer makes a great handle for a pair of pliers. Using the pliers, grab the screw and with a gentle pull and a slight rocking motion, pull the retainer outward. You can gently flatten and repair the retainer face with a small flat-faced nail punch. Once the retainers are out, remove the seals.

Remove any drains or plugs at the bottom of the bowl, then remove the venturi mixture nozzle (also known as a main jet mixture nozzle). The venturi nozzle is the long brass nozzle that extends into the main throat of the carburetor and feeds fuel into the air stream from the fuel bowl. It is threaded, so simply loosen to remove. A gasket fits between the base of the nozzle and the carburetor body. Note the size and shape, and check to see if this gasket is in the rebuild kit. If not, be sure to hang on to it for cleaning and refitting. By the way, there is a throat drain in the bottom of the carburetor that looks like a small plug of

Now start with the bottom half of the carburetor. First remove the main mixture nozzle. This usually requires a thin-wall, deep socket. Be sure to remove the gasket, if it sticks to the body of the carburetor.

bunched wires pressed into a 3/8- or 1/2-inch hole. This drain is nonremovable and does not require servicing.

Carburetor Cleaning

After complete disassembly, clean the carburetor to remove loose paint and excess dirt and grime. Removing as much paint as possible is particularly helpful, since the paint dissolves much more slowly and increases the time you must soak the carburetor. Leaving paint on the carburetor causes other problems as well. During the soak, the paint may leave behind a gummy residue that might find its way into important passageways in the carburetor. In addition, newer paint may not completely dissolve in the cleaner. Be sure to use a new container of carburetor cleaner for each carburetor. The solution can later be used for degreasing other less critical parts. The brand of cleaner you use isn't important, as I have found all widely available brands work well. The cleaner is available at auto parts stores; rely on the clerk to recommend a brand.

The carb and parts should soak for the duration recommended on the container of cleaner, though a longer soak is not harmful and may be helpful. Be sure to gently

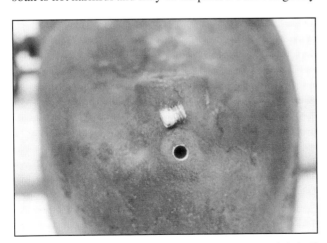

Often there is a small brass plug, or more than one plug, in the bottom, which should be removed to increase circulation of the cleaning fluid.

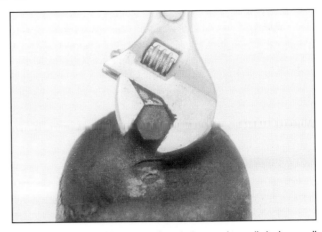

Remove the drain plug, if there is one, from the bottom. There will also be a small drain in the bottom that is packed with what appears to be fine brass wire (sintered bronze, actually). This should not be removed.

move the parts around from time to time to help speed the cleaning process. After soaking, most carburetor cleaners require a very thorough rinsing to remove all traces of cleaner and grime. Be particularly thorough during this step, then dry the parts quickly, especially the carburetor body. Most antique carburetor bodies contain some iron, and some are completely cast-iron. The body will rust if not dried thoroughly. I use compressed air to blow out all

Now that the carburetor is disassembled, soak all the parts in a new bucket of carburetor cleaner. Usually the carburetor will be clean in a few minutes, but if your carburetor has paint on it, the paint will take hours to soften before it can be removed. If your carburetor rebuild kit came with assembly and adjustment instructions, as seen here, take time to review them now. A review of your service manual is a good idea at this point too.

the passages and remove most of the water, then use a hair dryer to dry it completely.

At this point, some rebuilders will "media blast" the carburetor body using glass beads (as opposed to sand). This supposedly cleans the carburetor body more thoroughly, but I worry about contaminants and damaging particles working their way into the passages and orifices, so I don't do it. I also find it's almost always unnecessary unless the body is extensively rusted, as the biggest carburetor problems are worn or ruined jets and foreign material in passageways—neither of which can be cured through media blasting.

The best way to clean passageways and to be sure they are free, is to use compressed air. Blow the passageways out in the direction opposite the fuel flow. This often dislodges any grime or particles lodged in the passageways. To be sure they are free, and to loosen stubborn dirt and particles, I use monofilament fishing line, in 30- to 50-pound test size, and push the line through the passageways. Don't use mechanic's wire or any other hard wire to clean the passageways. The risk that the wire will damage the jets and passageways is just too high.

Assembly and Adjustment

Assembly is the reverse of disassembly, with the addition of a few adjustments and precautions. First, double-check your cleaning work. This is the last chance to make sure all the passageways in the carburetor are clear and to make sure that no trace of cleaning residue, dirt, grime, or water is left behind. Lay out all the components on a clean work area, matching original components with replacement parts from the rebuild kit and other sources. Carburetor kits are often packaged for rebuilding several different models of carburetors. If that is case with your rebuild kit, several parts will be left over. That is why I advised you to throw nothing away during disassembly. The only way to choose the proper part from two or three similar ones is to match it up with the old part.

Carefully reassemble the carburetor, being sure to orient gaskets properly and to keep dirt and dust out of the carburetor. After replacing any drain plugs and the main jet adjusting needle, if present, in the bottom half of the carburetor, install the main mixture nozzle. The mixture needle should be tightened all the way against its seat (gently!), then loosened the number of turns specified in your manual or your disassembly notes. Set the bottom half of the carburetor aside.

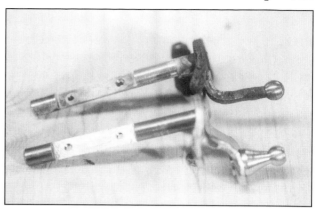

Here the new throttle shaft that came with the rebuild kit is compared with the old one. The old one (top) is more "original," with its unique governor linkage arm and ball. Unfortunately, the shaft is worn and scored, which means air can pass through the shaft seal, affecting the fuel/air mixture. (The worn area appears as a bright strip just to the left of the arm and ball for the governor linkage.) The new throttle shaft will have to be used.

Now install the throttle and choke shafts and baffles in the top half of the carburetor. Remember to install the shaft seals and seal retainers. While the original seal may be made of felt, the modern replacement is usually an O-ring. In fact, if a throttle shaft seal is not included in the carburetor rebuild kit, you can safely use a fuel-rated O-ring as a replacement. Be sure to size the O-ring so that the assembly is airtight, but the O-ring does not prevent the shaft from operating smoothly. After the seals, replace the retainers by gently driving them in with a small wooden dowel and light hammer. Check for smooth operation. Refer to your manual for adjustment of the throttle shaft. Typically, carburetors are designed so the throttle baffle does not quite close when the throttle is in the idle position.

The float should be installed and adjusted next. To adjust, turn the top half of the carburetor body upside down, and lay the main body gasket in place. Measure the clearance between the top of the float and the top of the gasket. Compare this measurement with the values found in the service manual. Lacking this specification, the carburetor rebuild kit may provide the measurement. Use the service manual's measurement over the kit's dimension if they differ. To adjust the float height, carefully bend the support arms that that connect the float(s) to the hinge. Make sure the bend(s) are not sharp, but rather are smooth and extend the entire length of the support. Also make sure the bend(s) do not extend to the landing at the hinge that operates the fuel inlet needle valve. This landing should be flat and square to ensure a positive fuel cut-out.

Assemble the two carburetor halves, making sure the gasket is properly oriented. Install the idle speed mixture screw, by turning it in and then loosening it the prescribed number of turns as outlined by the service manual or by your disassembly notes. If your carburetor has one, make sure the main jet needle, also known as a "power needle,"

Float height is an important measurement to take, and the correct measurement should be in the rebuild kit or your service manual. Here the carburetor top is inverted, and the distance between the top of the float (the "bottom" in this picture, as the carburetor top has been inverted) and the gasket surface. Please note that this measurement must be taken with the gasket in place. Bend the float arms near the hinge to adjust this distance.

or "economizer needle" is seated and adjusted properly. Likewise, there is often a main jet cut-off valve situated at the bottom of many carburetors; this needle valve must be properly installed and set to the "off" position.

That's it! Carburetor rebuilding is not difficult. You just need to be nearly fanatical about cleanliness, have a measure of patience, and be sure to document and note all the particulars of your carburetor during disassembly for problem-free assembly and adjustment. If you plan on painting the carburetor (some makes did this and an accurate restoration would not be complete without this step), I would wait until the engine is installed and you are done testing and adjusting the carburetor before painting.

DIESEL FUEL INJECTION

Diesels work on a different principle than carbureted engines, and require a completely different approach during fuel system restoration. Before we get too far, let's review basic diesel engine operation. Diesel fuel is a much heavier fuel than gasoline, and as such, has different burning characteristics. Diesel is very combustible, but not as flammable as gasoline. That means, under certain circumstances, diesel will burn after simply being compressed. Diesel engines, therefore, have no ignition systems, and require no spark—just high compression—to run. Because diesel is a heavy fuel with poor vaporization characteristics, carburetion systems are ineffective at delivering diesel fuel to the air stream. Therefore, a pump injects diesel fuel through an injector nozzle into the cylinder at the right time.

If your diesel fuel delivery system needs work, you should do it now while the engine is being rebuilt. Unless you have some special training or experience in this area, I do not recommend trying to rebuild your own fuel injec-

tion system. While some of the light work, such as injection nozzle replacement, is certainly within everyone's grasp, rebuilding the pump, metering head, and fuel lines require a professional shop. In addition, virtually all diesel testing equipment is specialized and expensive. If that's not enough, parts for these systems (with some exceptions) are virtually unavailable, and only professional shops with access to specialty suppliers can easily obtain parts. Therefore, we will simply outline removal and installation of the diesel fuel system.

Removing Injectors

The first thing to remove, save the fuel filters mentioned earlier in the book, are the injection nozzles. These are found at each cylinder and atomize the fuel for complete and even burning. The fuel line is connected to each injector with compression fittings, and removing the lines is straightforward. The fuel lines can be reused if there is no damage or rust.

The injectors are almost always bolted in place and easily removed. The mounting bolts go through holes in the injector flange or through a separate mounting plate that fits over the injector base. O-rings or gaskets seal the injectors, and these must be removed and saved for later reuse or comparison when new parts are obtained.

The fuel pump, fuel metering assemblies, and often the governor are almost always combined within the same unit. Once the fuel delivery system is removed, further disassembly is not usually required. You should note that regardless of the combination of subsystems and how they work together, the fuel delivery system must be synchronized to the engine. Synchronization varies widely, so any generalizations I could make wouldn't be helpful here. Fortunately you can count on the service manual having complete information for synchronization, the location of registration marks, and how you should remove the unit

Diesel fuel injection restoration starts with diesel fuel filter maintenance and replacement. Here are three filters on a John Deere diesel. From left, they are water separator, primary filter, and secondary filter.

from the engine. Be sure to read through your manual's directions thoroughly before you start.

Next, find a rebuild shop that seems knowledgeable and professional. The shops mentioned in the appendices of these book all specialize in, or actively seek, antique tractor fuel injection system restorations. Ask them exactly how complete units submitted for restoration should be for rebuilding. For example, while on the surface it makes sense to remove the governor or throttle linkage and rebuild them yourself, you will find most shops expect those items to be present to properly credit you for a core exchange if your unit cannot be rebuilt. If they can rebuild your unit, often you will find these shops include rebuilding the entire unit in their price. Removing and rebuilding those subsystems yourself may not save any money.

Most of the folks at these shops are very helpful and diligent, and can steer you in the right direction for parts and guidance, should it make sense to rebuild these subsystems yourself. Remember that dirt and contaminants are the worst thing in the world for your diesel fuel delivery system. Immediately cap all fuel inlet and outlet ports with rubber caps or thick cloth tape before storage or while shipping the unit to a rebuilding shop.

INTAKE MANIFOLDS

Manifolds seem to be a common problem area for antique tractors. Often they are rusted or worn through, or they are warped beyond reuse. Close inspection is important during any engine rebuild.

Removal Problems

Your problems will start right off the bat when you remove the manifold. Usually, the nuts and stud that fasten the manifold to the engine are rusted beyond recognition and defy all methods of loosening. Often you can count on breaking at least one stud off at the block or head and having to drill it out. If that isn't enough, you can also bet that the manifold gasket has completely metamorphosed into some weird unrecognizable alien material that defies description and requires lots of elbow grease to remove. In short, manifold removal isn't the most enjoyable part of engine rebuilding.

To remove, first soak the nuts with penetrating fluid, and heat them thoroughly after the volatile (and flammable!) compounds in the penetrating fluid have evaporated. Then try loosening the nut with an air impact wrench set on one of the lower settings. It helps to repeat this a few times. If the impact wrench doesn't work, you have two choices: continue this method until it works, or break them off intentionally. I usually cut them off with a torch if they are readily accessible, or I set the impact wrench on a high setting and break them off with the wrench. The nut may deform instead of the stud breaking, at which point you have to use a torch. Another tool that can help is a nut splitter. Occasionally the nuts are not exposed enough to allow

Manifold work begins with exhaust pipe and muffler removal. Must of these bolts and nuts are rusted tight, and may require heat or destruction to remove.

Removing manifolds may be quite a challenge. This manifold is in terrible shape. It has a large crack, the air warmer chamber (not visible in this photograph) is rusted through in spots, and the nuts are stuck tight.

After trying all sorts of less-destructive methods, a gas torch is used to remove the nuts from a tight area. A nut splitter will work, if you can get it on the nuts.

RESTORING DIESEL FUEL DELIVERY SYSTEMS

If you are restoring a diesel farm tractor engine, odds are you'll need to restore the diesel fuel delivery system at the same time. This requires specialized diagnostic equipment and shop tools and professional expertise. While this job may be beyond the reach of the average farm and weekend mechanic, this section will outline the process and help you understand what happens to your diesel fuel system components when they are sent out for repair.

A diesel fuel delivery system has three primary subsystems: injection, metering, and timing. As mentioned in the text, an injection pump delivers diesel fuel to an injector at each cylinder under high pressure. The nozzles atomize the fuel so it's a fine mist—much like a perfume sprayer. The nozzle must also deliver the atomized fuel in the proper pattern to burn the fuel efficiently. The injection system, because of the pressure and because of dirt, deposits and rust that may have accumulated over the years, usually needs attention. At the restoration shop, the injection system will be tested for proper pressure and fuel atomization.

The fuel metering system delivers the proper amount of fuel to the injection system, based on governor response. The metering system differs the most among the different makes. There are two primary designs: multi-port delivery and single port delivery. In multi-port delivery systems, each cylinder has its own fuel meter. In other words, the fuel meters are stationary under each cylinder's fuel injection line, and individual fuel pumps rotate and activate each meter. Single port injection systems use a single pump and meter that rotate as a unit, under each fuel injection line.

As you can imagine, timing is also important in the diesel fuel delivery system. The atomized fuel must be delivered at exactly the right time for a complete burn. While the fuel pump and meter are synchronized during installation, the restoration shop that does this work for you can provide any guidance or specs you need to install the system on your engine. The governor components serve the same purpose as on gas engines, but in diesel engines the governor is integral to, and is restored as part of, the diesel fuel delivery system. Throttle linkages and the fuel cut-off line are usually removed from the unit before sending off for repair.

The photos in this sidebar were taken at Central Fuel Injection in Estherville, Iowa, a leading antique tractor diesel fuel system restoration vendor.

Unless your diesel engine is rare, or unless you are a fanatic about originality and want to make sure you reuse the same unit that came off your tractor, most diesel repair shops simply exchange your unit for a rebuilt one. Most good diesel fuel restoration shops will have a full selection of rebuilt units available for immediate shipment, along with all the parts necessary to rebuild them. Here Central Fuel Injection's shelf of rebuilt units show the selection of injection units available. *Central Fuel Injection*

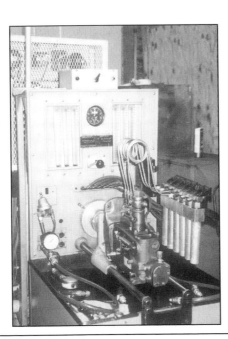

One of the last tests run on a rebuilt diesel fuel delivery system is a complete running load test on a test stand. This test makes sure a newly rebuilt units provides the proper amount of fuel and the proper amount of pump pressure under all throttle and governor settings, and does so by matching or exceeding all specifications for the unit. *Photo by Central Fuel Injection*

This disassembled diesel fuel delivery system is from an antique Oliver 88. As this picture shows, diesel fuel systems rank pretty high on the mechanical difficulty scale. Adding to the degree of difficulty is the fact they require tremendous precision during assembly, and incredibly close tolerances between many parts for proper operation. *Photo by Central Fuel Injection*

the use of a nut splitter, but some may be and this beats ruining the stud. After the nuts are removed, or after you have torched or broken them, the manifold will slide off.

Manifold Inspection

Now that the manifold is off, you will need to inspect it closely. The first thing to do is remove all loose rust with a wire brush on an angle grinder or bench grinder. While complete rust removal isn't necessary at this point, you do need to remove all loose rust. Afterward, inspect for any areas that are rusted through. The loose rust may have hidden a problem you couldn't see on the tractor. If the manifold has no perforations, a small test will help to find thin areas in the manifold that may give you problems in the near future. To perform this test, simply hold a small wrench in your hands much like you would hold a tuning fork, and gently tap the manifold all over. The wrench will make a metallic ringing sound as you tap the manifold. If the manifold has a thin area, the pitch will change noticeably, and really bad areas will return dull thuds. Be sure to check everywhere the casting has an exposed corner, and the undersides, which rust more significantly than the top.

Mating Surfaces

Next, check to see if the mating surface of the manifold is flat and true. This test was discussed earlier. Simply take a straightedge metal ruler, and place the ruler edgewise across the manifold mating surface along several different orientations and positions. If you can slip a business card anywhere between the ruler and the manifold, then the manifold surface must be machined back to true. Also look to see if any of the outside edges of the manifold mating surface are eroded or damaged.

Porting and Polishing

Modifying the intake and exhaust runners, commonly known as porting and polishing, is a good idea. While many consider this a performance step, I think of it more as a standard rebuild step. While true porting and polishing is an elaborate procedure filled with exacting ideas as to the correct size and profiles of the ports, we are doing more of a port "clean-up." To port and polish, simply chuck a carborundum grinding head to a die grinder, don the safety glasses, and remove all the excess carbon, factory defects, and rough edges from around all the intake and exhaust ports in the manifold. Make the inside surfaces of the ports as smooth as possible, as far in as possible. Move to a slightly less abrasive grinding head to finish your work. After porting and polishing, you should carefully match the manifold gasket holes with the port holes in both the engine and the manifold, You'll be surprised how common it is for the manifold gasket holes to be smaller than either set of port holes. Use an X-acto knife to enlarge the gasket holes to match the port holes.

Don't forget to restore your fuel tanks, sediment bowls, and diesel fuel filter while restoring the fuel system.

Manifold Installation

Installation is the reverse of assembly, and requires no special care or instruction. The manifold studs should be installed with thread sealant around the ends to facilitate removal in the future. The gaskets go on next, and are difficult if not impossible on some models to reverse or install wrong. Likewise, the manifold can only go on one way. Install the gasket dry, with no sealants. Mount the manifold, then install brass stud nuts with plenty of brass washers. The brass fights corrosion and facilitates removal. If the torque specifications preclude using brass nuts, then use hardened steel nuts, which corrode less quickly, and coat the outside thread of the stud with thread sealant. This will help with future removal.

AIR INTAKE WARMERS

These are known collectively as heat risers, and now is the time to check and replace any rusted heat risers, and heat riser springs. Heat risers warm the air stream entering the engine while the engine is cold. As the engine warms up, the valve opens or closes, depending on the design or your perspective, allowing the intake air to bypass the warming chamber in the manifold. Riser springs are usually so rusted they no longer exist, and riser valves are usually stuck fast. The valves required frequent maintenance, which they rarely got, to remain unstuck.

John Deere numbered series tractors have a "heat exchanger" (same principle as the heat riser) and Minneapolis-Moline and Case are two other makes that often had manifolds with a heat riser. If your heat riser is stuck, and disassembly is not possible, the usual approach for rusted parts may work: penetrating oil, heat, and patience.

If that doesn't work, you have two choices. First, you may leave the riser alone. Most riser valves are stuck in the "open" or "engine warm" position; these valves can be left stuck, and the manifold can be reused. Second, you can destroy and remove the part and replace it. If individual valves are not available and an operating heat riser is important in your climate, you must replace the entire manifold. Heat risers, while they serve an important purpose in very cold climates and are helpful in others, are not critical to the engine operation. Just realize that running the tractor this way, or with the valve removed, increases the need for a thorough engine warm-up before use, and may cause poor idling in very cold temperatures.

FUEL TANK

No fuel system restoration is complete without completely restoring the fuel tank and any associated lines, fittings, hoses, sediment traps, and bowls. After removing the fuel tank from the tractor, be sure to first empty all fuel into a safe container. Then turn the tank upside down and let it drain for 15 to 30 minutes to remove all remaining fuel.

Inspection and Cleaning

Inspecting the tank requires some careful looking with a flashlight, preferably a fluorescent work light, as they're less likely to start a fire if the bulb breaks. If the tank shows only slight traces of rust, you can safely reuse the tank after cleaning it thoroughly with a lye solution, and then rinsing and drying. If the rust buildup is more than a trace, then you need to scour the tank of accumulated rust and coat the inside of the tank with a sealer designed specifically for the purpose. Also be on the lookout for pinholes, dents, creases, and other problem areas that need repair. Have a qualified welding shop advise you on the feasibility of repair before going any further.

To scour the tank, put some clear water and a handful of small smooth creek pebbles or roofing nails in the tank. (Roofing nails are made of aluminum, hard enough to remove rust but not hard enough to damage the tank.) Then begin agitating the mixture, alternating sides and rinsing often, until all traces of rust are gone. This is a tedious and time-consuming process, and there are no shortcuts here.

Making a tumbling apparatus that is easily turned by hand, or better yet, electrically powered, will help alleviate the drudgery of this job, or you can put it on a small cart and just push it back and forth. The job is finished when the rinse water shows no appreciable signs of rust. Next follow with a solution of water and a small amount of a strong cleaner and repeat. Change the solution two or three times. This will remove any last traces of gasoline, sludge, and fuel varnish. Rinse and dry the tank completely. The exhaust of a vacuum cleaner pumped into the tank helps dry it quickly to eliminate flash rust.

Fuel Tank Repair

At this point, you are ready to prep and coat the interior of the tank. First, inspect the tank again for any pinholes that

TIP

Manifolds without leaks equal a smooth-idling, smooth-running engine. Make sure every manifold mating surface is square and true and the manifold itself is solid without rust holes before installing it.

may have opened up during rust removal. Any holes larger than a thick pencil point (smaller holes will be filled by the coating process described next) will have to be repaired by a certified tank welder who will weld or braze the hole closed. If there are numerous pinholes congregated in one area, that area should be cut out and a patch welded or brazed in. Again, a welding shop well versed in tank repair can help you here. One note on welding shops: Do be aware that many shops no longer do fuel tanks because of the safety and liability issues, so you may have trouble finding someone to do the work. *Under no circumstances should you attempt to weld or braze a fuel tank yourself without special training!* The risk of harm or death is simply too great. If you can't find a shop to repair your tank, then a replacement tank is cheap insurance against death and dismemberment.

Fuel Tank Coatings

Local automotive stores and the appendices are sources for tank coating products. They come as a two- or three-step process, with two or three chemicals. The first step is usually a lye-based cleaner, and if you feel your own cleaning process was sufficient in removing all traces of fuel, residue, and rust, this step can be skipped. The second step is an acid bath that etches the metal. This is important, and requires a full and complete coating. Be sure to follow any instructions on the product for proper drying after this step. The last step is applying the coating. Interestingly, this product bridges and fills small pinholes. The product label will tell you the largest-size hole it will bridge. The coating takes several days in a warm shop to cure completely, and adding fuel prematurely will ruin the coating. Be patient, and make sure the coating has cured before fueling the tank.

The last steps include replacing the sediment bowl assembly, because most old ones leak, due to worn valve seats and valves. While buying individual valves and seats may be possible at your local stores, their availability is sporadic, so plan on buying the whole assembly. When installing the sediment bowl on the tank, be sure to coat the threads with a fuel-resistant thread sealant. Fuel lines should now be reproduced (the lines can be bent by hand), and new flare nuts and compression fittings bought and installed. See the sidebar on proper pipe flaring tools and techniques.

Proper fuel system restoration is important to ensure your newly rebuilt engine's operating performance and efficiency. Because fuel system restoration seems tangential to your main goal of engine rebuilding, it is easy to overlook this important step when rebuilding the engine, and it's common to rush through this and do the job poorly. A properly rebuilt fuel system—including carburetor or diesel fuel pump, fuel tank, lines, sediment bowls, and filter—is a critical part of a well-done engine rebuild.

MAKING TUBE FLARES

Any time you have to recreate a fuel or oil line, you must create a seat at each end of the line. The seat is called a "flared seat," and there are two types. The first is called a single flare, and this type of seat is not used in engine restoration. The second is called a double flare and is used in engine restoration. The idea behind a double flare is simple: First, fold and crush the end of the line inward toward the center of the tube. Then expand the end of the tube, causing the first fold to flatten

and seat against the shoulder. Double flares make strong, stiff, leak-free seats that compression nuts of various oil and gas inlets and line couplings can seal against.

Creating the flare, however, is a little more involved than the concept. First, get a steel tube, preferably plated against corrosion. Never use copper for any type of fuel or oil line in an antique tractor. Copper lines will crack as they fatigue from vibration. Using a tubing bender and a tubing or

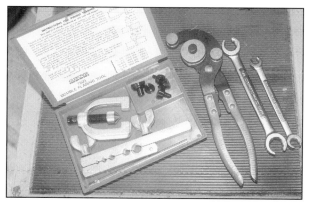

1 Making new fuel and oil lines is something every engine restorer will one day have to do. Like most skills associated with engine rebuilding, a little care, patience, and practice will have you making excellent flares in no time. Shown here is a kit with the tools needed to actually create a double-flared end on an oil or fuel line. Also shown with the kit is a tubing bender and flare nut wrenches.

2 The first step is to fabricate a line that is identical to the line you are replacing. This includes replicating all the bends with the tubing bender. The tube is cut with a tubing cutter, which is nothing more than a smaller version of the plumber's pipe cutter. In fact, a plumber's copper pipe cutter will work in a pinch. This rolling-cam tube bender does 3/8- and 1/2-inch lines; a smaller bender (on the bench) handles 1/4- and 5/16-inch lines.

3 To create the first half of the double flare, file away a small bevel in the end of the tube, according to the double flare kit instructions. This material removal facilitates the first step in this process. After this, set the tube in the small vise included with the kit, being sure to extend the pipe past the top of the vise a small bit. The ridge at the bottom of the anvil is the proper height and can be used, as shown here, to make sure the pipe extends past the top the proper amount.

4 Then, using the press that comes with the kit, drive the anvil down onto the tubing. You want to press firmly, but don't overdo it. Note: Don't forget to slip the threaded brass fitting on the line before you make the flare!

MAKING TUBE FLARES *continued*

pipe cutter, cut and form the line to replicate the original. Shallow and wide bends can usually be made manually, although manual bending will kink the tubing if the bend is tight.

After cutting the tube to length using a tubing cutter, ream the inside of the cuts to remove any burrs and smooth the edges. You can buy a small cutter made for small tubes to make this cut, but a regular plumber's pipe cutter works fine too. When tubing is flared, it may crack from the stress. Therefore, the outside edge of the end of the line must be beveled with a file. This will remove enough material to make the ends of the lines a little more flexible, minimizing the risk of cracking. To create the first part of the flare, you set the tubing in the hand-held flaring vise, being sure to set the tube so it extends the proper amount through the top of the vise. (Don't forget to install the fitting on the tube before you make the flare!) The flaring kit and the

accompanying photographs show how this is done. Next, using the die for the size of tubing you are using, and the press that comes with the kit, set the first part of the flare. Then remove the die, and set the second part of the flare using the anvil of the press. That's it. The flare is complete.

Now that you are finished, remove the tubing from the vise and inspect the flare for cracks and other flaws, such as low spots, out of round, etc. Creating imperfect flares is easy to do, even for those of us who have made quite a few. Here are a couple of other tips for creating flares: Always apply pressure with the press slowly. This will minimize cracking. Setting the tubing in the vise is important. If you set it too high, the flare will be out of round or crack. If you set it too low, the flare will be incomplete or malformed. Last, tubing is cheap. Feel free to practice a lot, as practice is the only way to become proficient.

5 This step creates an inward-pointing fold in the tube's end, as shown here. The "bell" created on the end of the tube should be uniform and concentric. If it isn't, the finished flare might not seal.

6 Now, using the press directly, press down on the end of the tubing with the cone-shaped driver. This completes the inward-pointing fold, and presses it flat on the inside of the tubing, while at the same time expanding the end of the tubing.

7 This last photo shows the finished product: A double flare creates a wide flat end in the tube suitable for use in compression fittings. A well-made double-flared end will seat correctly the first time and never leak a drop of fluid.

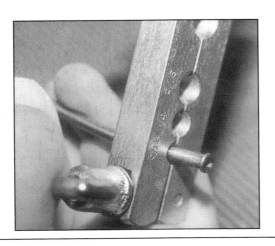

AUXILIARY SYSTEMS

OIL PUMP

The oil pump is the heart of your engine, pumping oil continuously to the critical areas of your engine. With a worn oil pump, oil pressure may drop to the point where it no longer protects parts, such as bearings, under heavy load. Every engine rebuild should include a close inspection of the oil pump, and restoration or replacement should be completed as a matter of course for any pump that shows damage or wear. Likewise, if an engine exhibited poor oil pressure that could not be explained through bearing wear or open galleys, the oil pump should be rebuilt.

Removal

The oil pump is almost always driven off the camshaft, and is almost always of a gear pump variety. This means the oil is pumped by two gears driven in opposition (one spins counterclockwise while the other is driven clockwise), driving oil from the pickup side of the pump and into the oil distribution system. The system works just like an eggbeater, and

performs well. Removal is simple; usually just a few mounting bolts hold the pump in place. The gear that drives the pump may be helically cut, or rarely, a worm gear. To remove these pumps, the camshaft has to be turned as the pump is pulled down. Once it's removed, you can work on the pump at a workbench.

Inspection and Overhaul

Overhaul begins by inspecting the pump's drive gear and the camshaft gear that drives it. There should be no appreciable wear or damage on any of these parts. If there is any damage, you should replace the camshaft or oil pump. After this initial inspection, disassemble the oil pickup screen and related tubes, plates, and housings. Any gaskets between any cover, the enclosed gears, and the housing of the pump will be thin, and their thickness is important, because the gaskets also act as a spacer or shim. Be sure you keep this gasket for comparison later on. Next, remove the pump gear cover. Inspect the inside of the cover for wear. In highly worn pumps, you'll see striations and wear on this inside surface. Then inspect the gears for any abnormal wear or damage.

Oil pump restoration begins by thoroughly cleaning the oil pickup assembly. Here the oil screen of an Allis-Chalmers WC shows all the really nasty stuff you'll likely find on your oil pickup screen. The screen is often rusted as well, requiring replacement. Usually a piece of stainless-steel wire screen of the same mesh will work fine.

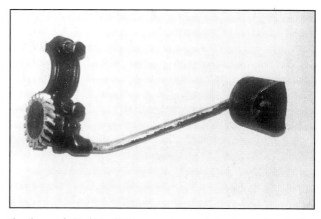

The oil pump of a Ford 8N, which is mounted on a main bearing cap. The oil pickup housing does not have a screen of its own; it sits in a small screen that attaches to the oil drain plug. This screen can then be cleaned at every oil change.

This oil pump came from a Farmall F-20. The protrusion from the base that looks like a hot dog is the oil pressure relieve valve.

After initial visual inspection, measure the pump gear clearance. This specification tells how close the teeth of the pump come to the side wall of the main pump body. Next, measure the clearance between the bottom of the pump gears (the part of the gears that are exposed), and the inside of the pump cover. The best way to take this measurement is to measure the clearance between the gears and a stiff straightedge held against the edges of the pump body. Both of these dimensions are fairly critical, and just a little bit of wear affects oil pressure. Your service manual should have these specifications. If not, I advise replacing a pump if the clearance between the drive gears and the pump body exceeds .005 inch or so, or the gear to bottom cover exceeds .010 inch. These are absolute maximums, and most antique tractor manufacturers called for much closer specifications.

After inspection, the drive gear and drive shaft to the pump gears. The drive gear is often pinned into place and the pin must be extracted first, usually pressed out with a thin punch. After the drive gear is removed, pull the pump drive shaft, and one of the pump gears will come with it. The other pump gear is usually on an idler stud and can be removed directly or after removing a keeper clip. The pump gears—sometimes one, sometimes both—are held onto their shafts with a retaining clip, and the pump gear on the end of the drive shaft usually has a woodruff key.

After disassembly, check the fit and finish of the shafts and the bores the shafts ride in. The shafts should be clean, bright, and show no excessive wear or damage. The bore should also be free of any marks or damage, and should be round with no elliptical wear. Occasionally, the bores in the pump body are bushed, and these bushings can be removed and replaced. Last, inspect the pump body for any deformation or cracking. Any damage calls for housing replacement, as repair is difficult, and once made, repairs are not typically long-lived.

The F-20's oil pump has a serious problem. A small piece of metal broke off the camshaft drive gear and wedged between the teeth of the two gears, bending the oil pump drive shaft.

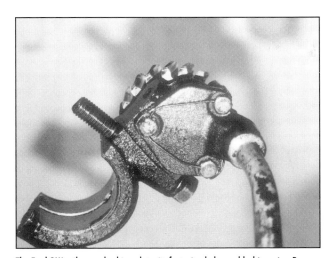

The Ford 8N's oil pump backing plate, its fastening bolts, and locking wire. Removing this plate will expose the pump gears. Engine rebuild kits often come with an oil pump rebuild kit that includes new shafts and at least a new drive gear.

If you didn't rebuild the oil pressure relief valve during block conditioning, do so now while working on the oil pump.

Reassembly and Installation

Assembly of the oil pump is the reverse of disassembly, and is not too terribly difficult. Because of the importance of oil pressure to the engine, care and thoroughness during assembly are important. Make sure all keeper clips and pins are installed. Your service manual should outline some basics steps, but they often neglect the pin that holds the pump drive gear in place. You must replace this pin so that it's tight. That means using a slightly oversized pin (or a knurled one) and pressing it into place so it won't back out during use.

The next important thing to remember is the gasket between the pump's bottom cover and the housing. This gasket must be precise in its thickness, so get the right gasket material. If the proper material cannot be found, very thin card stock, or even thin plastic, such as overhead transparency film, will work. After assembly, check the pump's operation; it should be smooth with no binding or slop. During assembly, fill the pump's interior cavities with fresh 30-weight engine oil. This will minimize the time it takes to prime the engine with oil during initial spin up.

MAGNETO

While a very thorough and complete rebuilding of your magneto is beyond the scope of this book, you can often bring a magneto back to life with a simple cleaning, a little oil, and a tune-up. That's what we'll cover here. A complete magneto restoration should be trusted to a professional shop; at the very least, it will require some outside reading and training on your part before you tackle the job. The reasons are many. A professional shop has test equipment that is not readily available to the hobbyist mechanic. In addition, the shop will have access to parts that will help keep your magneto original. Most important, if there is not a part available, the professionals will have the know-how to substitute other parts or improvise with modern parts. Most of these improvisations and substitution judgment calls can only come from shops that know magnetos well.

Removal

To begin your magneto refurbishing, you will need to remove the magneto; it is usually attached with a few bolts. Before you remove it, though, you will want to check your service manual for timing information and instructions. These instructions will tell how to identify any timing or registration marks, and possibly where to position one of the pistons, probably the first, in respect to its firing cycle. Also, before you remove the magneto, mark, remove, and clear all

Magneto rebuilding starts by removing the mag from the engine. This Wico Model X came from a John Deere B.

of the spark plug wires and coil wires. (Some magnetos feed the rotor cap via a wire, some feed the cap internally.) Remove the magneto without disassembling any part of it beforehand, if possible. After removal, take the unit to a workbench for rebuilding.

Rebuilding the Magneto

The range of magneto designs is wide, and while I can't take you through each magneto, I can make several valuable generalizations. First, virtually all but the very oldest magnetos have something called an "impulse coupling." The impulse coupling delays each spark during slow engine revolutions, such as when the engine is starting. This is done because of an interesting phenomenon of engine fuel burning. There is a very small delay between the time the magneto creates the spark and when the fuel starts burning in earnest. Since you want the fuel to begin burning when the piston is at the top of its compression stroke, the magneto, because of the delay, must initiate the spark *before* the piston has reached the top of the compression stroke. That is why all engines are timed so the ignition begins firing a few degrees BTDC (before top dead center).

Now, back to our impulse coupling. During very slow engine rpm, this advanced timing creates problems. The spark arrives in the cylinder before the piston has reached top dead center, resulting in engine kickback. To prevent this, the impulse coupling retards the timing during slow rpm. The coupling serves two purposes. First, it accelerates the speed at which the magneto turns during starting, helping to generate a stronger spark. Once the engine starts, the impulse coupling disengages, and the timing returns to normal once the engine reaches idle speed.

A strong, smoothly operating impulse coupling is important to an easy-starting engine, so we want to first

This is the driven lug at the rear of the magneto. This lug makes synchronization at installation easier than the usual cut gears found on some other tractors. Note that the full advance lag angle is stamped on the lug. The V-shaped metal anchor positioned at two o'clock is the device that powers the impulse coupling. The drive pawl that engages against this metal anchor, thereby winding the impulse coupling, is barely visible immediately above the anchor.

check its operational status. How quickly the impulse coupling spins the magneto stator determines how strong the spark is when starting the engine, so many starting problems can be traced to a faulty impulse coupling. First, before disassembly, hand spin the magneto in the normal direction of rotation, testing for a very definite "snap" from the impulse coupling. If you aren't sure if you heard one, then you didn't. This noise is distinct and quite noticeable. *Be sure to keep your hands free of the coil or coil output terminal as you do this!* If your impulse coupling and magneto are working, you will get a nasty shock if you don't.

Next, test the voltage from the coil. You will want to see at least 20,000 volts. Many magnetos create more than 30,000 volts. To test, you will need a digital multimeter that measures direct current voltage in excess of 30,000 volts and stores the highest value obtained. The reason the multimeter must store the value is because the magneto's voltage release is momentary. In fact, it's fast enough that the multimeter's display can't react completely to a very high value, plus, you will not be able to read the display quickly enough. This is not your average off-the-shelf multimeter, but it can be obtained through industrial supply houses such as Grainger, Inc. An alternative procedure to using a multimeter is to simply wire a spark plug

TIP

Whenever you work on a magneto, be mindful of the high-voltage output terminal. Spin the magneto with your hand too close to the high-voltage output and you'll get a nasty shock.

to the coil output terminal, then ground the spark plug to the base of the magneto and test for a spark. This method is not foolproof, since many borderline magnetos will throw a spark that's not hot enough or long enough to fire a cylinder during running conditions. However, the presence of a spark is enough to justify tuning and cleaning the magneto to see if it will work or if it needs a professional rebuild.

To clean and oil the impulse coupling, the magneto must be disassembled. There are various designs, but most have a spring-loaded shaft that accepts the input from the magneto drive gears, and stores that energy in the spring. As the spring tightens, it eventually retracts the pawls that free the spring to turn the magneto drive shaft or stator. This entire assembly must be cleaned and lightly coated with oil. The spring must be free of any rust.

Next, inspect all the gaskets and insulators, paying particular attention to the insulators that isolate the components that generate the spark from the base and body of the magneto. These insulators break down or fracture over time, especially the old-style mica insulators. Of course, replacing weatherproofing gaskets is a standard practice during refurbishing. To clean dirt, dust, and other grime from inside the magneto, first use compressed air, then gently wipe with a swab and electrical parts cleaner (available in spray cans). For stubborn grease and dirt, spray the electrical cleaner straight from the can.

At the drive end of the magneto, inspect and replace the oil seal if one is present. Replacement is advisable if it looks as if the original seal is still in place. After pulling the seal, inspect the drive shaft for any scoring caused by the seal. This would also be the time to replace the bearing if it looks worn.

Take the time to recharge the magneto's magnets if someone locally can do the work. Some magnetos have the magnets built into the stator, instead of the housing. (Housing magnets are the horseshoe-shaped magnets we are all used

Light refurbishing of the magneto includes dressing the points with a points file. The points will have to be loosened and spread apart to fit the file between them.

to seeing.) Pulling the stator is necessary to recharge these magnets. Finding someone to recharge magnets can be tough. Call local electric motor repair shops. They often don't do it, but will usually know of someone that can. If a magnet recharger can't be found, skip the recharging for now and see how well your magneto works on the engine.

Assembly

Next, assemble the magneto. Apply a light coat of oil to any drive parts and bushings. Too much oil is a bad thing, so be sparing when oiling magneto drive parts. Don't fill the oil cups yet, though, we'll do that after the magneto is installed. Also, replace any tune-up components, including points, condenser, the magneto cover (rotor cap), the rotor tower cap, and spark plug wires. Replacing these parts is no different than a standard tune-up, so follow all the same procedures, including point gap adjustment, greasing the point cam and double-checking your connections, particularly the connection between the condenser and the points. Leave the rotor cap off for now.

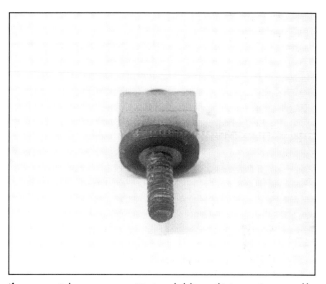

Replacing the points and setting the point gap is something you should do at every engine rebuild. Here, while the points arm is resting on the highest point on the drive rotor cam, set the distance between the points with a feeler gauge. Both large screws seen here will have to be loosened to move the points backing plate back or forth as needed for adjustment.

If your magneto has poor or nonexistent spark delivery, this is sometimes caused by old, rotted insulators. This screw protrudes from the magneto body, but cannot be in contact with the body of the magneto, or the system will short circuit. The insulators you see around this bolt are often old, cracked, or otherwise damaged. This means the magneto will ground against itself, causing the magneto to appear "dead."

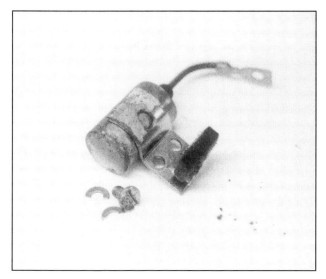

Condensers are easily replaced, and they're usually pretty cheap. Replace the condenser, along with the points, whenever you rebuild an engine.

If you will look closely at the points, you will see a whitish material surrounding the contacts. This corrosion will eventually foul the points, causing the magneto to misfire, if it will fire at all. Points replacement or filing is the sure fix for this problem.

Chapter 11

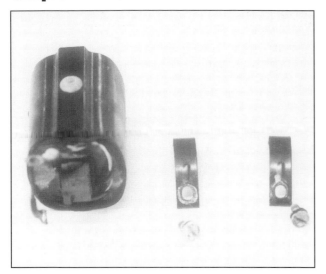

If after all your maintenance and light refurbishing your magneto will not fire, sus-pect the coil. (Assuming you have double-checked your mounting of the magneto and its static timing!) Coils are usually easy to replace, though they can be hard to find. This coil is ready for replacement. Shown with it are the two retaining straps used to mount it.

Magneto Installation and Timing

Installing the magneto begins with positioning the engine properly. The exact procedures vary somewhat, but virtu-ally all of them require that the Number 1 piston (left cylinder in John Deere engines, the front cylinder in most in-line engines), be at top dead center (TDC) of the com-pression stroke. Place your finger or a small tissue over the Number 1 spark plug hole to determine when the Number 1 piston is initiating its compression stroke. Continue turn-ing until the engine TDC mark reaches the index pin or, in the case of John Deere horizontal engines, the impulse mark on the flywheel reaches its proper index mark. (Loca-tion of the index mark varies; check your manual.) Now, turn the magneto drive gear, in the direction of rotation, until either the registration mark of the magneto's drive gear lines up with the marks on the engine's drive gear or the impulse coupling snaps while the rotor is under the Number 1 cylinder spark plug terminal. The drive gear of the magneto and drive gear of the engine should line up. Loosely mount the magneto to the engine. Now rotate the entire magneto *opposite* the normal rotation of the magneto drive gearing. In other words, turn the magneto the same direction (when looking at the top of the rotor tower) of the rotor tower. This is difficult to visualize, but some close

Don't forget new spark plugs and spark plug wires while rebuilding your engine.

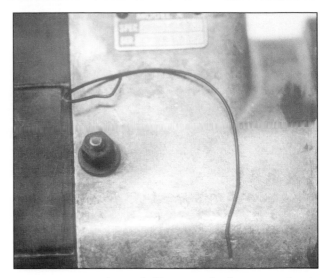

To test your magneto, make a wire lead from a piece of mechanic's wire. Fashion the end so the wire fits snugly in the Number 1 spark plug wire hole in the distributor cover. Then bend the wire so the loose end is just a fraction of an inch from any metal part of the magneto body. Mount the magneto in a wood-lined vise (don't tighten it down too hard!) and then spin the magneto drive lug. After the impulse coupling snaps, you should see a bright blue spark between the wire and the magneto body. If not, double-check your work. Still perplexed? That's all right. These devices are tricky, and there is no shame in sending one out to a professional magneto rebuild shop for a complete overhaul.

study of the manual and some mental gymnastics should build a picture in your mind.

Continue turning the magneto until you reach the end of possible travel. Now turn the engine until the next cylinder in the firing order reaches TDC during its compression stroke. This extra turn of the engine is necessary to wind the impulse coupling. Now, turn the magneto back slowly, until the impulse coupling trips. The magneto is now perfectly timed! If you don't hear the impulse coupling trip, or you hear it trip during the first turn, then you are turning incor-rectly, and you need to reverse directions and follow this step again. Finish up the installation by tightening the fas-teners completely, installing the rotor cap, and installing new spark plugs and spark plug wires.

DISTRIBUTOR

Restoring a distributor is much like restoring a magneto, but simpler. With distributor ignitions, much of the difficult componentry has been simplified, and the spark advance mechanisms are more easily serviced and tend to be more robust. Removal and installation are nearly identical, as are tune-up issues. There are a few differences. First, the spark advance mechanism is inertial. Most use a system of weights and springs, much like a governor, to advance and retard spark. In addition, vacuum advance technology became common in later distributors, something magnetos never had. Timing procedures are a little different, as taking a true running timing (timing the distributor to the engine while the engine is running) is critical with a distributor, but typically unnecessary with a magneto.

Removal

First, mark and clear all spark plug and coil wires. Be sure to mark the rotor cap terminals as well. Like the magneto, a distributor is usually only held to the engine with a bolt or two. Refer to the service manual before beginning these steps in case identification of timing and synchronization marks is necessary.

Take the distributor to the workbench for further work. Start the disassembly with the rotor cap and tower, and then remove any dust plates covering the point set. Grab the drive end of the distributor and turn it, feeling for any roughness or looseness of the drive shaft within the bushings. If either of these conditions exist, the distributor will have to be completely disassembled and new bushings will have to be installed.

Disassembly

To completely disassemble the distributor, first loosen the points backing plate from the distributor body. Next remove the advance mechanism. At this point, the drive gear must be removed. The gear is usually pinned in place, and removing the pin will allow removal of the drive gear. After the drive gear is removed, the drive shaft, along with part or all of the advance mechanism, can be pulled from the distributor body.

If the distributor drive shaft bushings need attention, now is the time to drive them out and replace them. If the bushings have helical grooves for oil distribution, be sure the new bushings have the same types of oil feed grooves. Often the grooves are in the drive shaft, and plain bushings were used that can be replaced with plain bushings.

Before inserting the drive shaft, inspect and reassemble the advance mechanisms. The springs in the inertial weight advance system are very specific springs that cannot be replaced with just any old springs. The composition and tension are balanced for the weights and intended engine operating speed. Therefore, reusing the original springs is advised in all circumstances, unless they are clearly damaged or otherwise beyond reuse. If springs must be replaced, you should only use springs you know to be certified for use in that distributor. Unfortunately, finding them is often next to impossible, so finding a used distributor to rob them from is the only way to obtain them. If that isn't possible, you'll have to purchase a professionally rebuilt distributor.

Next replace the vacuum advance mechanism. While some earlier distributors had serviceable vacuum advance mechanisms, replacing the entire vacuum advance unit is preferable and cheaper in the long run. After assembly of the advance mechanism and the points backing plate, the drive shaft and drive gear can be

TIP

> Be sure to refer to your service manual for a complete explanation of synchronizing your magneto or distributor to the engine.

installed and assembled, after lightly oiling the drive shaft. Fasten the points backing plate and test the operation of the drive shaft, the rotor drive shaft, and the advance mechanisms. Everything should feel smooth and precise, with no noticeable looseness.

Next assemble the point set and condenser, using new components; adjust the point gap, and lube the points cam arm. Just a little dab of grease behind the arm is all it takes—don't overgrease it. Double-check all your connections and fasteners, then install the points dust plate, replacing all gaskets, insulators, or dust seals beforehand. Refrain from adding any oil to the oil cup (if present) until installation.

Installation and Timing

Installation and timing a distributor is also similar to a magneto. We first statically time the distributor to the engine. This will at least ensure the engine will run until we can fine-tune it with a running timing. To install the distributor, turn it until the points are open and the rotor tower is under the Number 1 cylinder terminal in the rotor cap. I like to install the rotor cap, and then mark the distributor body with the location of the Number 1 terminal. I then remove the cap and line up the rotor with that mark. Some engines have marks on the distributor housing and engine or engine driving gears that will help synchronize the distributor to the engine. Occasionally that isn't the case, though, so you must turn the engine so the Number 1 piston, while on its compression stroke, is lined up with the idle timing mark (not TDC). The drive lug and recess between the distributor and the gear in the engine that drives it should line up perfectly. Then hold the rotor firmly, install the distributor, and fasten the base to the engine. Unlike a magneto, the base of the distributor usually doesn't turn, just the body does.

Static-timing the distributor is the same, except in this case you can't listen for an impulse coupling snap, and you don't need to turn the engine a second time after the distributor is installed. You will have to hook up a spark plug (a spark tester helps here) to the Number 1 cylinder, and look for a spark. To get a spark, hook the coil to a suitable battery. Don't hook the coil to the distributor just yet. Next, turn the distributor body in the direction of rotor tower rotation until it will turn no more. Now hook up the coil to the distributor, then slowly turn the distributor body opposite the direction that the rotor tower turns until you get a spark at the spark plug. As soon as you get a spark, firmly hold the distributor

TIP

> Even if your radiator doesn't leak or need rebuilding, having a professional shop soak the radiator in a cleaner that aggressively removes scale and rust can dramatically improve its efficiency. Some mechanics recommend against this, since the corrosion and rust may have been masking a leak, and the leak may develop after cleaning. I recommend that production tractors have the radiator cleaned and then repaired if a leak develops. Show tractors don't need the extra cooling efficiency, and the risk of leaks isn't worth efficiencies you don't need.

body while you lock it down. Your distributor is now statically timed. Some folks will tell you to position the Number 1 cylinder to TDC, as you would a magneto, but a distributor must be statically timed to the timing mark and not TDC.

HYDRAULIC PUMPS

Full and complete hydraulic pump restoration is beyond the scope of this book, but usually a few minor maintenance and restoration procedures need to be tackled during an engine rebuild. First of all, this book assumes an engine-mounted hydraulic pump–it will not cover pumps integral to the transmission.

Hydraulic pumps cause only one problem for rebuilders: leaks. The most notorious leak allows hydraulic oil to bypass the pump's oil seal and dump hydraulic fluid into the engine. This is particularly common and should be sought out and addressed now. This type of leak can be repaired with a new seal, but more likely the old seal has scored the pump's drive shaft, and the shaft will have to be repaired before a new seal will work.

Repair Options

There are three common repairs: chroming the shaft, installing a sleeve, and filling the scoring with epoxy designed for this purpose. The most common and easiest solution is to sleeve the shaft. Sleeves are available from any bearing supply source. Bring the pump with you, as they will need to measure the shaft to correctly outfit you with the proper sleeve.

Epoxy works well, too, and can also be found at your bearing supply center. Simply fill in the groves and scoring, after painstakingly cleaning the shaft to remove all trace of oil and dirt, leaving a little too much epoxy in each scored area. After it cures, the excess epoxy is then sanded, "shoe polish"-style, with long strips of successively finer

grades of wet or dry sandpaper. You end with 1,500-grit or finer sandpaper that polishes, more than sands, the epoxy. The sanding should be done so the entire circumference of the shaft is sanded evenly. Plating the shaft is also an option, though it tends to be the most expensive, and finding someone that will do this work can be tough, especially in smaller towns. I recommend sleeving or filling the scoring.

Gaskets

Other common repairs that should be addressed at this time are bearing and gasket replacement. To inspect and replace the bearing, the pump body is usually split in half. The pump body halves are usually bolted together. Be careful when splitting the body, and lift the halves apart slowly, because there are often spring-loaded relief valves that love to launch themselves into orbit if the halves are carelessly and quickly pulled apart. The bearing is usually of the ball type, and can be easily pressed off so a new bearing can be driven on. Between the body halves, a very thin gasket acts as a spacer; when you replace this gasket, be sure to use gasket material of identical composition and thickness. Many hydraulic repair shops can obtain this material for you. Occasionally this material is difficult to find, so be careful with the old gasket, because you may need to reuse it.

To wrap up pump repairs, inspect for drive gear wear, pump body cracks, and other problems. Other concerns include engine proofmeters, which are occasionally mounted to engine-driven hydraulic pumps. Be sure to inspect and repair any problems with the proofmeter cable coupling before installing the pump. Last, but not least, occasionally the pump shares a drive design with a governor, diesel fuel pump, or other engine auxiliary device. If that is the case, check the shared gearing to make sure any installation and repair issues are addressed before mounting the pump.

COOLING SYSTEM
Water Pump

The cooling devices on the engine should also be rebuilt during an engine restoration. Unless you know the water pump has been recently rebuilt, rebuild or replace it as a matter of course. A rebuilt water pump is usually inexpensive, with a trade-in, and usually it is time consuming to remove after the engine is back together and installed. The prospect of going through these steps just six months after finishing your tractor is sufficient to warrant a new water pump.

Unfortunately, rebuilding the water pump yourself, while possible, is usually not the greatest idea. Pulling the fan hubs and the impellers is difficult, and many hubs have been cracked and ruined by overzealous rebuilders confident that he or she can pull them with no problem. The proper drive shafts with their integral sealed bearings are not widely available, and when they are, they cost nearly as much as a completely rebuilt pump. Because of this, I think you will find professionally rebuilt water pumps are well worth your time and money. In addition to the mail order firms mentioned in the appendices, most full-service auto parts stores near you can subcontract this job out to a rebuilding firm for you.

Cooling Fan System

Your tractor's cooling fan drive system may be as simple as fan blades attached to a hub in the water pump, or it may be as involved as a supported fan shaft drive system, made famous by the John Deere horizontal-engine tractors. It may also be a hybrid design, mounted to the front of the engine and driven like a water pump. The latter type was made famous by early Farmall letter series tractors, though this design can also be found on other tractors. Fortunately, it's easy to refurbish any of these systems. In particular, on systems with a water pump-driven fan, there is nothing to be done to the fan and hub assembly except straighten and repair or replace damaged blades.

On supported fan shaft engines, such as the horizontal-engine John Deeres, the fan shaft drive assembly simply requires replacement of the bushings and bearings. These bushings and bearings are available on the replacement parts market. Please note that on the very early John Deere As, the fan shaft was exposed, and there was a support approximately halfway down the shaft. This support was not bushed and the fan shaft turned inside a bore in the support. Wear resulted in fan shaft movement, which created stress that often fractured the support. Be sure to inspect all supports in these models of tractors for the beginning of cracks. The worn bore is usually repaired by drilling the bore wider and pressing in a bushing. Other concerns are the front bearing for the fan shaft, which is typically worn. The driven end, in the governor assembly, is supported by a bearing, which may need to be replaced.

In the case of independent fan hub assemblies, two designs are in common use. The first is a support on the front of the engine that holds a shaft. Around this shaft is a hub with a bushed bore that's kept in place with a retaining clip or ring. The fan blades are attached to the hub, which is driven by the engine drive belt. Interestingly, this hub often doubles as an oil reservoir for the assembly, and a small filler hole in the hub is evident. In some of these systems, an oil seal was present behind the hub to control oil leakage. Keeping the hub filled with oil was often overlooked, and often the bushings or shaft must be replaced.

Radiator

Restoration of the radiator starts with assessment of its current condition. Is the radiator completely shot? Is the bottom tank rusted through? In the case of multipart radiators

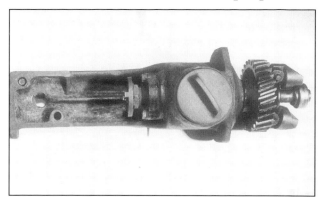

Rebuilding other auxiliary systems should also take place now. Governors, such as this Case CO governor and magneto drive mechanism, should be torn apart and inspected. Bearings, shafts, and bushings should be replaced or repaired as needed.

After assessment, clean the radiator thoroughly. Removal of chaff and dirt from between the fins of the core is the most important part of cleaning, and you'll want to be sure to do a good job here. While you are at it, straighten the core's cooling fins. The entire radiator, after removing the worst of the debris and dirt from the core, can be pressure washed. Exercise care with the core, because the pressure can bend the cooling fins.

There are two main types of radiators: one-piece radiators, with the tank soldered to the core, and multipart radiators, with the tank and core mechanically fastened to each other. You should have no trouble disassembling multipart radiators, except for some really rusty fasteners, and replacing the major components. If minor damage to the tanks is a problem, careful straightening is fully within the engine rebuilder's grasp. If you choose to replace the tanks, many reproduction and used tanks are available, although used tanks are not particularly common for older antique tractors. If the core of your multipart radiator is beyond hope, reproduction cores are occasionally available, or custom cores can be ordered from any automotive or construction industry radiator repair shop. New gaskets are simple enough to make and install to complete the job.

Radiator restoration gets tricky when it requires significant soldering. Problems that must be repaired through soldering include tank pinholes and cracks, holes in and damage to the core, and loose overflow pipes. Later-model tractors are more likely to have tanks soldered onto the radiator core into a complete one-piece unit. This makes tank removal and repair impossible unless you have brazing and soldering skills. While these skills are certainly not difficult, becoming proficient requires practice. If you are not inclined to acquire these skills, I recommend entire radiator replacement, or have a local radiator shop do the work for you.

ASSEMBLY, INSTALLATION AND TESTING

At this point, you are close enough to the end of the project that the sense of completion is palpable. Like a horse after a hard day's work, we all can get a little case of "barn fever" and start rushing the last stage of engine rebuilding. And why not? The engine looks nearly complete, and everything on it is new or restored, and it's clear by now you have a nice little engine that should run well.

Unfortunately, because of this excitement, and in the rush to finish things up, we tend to slap the engine in the tractor and crank it up. During this rush, I have seen and made many mistakes. So I suggest you slow down, put things in perspective, and realize there is still enough work remaining to justify the same deliberate approach you had during the first part of the project. Plus, there are still several restoration steps you will need to complete, and the engine still has to be closed up, both of which are not two-minute affairs. After that, installing the engine, testing it, and then breaking it in are also not things that can be done quickly. With that in mind, let's round this corner to the home stretch with a plan and let's get your engine running.

BALANCING THE FLYWHEEL

The flywheel is the last thing you will install on the engine before final engine installation (if the engine was removed) and testing. One last thing that can be done to the flywheel that is a nice extra is balancing. It's not mandatory, so I didn't include it in flywheel restoration. Balancing the flywheel produces an engine free from vibration. This lack of vibration will help the engine bearings and seals nearest the flywheel last longer. Balancing a flywheel, however, requires the services of a machine shop with special equipment. The shop that surfaces the flywheel can probably balance it as well.

The procedure is similar to balancing a car tire. The shop will spin the flywheel on a balancing machine. In simple terms, the balancer identifies areas of the flywheel where metal can be drilled away to balance the side of the

flywheel with too much weight, which generates a wobble. Newer machines also identify how far from the center and how big the drilled hole must be. The shop will then drill holes at these spots to balance the flywheel. Large flywheels, such as those found on very old antique tractors and John Deere horizontal-engine tractors, may be too large for many automotive shops. In that case, look for a full-service machine shop.

FINAL CHECKLIST

The last procedures you perform during an engine restoration are cylinder head fastening and "buttoning up" the lower end of the engine—oil pan, seals, etc. This is your last chance to make sure you haven't forgotten anything, left any fasteners loose, and to double-check the other little details that can create an expensive detour later. Here is a list of commonly overlooked items that are important to check at the end of an engine rebuild:

- Check for cotter pins and mechanic's wire on all the fasteners that require them.

As you assemble the engine for test firing, be sure you double-check all connections. Seen here is an oil delivery line, one of many critical connections occasionally overlooked in the mechanic's rush to get the engine running.

- Look for missing oil galley plugs.
- Clean any dirt or contaminants that may have accumulated during the rebuild.
- Account for any extra parts—were they replaced, or did you forget to install them?
- Spin-test the engine by hand to visually check operational integrity and smoothness.
- Check for forgotten or missed freeze plugs, including the back of the engine.
- Visually check cylinder sleeve O-rings for adequate seating.
- Liberally apply oil to the surfaces that need them.
- Make sure Plastigage was removed from the crankshaft journals.
- Check for assembly lube on all bearing surfaces.
- Tighten and secure all oil lines.
- Check timing of diesel fuel pump. (Getting the timing right here is real important.)
- Repair bolts and threads left for later repair.
- *Double- and triple-check everything.*

INSTALLING THE ENGINE
Closing It Up

Install the cylinder head according to the instructions in the cylinder head chapter, if you haven't already. Be sure to double-check the torque specs as you install the head fasteners. Also remember to fasten your hoist brackets under your head bolts if your service manual recommends attaching brackets to the cylinder head (most do). At this point you should install the front timing cover, the water pump, if it attaches to the engine, and any auxiliary devices and parts or assemblies that may be difficult to install when the engine is mounted on the tractor. You can safely leave off things such as carburetors, magnetos, and so forth that are more easily installed when the engine is mounted to the tractor. You don't want to make the engine overly heavy for hoisting, nor do you want to attach things that could get in the way of the hoisting chains. If your hoisting brackets weren't under the head bolts, attach the hoisting brackets the same way you did to remove the engine at the beginning. If you have forgotten exactly how you did this, refer back to your service manual. If your manual doesn't specify, attach brackets under two head bolts.

Oil pan installation comes next. Take the time to flatten and straighten any rough flanges found on the oil pan. These flanges are notorious for becoming wavy over the years, creating a lot of leak points. Bar stock placed against the flange and beaten with a heavy hammer will do wonders for straightening them. High spots and rough spots can be minimized with a large mill file. A liberal dose of gasket sealant and a thick cork-style gasket will seal the oil pan, but because oil pans are so notorious for leaking, I recommend using modern gasket-forming products. These products apply like, and have the consistency of, silicone

Finish mounting all ignition and auxiliary systems in preparation for testing. Now is the time to double- and triple-check all connections and synchronization tasks. Synchronizing the magneto to the engine is an important step if you want the engine to start on the first try. (The lug that drives the magneto is seen here.)

While routing spark plug wires, the correct firing order of the cylinders may be as close as the engine block. Here the block of a Case CO clearly outlines the engine firing order.

caulking. (Don't use silicone caulking!) Apply it in a large bead all along the bed of the engine block where the oil pan will mate against it, being sure to completely encircle each bolt hole. Also apply caulking around corners, especially where the rubber oil pan seals meet the seal carriers. If you are using a cork gasket and sealant, apply the sealant to both sides as usual. Tighten the oil pan bolts, but stay on the low side of the torque specification. Try not to tighten the oil pan so much that all the gasket-forming compound is squeezed out from the seam.

Swinging the Engine

Attach the hoist chains to the brackets, and then lift the engine just enough to take the weight of the engine off the engine stand. Remove the bolts that attach the engine to the engine stand. Roll the hoist and engine until it is near the tractor, then install the flywheel and clutch if necessary. After the flywheel is in place, lower the engine, using a helper to guide the engine into place. In the case of vertical

TIP

I also suggest that you take the time to thoroughly clean, prime, and color-coat the engine before removing it from the engine stand. Getting the first coat of paint on the engine while it is still on the stand is so much easier than while it is on the tractor.

engines with a rear flywheel, lining up the tractor's drive shaft with the clutch pilot bushing in the flywheel will be your toughest job, and there is no way around trial and error and multiple attempts. Just be sure not to damage the pilot bushing in the process.

After lowering the engine in place, attach the engine to the frame of the tractor, using new, hardened bolts coated with thread sealant. This will minimize the risk that they'll back their way out from engine vibration. This is specially important where the engine crankcase is a structural part of the tractor. Double-check all your work. Finish assembling the engine, mounting the carburetor, the magneto, and any oil lines, filter, and starter. Don't forget the little things, such as the exhaust pipe. In the rush to test the engine, it's easy to forget something. If your tractor has a starter, install a freshly charged battery and connect only those connections necessary for the starter to turn, but leave the battery ungrounded for now.

TESTING AND THE MOMENT OF TRUTH

Since there is a possibility that something on the engine may need further attention or a problem may develop that requires clear engine access or removal, only install those systems necessary for engine startup and running. Since at this point we are more interested in assembling the tractor just enough to test the engine, some things are not installed right now. For instance, during testing we won't need a generator, and possibly some other items. The oil line has to be run to the oil pressure gauge to check oil pressure during our initial spin up. If your oil pressure gauge is inoperable, or your tractor has an old-style red head or "make or break" style gauge, you may want to temporarily attach a modern oil pressure gauge to get an accurate reading.

Magneto ignition systems do not need any further attention, though you may want to rig a ground wire so you can kill the engine easily from beside the tractor. Ignition wiring can be directly wired to the distributor from the battery via a patch wire with alligator clips, and the distributor can be grounded via a second patch wire, so make up two of these wires now (don't connect them yet, though). Fuel can be delivered to the carburetor or diesel fuel filters via a small temporary tank, such as a lawnmower tank, to avoid the extra work of installing the original tank.

However, I recommend installing the original tank for safety, and that is always the way I handle it myself. Use rubber fuel hose with clamps to avoid the work of making and installing gas lines at this time. While throttle connections are nice, they aren't necessary, as we will only idle the engine. You will need to connect the carburetor to the governor, and you'll want clear access to the choke. You also have to make sure the diesel fuel cutout plunger or switch is working properly.

As you assemble the tractor engine in such an incomplete way, make sure you are completely enclosing and installing the entire oil delivery and filtering system. Also make sure your electrical system mock-ups don't create a dangerous situation that could spark and set a temporary gas tank up in flames. In short, improvise, but be smart. If in doubt, completely and correctly install the systems.

Next, assemble enough of the tractor so the engine is completely and safely supported; the front axle must be installed. On some tractors, this means assembling virtually the entire tractor. On others, such as channel frame tractors, no additional work is needed here. Once again, double- and triple-check your work: make sure you haven't forgotten anything, you don't have a dangerous fuel leak, and that your electrical system is safe. *Now add oil to the engine!*

After everything is in place, *make sure the tractor is in neutral, and the wheels are chocked!* Without the spark plugs installed, and with the ignition off, engage the starter (or hand start).We don't want to start the engine; we just want to spin it up to prime it with oil. As an electric starter spins the engine, watch the oil gauge, looking for acceptable pressure readings. With these slow starting speeds, readings will probably be less than specification, but should

On the John Deere horizontal engine, synchronizing the distributor or magneto requires alignment of the flywheel marks with certain registers on the engine crankcase. (Seen here is a magneto impulse mark.) Check your service manuals for your specific model's timing procedures.

Getting the engine ready to run usually means getting the wiring in shape. Here the rat's nest of wiring is cleared, and only enough wiring is left to run the initial engine test. The rest of the wiring will be replaced after engine break-in or after painting.

at least be 8 to 12 psi. If you fail to get an oil pressure reading, you need to trace back through the oil delivery system to ascertain why. Usually the gauge or the oil pressure relief valve is the culprit. Otherwise, you must disassemble the engine to determine if a galley plug was missed, a bearing was installed incorrectly, or if there is dirt in one of the galleys.

After achieving oil pressure, you can attempt to start the engine. This initial starting is best done outside. Again, make sure the tractor is in neutral and the wheels are chocked. Also check for and fix any fuel leaks, then attach the ignition leads to the distributor if your engine has a distributor ignition. Install the spark plugs and spark plug wires. If your engine is a diesel, prime the injection system according to the service manual instructions. Give the engine a spin by hand crank, electric starter, or pony motor. If you are starting a diesel with a pony motor, give it a chance to warm up, then engage the pony motor clutch. As is usual with any engine so equipped, you should open up any compression release petcocks. You need to have a helper apply a little bit of throttle and choke the carburetor to get the engine to fire. Immediately stop if you get a backfire from a gasoline engine, or if you get flames or sooty black smoke from the exhaust of a diesel engine.

If the engine doesn't start, or runs poorly, immediate disconnect the ignition wires or close the diesel fuel shut-off valve. Double-check all your timing and synchronization work, making sure the magneto or distributor is correctly timed, and your diesel fuel injection pump is synchronized. Do not rush this. Go through everything with a fine-tooth comb, repairing any problem you see and making any adjustments you feel are necessary.

After a few fits and Chinese firedrills (getting ignition timing 180 degrees off is my most common mistake), your

TIP

During the initial powered spin-up to oil prime the engine, a hand-started engine can be spun up via its belt pulley connected to another tractor, or it can be spun up via the PTO, connected with a PTO drive shaft to a tractor with a backward-turning PTO, such as a Farmall Cub.

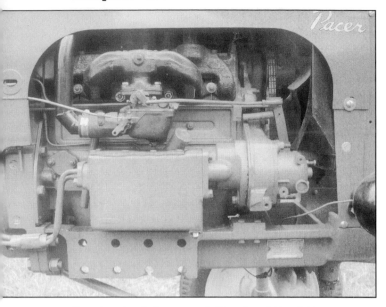

This is the end result of an engine rebuild—a dependable, reliable, sweet-running engine. After painting, this Continental Y91, installed in a Massey-Harris Pacer, looks as good as it runs.

engine should start and idle on its own. There is no need to run the engine long—maybe 15–45 seconds—especially if you did not install the cooling system. Right now we only want to assure ourselves that completely assembling the tractor is not a monumental waste of time.

If this initial test runs smoothly, you can bask in the glow of a rebuilt engine. While there are still a few hours of busy work left to do, and there will still be a bug or two (maybe even a big bug or two) to work out, you really have done it! You have rebuilt your engine, and gotten it to fire and run on its own. A congratulatory pat on your own back is appropriate, and maybe a phone call to a friend or two to invite them over for a little celebration is in order. While you are waiting for them to arrive, go ahead and disconnect the fuel and battery, close all the fuel storage

TIP

If your engine is a diesel engine and the pony motor has been rebuilt, be sure to spin up, test, and break in the pony motor according to the instructions before using it to spin up, test, and break in the diesel.

valves, and disassemble any mock-ups you created for the test. Now is the time to completely assemble the engine and all the fuel, cooling, oil, and electrical systems in preparation for the initial engine break-in.

INITIAL BREAK-IN

After you have assembled the engine and electrical, fuel, air intake, and cooling systems (don't forget to add coolant, but leave the radiator cap off), start the engine and let it run in earnest, beginning the break-in period. The first step to breaking in an engine is an initial 15-minute run. While 15 minutes is conventional wisdom, we actually want the engine to warm up to full operating temperature and stay there for several minutes. This may take 10 minutes or it may take 20. Simply make sure the engine reaches full operating temperature. A thermometer installed in the open radiator will help you judge this. Immediately after starting the engine, check for oil pressure, and then check for oil or bubbles (a compression leak) in the coolant. If these all look OK, let the engine idle for a moment or two, then vary the engine speed frequently during the rest of the initial run.

Also during this 15-minute period, make any necessary carburetor adjustments to allow smooth and even running and good throttle response. Continue to look diligently for oil leaks (especially at the head gasket on overhead valve engines) or a loss of oil pressure. If you see a significant drop in coolant level, or any signs that oil and coolant may be mixing, shut the engine down and retorque the cylinder head fasteners. Also be ready to immediately shut down the engine should any abnormal sounds show up. After 15 minutes, shut down the engine and let it cool. After the cool down, you should readjust the valve lash, retorque the cylinder head fasteners, and drain the oil, looking for abnormal metal particles, the presence of engine coolant, or trash in the oil that may indicate a failing internal part. Also check the coolant again for any presence of oil.

If anything concerns you at this point, don't hope that the problem will solve itself. No matter how disheartening it may seem, take the time to repair any problems immediately, even if it means removing the engine and putting it back on the stand. Rare is the hobbyist who can claim he has batted 1,000 and produced a flawless engine on every try. Realize though, that some minor problems may in fact cure themselves, and don't jump to doomsday conclusions. For example, while coolant leaks into the oil or vice versa may represent a significant problem, it may simply be that the head has not seated tightly enough against the head gasket, and the second tightening after the 15-minute initial break-in may cure the problem. I would wait until you retorque before becoming convinced you have a problem, especially if the oil/coolant leaks are minor.

Other problems that often work themselves out:

- Oil leak at the engine seals (depending on the type of seal, it may take 30 minutes to an hour of running time to seal completely).
- Unusual smells. This is very common, as new paint and sealants heat up or cure, and will pass in time.
- Coolant coming from the exhaust stack. Place your hand in the exhaust stream, letting some of the moisture cover your hand. I think you will find this is condensation and not coolant. If it is coolant, wait until the second cylinder head tightening before jumping to conclusions.
- Rough idle. Torque the manifold fasteners one more time, and double-check your carburetor rebuild.
- Big one-time drop in coolant. Probably an air pocket in the engine coolant jacket. Fill up the radiator and check for continued falling levels.

EXTENDED BREAK-IN

After the 15-minute break-in, and after all problems are fixed, break the new engine in with a wide variety of activities. This includes lugging the engine from time to time, and running the engine at maximum rpm with no load in addition to occasional periods of idling. All of these different operating conditions are important to the future health of your engine. The easiest way to lug your engine is to belt it up to a heavy load or simply negotiate a steep hill in road gear with the brakes applied. Again, never lug or idle it for an extended period of time. Most of the time should be spent on a moderate load, maybe pulling a wagon loaded appropriately for the size of your tractor, or powering a mill or grain auger that isn't loaded too quickly. In short, just have fun with the tractor, putting it through its paces.

After the extended break-in, perform a complete service of the engine. Change the oil and filter, check for leaks, lubricate all oil cups and lubrication points, and change the coolant if initially you have some problems with oil or combustion gases passing into the coolant. Also check all engine mounting bolts, finishing your adjustments of the carburetor and throttle links, and clean the spark plugs. Check the points to make sure they aren't pitting, and make sure oil from the engine isn't passing into the points chamber. Time the engine and you are finished!

WHAT'S NEXT?

If you plan on modifying the engine, such as converting to 12 volts or adding a front-mounted auxiliary hydraulic pump, now is the time to take care of these chores.

The rebuild has also left you with a large supply of broken, rusty, and barely usable parts, but it has also left you with a supply of parts that may be reusable by someone

Whatever reasons you had for rebuilding your antique tractor's engine, the sense of pride rushes over you as soon as it starts for the first time. Enjoying a complete sense of accomplishment, however, usually comes the first time you really need the tractor, and having it perform flawlessly. As your tractor quietly purrs on a snowy morning clearing the drive to the blacktop, you suddenly realize you aren't worrying if the tractor will spit, sputter, cough, or die, as you did for years before the rebuild. That is when the sense of your accomplishment will really kick in.

whose goals for rebuilding an engine are more austere. For instance, organizations, such as 4-H clubs, rebuild tractors regularly, but financial constraints force them to make do with used parts whenever possible. Box up your reusable parts and give them to someone who might need them.

Maybe now that you have rebuilt the engine, you are ready to tackle the restoration of the entire tractor. If you decide to tackle this next logical step, now is the time to begin, while your newly learned skills and confidence are fresh.

Of course, you can always start looking for that next tractor that needs an engine rebuild!

APPENDIX 1

You are probably reading this section months after you bought this book, and have learned more that you ever thought you would and gained much in the process. I hope this has been a thoroughly enjoyable journey for you, as I know writing this book has been for me. I hope you have accomplished the goals for your engine without too many expensive lessons, unbearable frustrations or hard-won wisdom; but the fact of the matter is you probably did, or will if you rebuild engines long enough. I know I have certainly slung down a wrench in frustration and ruined a $20 part more often than I have jumped and hollered in triumph. It is the triumphs though, that keep me coming back for more.

Of course, I wouldn't leave you unsupported in either case of frustration or triumph. There is help on the Internet at the Web site I own. All you need is a Web browser and an e-mail software to take advantage of this. This support comes in the form of a free electronic mailing list dedicated to antique tractor engine rebuilding called AT-engine. To subscribe (it's free), simply follow these instructions:

Go to the Web site www.atis.net, and click on the mailing list button.

Click on the link that reads: "AT-engine."

Fill out the form, submit it, then completely read the e-mail that returns to your e-mail box. These e-mail messages describe the list, but more important, they outline one more specific step you have to take to confirm your subscription. This extra step ensures the data you entered was correct and you were not subscribed accidentally. Rest assured that no junk e-mail originates from ATIS, and I do not sell your e-mail address. If you have any troubles with the subscription process, feel free to e-mail me at yostsw@atis.net

There are hundreds of subscribers to this list, many (probably most) more talented than I at engine restoration. They can steer you through the long process of engine restoration. All of these people, in addition to me, use the list as a way to support each other with advice, guidance, parts acquisition, and sometimes just a listening ear when we need to throw that virtual wrench in frustration.

Good luck, and be sure to join the mailing list for the only place in the world you can talk with hundreds of other rebuilders simultaneously.

APPENDIX 2: Restoration Parts and Service

Here is a list of all the parts sources and services that I know of. I have not personally done business with all of them, but they've been referred to me by others who have used them. Please note the following when using this list:

Increasingly the Internet is the most powerful way to find parts and help. Point your Web browser to www.atis.net for mailing lists, bulletin boards, classified ads, nationwide meetings, and a show schedule that should help you locate the advice or part you need.

Don't overlook the manufacturer's national chain of dealers. John Deere is still a great source of parts for antique John Deere tractors. New Holland often has antique Ford parts, and Case (IHC and Farmall, as well as Case) and AgCo are likewise helpful. Please note that at the time of this writing, plans were under way to merge New Holland and Case/IH.

Local farm equipment stores frequently have some parts and services for antique tractors. Of particular mention is the brand of tractor parts named TISCO. TISCO parts are sold through these local stores, and they distribute a good selection of antique tractor parts.

Sometime your closest parts source is your local auto parts store (not one of the discount chains, but the locally owned full-service stores, like NAPA). For example, I can buy a nearly complete engine rebuild kit for many obsolete Continental engines through NAPA, and through the local NAPA, I can also send brake bands, clutch plates, and water pumps out for rebuilding.

I list a lot of salvage yards for hard-to-find used parts, such as engine blocks, cylinder heads, usable water pumps, camshafts, etc. While some of them may also have a stock of NOS parts, most of these yards do not stock any new or reproduction parts unless I list otherwise.

Companies and individuals that sell engine rebuild parts almost always advertise in the collector's periodical devoted to the antique tractor you are working on. Therefore, the best current sources of information on who has engine rebuild kits are the periodicals I list here. For example, if you are looking for Ford engine parts, subscribe to the 9N-2N-8N Newsletter. In addition to advertisements for parts, the technical articles in these magazines are of great help.

As in my last book, I sincerely thank Jim Poole, who was responsible for putting together most of this list. Please remember that many of these are small sideline businesses for the owners, who have other and more pressing priorities, such as a day job or farm work. In short, persistence and patience will go a long way toward establishing contact and a rewarding relationship with these companies.

Where possible, I have included all contact information, though on many entries some or part of the information is missing. Be aware also that area codes in the United States have been changing rapidly, and some of these might be outdated by the time the book goes to print and gets in your hand.

IMPLEMENTS
Tractor Buddies, Inc.
P.O. Box 36
Genesee Depot, Wisconsin 53127-0036
(414) 968-9724
e-mail: Sales@tractorbuddies.com
Web site: www.TractorBuddies.com
Tractor Buddies specializes in selling Woods brand implements and mowers that fit antique tractors.

INTERNET RESOURCES
Antique Tractor Internet Services
3160 MacBrandon Lane
Pfafftown, North Carolina 27040
(910) 924-6109
e-mail: Sales@atis.net
Web site: www.atis.net
This Web site is owned by the author. It was the first, and is still the largest and most complete site on the Internet for antique tractors. We specialize in providing World Wide Web services for antique tractor businesses, collectors, and clubs.

MAGAZINES AND PERIODICALS
9N-2N-8N Newsletter
P.O. Box 235
Chelsea, Vermont 05038-0235
Publisher: Gerard W. Rinaldi
For Ford enthusiasts.

Antique Power
Box 562
Yellow Springs, Ohio 45387
(800) 767-5828
Publisher/Editor: Pat Ertl
All brands tractor magazine. Free classifieds to subscribers.

The Belt Pulley
Box 83
Nokomis, Illinois 62075
All brands tractor magazine.

Cockshutt Quarterly
International Cockshutt Club
Diana Myers
2910 Essex Road
LaRue, Ohio 43332-8830
For Cockshutt, Co-op, Blackhawk, and Gambles Farmcrest enthusiasts.

Engineers and Engines
P.O. Box 2757
Joliet, Illinois 60434-2757
All brands, emphasis on steam engines.

The Ferguson Journal
Denehurst, Rosehill Road
Stoke Heath
Market Drayton TF9 2JU
United Kingdom
For Massey Ferguson enthusiasts.

Gas Engine Magazine
P.O. Box 328
Lancaster, Pennsylvania 17608
For enthusiasts and collectors of all types of gas engines.

The Golden Arrow
John Kasmiski
N7209 State Highway 67
Mayville, Wisconsin 53050
For Cockshutt, Co-op, Blackhawk, and Gambles Farmcrest enthusiasts.

Green Magazine
RR 1, Box 7
Bee, Nebraska 68314
For John Deere enthusiasts.

MM Corresponder
Rt. 1, Box 153
Vail, Iowa 51465
For Minneapolis-Moline enthusiasts.

Old Abe's News
(J. I. Case Collectors Association, Inc.)
400 Carriage Drive
Plain City, Ohio 42064
For Case enthusiasts.

The Old Allis News
Pleasant Knoll 10925 Love Road
Bellevue, Michigan 49021
For Allis Chalmers enthusiasts.

Oliver Collector's News
Manvel, North Dakota 58256-0044
For Oliver enthusiasts.

Polk's
72435 SR 15
New Paris, Indiana 46553
All brands tractor magazine.

The Prairie Gold Rush
Rt. 1, Box 119
Francesville, Indiana 47946
For Minneapolis-Moline enthusiasts.

Red Power Newsletter
Box 277
Battle Creek, Iowa 51006
Editor and Publisher: Daryl A. Miller
For all IHC (Farmall) enthusiasts.

The Rumely Newsletter
P.O. Box 12
Moline, Illinois 61265
For Rummy enthusiasts.

Tractor Digest
P.O. Box 31
Eldora, Iowa 50627-0031
For John Deere enthusiasts.

Two-Cylinder Club
310 East G Avenue
Grundy Center, Iowa 50638
Annual membership includes magazine.
For John Deere enthusiasts.

Turtle River Toy News
Rt. 1
Manvel, North Dakota 58256
For Oliver enthusiasts.

Wild Harvest: Massey Collectors' News
Box 529
Denver, Iowa 50622
Publisher/Editor: Keith Oltrogge
For Massey, Massey-Harris, and Wallis enthusiasts.

MANUALS AND BOOKS
American Society of Agricultural Engineers
Dept 3670
St.©202
Joseph, Michigan 49085
(800) 895-4616
ASAE creates and support standards in agriculture. It sells copies of the standards and has several books about antique tractors.

Binder Books
P.O. Box 230269
Tigard, Oregon 97281-0269
(503) 684-2024
e-mail: sac@binderbooks.com
Web site: www.binderbooks.com
They specialize in providing manuals for all kinds of International Harvester products, though they have manuals for other brands.

Broken Kettle Books
702 East Madison
Fairfield, Iowa

Homer's Mechanical Literature
1-888-5HOMERS
e-mail: Sales@homersbooks.com
Web site: www.homersbooks.com
Offering a wide variety of new and old, popular and hard-to-find mechanical books. Also buys books.

John Deere Distribution Service
1400 13th Street
East Moline, Illinois 61244
(800) 522-7448
Manuals direct from John Deere.

King's Books
P.O. Box 86
Radnor, Ohio 43006-0086
A good selection of books pertaining to antique equipment.

Warren D. Jensen
P.O. Box 1203
Albert Lea, Minnesota 56007
(800) 443-0625
e-mail: jensales@jensales.com
Web site: http://deskmedia.com/jensales
A large selection of manuals and farm toys.

NOS, NEW, REPRODUCTION, AND SALVAGE PARTS
2 Cylinder Plus Salvage
Rt. 2, Box 123
Conway, Missouri 65632
(417) 589-2634
John Deere parts.

ABC Company
Letcher, South Dakota 57359
(800) 843-3721

Abilene Machine
P.O. Box 281
Solomon, Kansas 67480
(800) 253-0337

Agri-services
13899 North Road
Alden, New York 14004
(716) 937-6618
Wiring harnesses.

AGTIQUE Tractor
P.O. Box 279
Leaf River, Illinois 61047
(815) 738-2251
Web site: www.agtique.com

Albert Lea Tractor Parts
County Road 56, Route 3, Box 335
Albert Lea, Minnesota 56007
(507) 373-1265

Alexander Tractors Parts
Winnsborro, Texas
(800) 231-6876

Alvin Kaddatz Auctioneering & Farm Equip.
Rt. 1, Box 113
Hillsboro, Texas 76645
(254) 582-3071

American Radiator
(800) 621-6067

Anderson Tractor Supply
Bluffton, Ohio
(419) 358-3015

Antique Gauges Inc.
12287 Old Skipton Road
Cordova, Maryland 21625
(410) 822-4963
John Deere authorized source of replacement gauges. They carry other gauges as well.

Arnold's of Kimble
Minnesota
(612) 398-3800
Several dealerships, all in Minnesota.

Athens Tractors Salvage
Rt. 2, Box 143A
Madison, Alabama
(800) 633-3223

Audobon Tractor Parts
Audobon, Iowa
(888) 831-5730

Austin Farm Salvage
Butler, Missouri
(816) 679-4080

Austin Ignition Co.
(800) 686-6366

Auswell Stauffer
Kansas
(913) 364-2546

B&M Parts Inc.
(800) 356-7155

B&M Tractor
Highway 59
Taylor, Texas
(512) 352-8515

Baker Salvage
Bishopville, South Carolina
(803) 428-5497

Balcom Implement
Fairmont, Minnesota
(800) 658-2309
Minneapolis-Moline and others.

Bannon Tractor
Denton, Texas
(817) 566-0091

Bates
Indiana
(219) 342-2955

Bates Corporation
Bourdon, Indiana
(800) 248-2955

Belkins Tractor
Georgetown, Massachusetts
(508) 352-7777
Gravely specialist.

Bettis Tractor Parts
Cranfordsville, Arkansas
(870) 823-5546

Biewer's Tractor and Machinery Salvage
Barnesville, Minnesota
(218) 937-5627

Bill Knapp
Penemite Road
Livonia, New York 14487
(716) 346-5777

Bob Logan's Discount Tractor Supply
Illinois
(815) 288-1818

Bob Martin Antique Tractor Parts
5 Ogle Industrial Drive
Vevay, Indiana 47043
(812) 427-2622
Web site: venus.net/~rmartin

Bowman Bros.
Mt. Jackson, Virginia
(540) 477-3105

Bozeman Machinery Tractor
122 Idalou Road
Lubbock, Texas 79403
(800) 766-2076

C T Farm & Family
P.O. Box 3330
Des Moines, Iowa 50316
(800) 247-7508

Campbell's Used Tractor Parts
Lawrenceburg, Tennessee
(931) 762-7185

Central Michigan Tractor & Parts
2713 N. U.S. 27
St. Johns, Michigan 48879
(800) 248-9263

Christian's Tractor Salvage
Rt. 29, Box 29025
Tyler, Texas 75706
(800) 527-2668

Colfax Tractor Parts
Rt. 1, Box 119
Colfax, Iowa 50054
(800) 284-3001

Conroy Truck and Tractor
(800) 895-7209

Coulter's Salvage
Kentucky
(606) 236-3745

Country Tractor
Washington
(206) 748-3110
A-C Farmall, Ford, Oliver.

Cross Creek Tractor Co.
Cullman, Alabama
(800) 462-7335

D & S Salvage
Sikestown, Missouri
(800) 833-9488

Dale Canterbury
3326N 3300E
Kimberly, Idaho 83341
(208) 736-8341
JD-Case-Oliver-AC-MM.

David Moore Repair & Salvage
1540 Joe Quick Road
New Market, Alabama 35761
(205) 828-3884

Dengler's
Middletown, Ohio
(513) 423-4000

Dennis Polk Equipment
72435 SR 15
New Paris, Indiana 46553
(800) 795-3501
Polk's is also one of the nation's largest auction-eers of antique farm equipment.

Dennler Supply
Rt. 1, Box 115
Juliaetta, Idaho 83535
(208) 276-3771

Discount Tractor Supply
Box 265
Franklin Grove, Illinois 61031
(800) 433-5805

Draper Tractor Parts, Inc.
Rt. 1, Box 41
Garfield, Washington 99130
(509) 397-2666

Dunmire Literature
Wichita, Kansas
(316) 942-2938
Garden tractor literature.

Ed Axthelm
5071 Ashley Road
Cardington, Ohio 43315
(419) 864-4959

Evansville Tractor Parts
Evansville, Wisconsin
(888) 525-7278

Everett Brothers
6771 Everett Valley Road
Gnadenhutten, Ohio 44629
(614) 922-3335
Good source for Minneapolis-Moline.

Farmer's Tractor Parts
Ellendale, North Dakota
(800) 497-3536

Farmland Tractor
Oregon
(503) 928-1646

Fennesy Tractor Salvage
R.R. #1
Springville, Indiana 47462
(821) 825-9130

Fergiland
The Gateway, Highfields
Melbourne, Derby DE3 1DG
United Kingdom
Telephone: 1332 862972
Ferguson, especially T20s.

Florin Tractor Parts
8345 Florin Road
Sacramento, California 95828
(800) 223-9916

Forrest Oakley
Oxford, North Carolina
(919) 693-4367

Frontier Tractor
50 miles north of Houston, Texas
(800) 586-7900

G. Milnarik
Nebraska
(402) 986-1352
IH-Farmall-McCormick Deering.

Gap Tractor
P.O. Box 97
Cranfills Gap, Texas 76637
(818) 597-2217

Gary's Implement Inc.
Junction 26 & 385
Bridgeport, Nebraska 69236
(308) 262-1242

General Equipment Co.
Debins, Iowa
(800) 247-2472

General Gear
Boise, Idaho
(208) 342-8911
e-mail: webmaster@tractorparts.com
Web site: www.tractorparts.com
Crawlers and antique construction and industrial equipment. This is a great source for crawler information. John Parks, the owner, is extremely knowledgeable.

G. K. Argent
North Fields Farm
Great Waldinfield, Sudbury,
Suffolk, England
Telephone: 1787 372885
Ferguson.

Gordon Shelton
P.O. Box 66
Hartwood, Virginia 22471
(540) 752-2720

Gratton Coulee Truck & Agri Parts Ltd.
Irma, Alberta
(403) 754-2303

Green Salvage
Fremont, North Carolina
(919) 242-6154
AC specialist.

H & R Construction
Buffalo, New York
(800) 333-0650

Hamilton Equipment
(800) 433-5802

Hill-T Eq.
Ohio
(513) 548-0718

Holt Agtractor Parts
Donalsonville, Georgia
(800) 290-1149

Iowa Falls Tractor Parts
Rt. 3, Box 330A
Iowa Falls, Iowa 50126
(800) 232-3276

J. P. Tractor Salvage
1347 Madison 426
Fredericktown, Missouri 63645
(573) 783-7055
Good source for International Harvester parts.

John Brillman
P.O. Box 333
Tatamy, Pennsylvania 18085
(610) 252-9828
Specialize in secondary ignition components (spark plugs, spark plug wires, etc).

Johnson Diesel
Michigan
(616) 877-4663

Jones Salvage
RR2, Box 171
Ainsworth, Nebraska 69210
(800) 286-2170
e-mail: jonsal@bloomnet.com
Web site: www.successmp.com/shops/jonessalvage

Junction Tractor Parts
2425 Utica Road
Johnstown, Ohio 43080
(740) 892-2889

King Tractor Parts
Kentucky
(606) 234-5748
About 50 miles south of Cincinnati, Ohio.

Knoxland
New Hampshire
(603) 529-2366
MF dealer, well known for parts.

Kyle Trusdell
Southern Ohio
(513) 549-4201

L & S Equipment
Berwick, Maine
(207) 698-1487

Lakeside Farm Implements
N6891 County Road B
Montello, Wisconsin
(800) 356-4863

Larry's Tractor
1515 W. 13th Street
Tipton, Iowa 52772
(319) 886-2469

Leibach Machinery
5000 Reynolda Road
Winston-Salem, North Carolina 27106
(336) 924-4115

Leesburg Tractor Parts
Rt. 2, Box 85
Leesburg, Indiana 46538
(800) 426-6960

Lindsay Used Tractor Parts
Lindsay, Ontario
Canada
(705) 324-8331
e-mail: tractors@nexicom.net

Lindstrom's JD Model H Parts
1275 NW 26th Road
Joseph, Missouri 64503
(816) 279-6262
The premier source of parts for the John Deere Model H.

Little Red Tractor Co.
RR 1, Box 129
Howells, Nebraska 68641

Lyles
Connecticut
(860) 889-0051
Tractors/ implements.

Lynch Farms
1624 Alexandria Road
Eaton, Ohio 45320
(937) 456-6686
Oliver Parts, including reproduction louvered engine side panels.

Manning Tractor
Manning, South Carolina
(803) 435-8368

Maplewood Eq.
(800) 234-9989
Combines, planters, hay tools, implements.

McLeads Parts Ltd.
Canada
(403) 476-1234

Meridian Equipment
Washington
(360) 398-2141
Ask for Dave; A-C Farmall, JD Case.

Meyer's Tractor and Combine Salvage
Aberdeen, South Dakota
(605) 225-0185

Meyers Tractor & Combine Parts
3190 South Elm Avenue
Fresno, California 93706
(800) 344-9494

Mid East Tractor Parts
Highway 70
Goldsboro, North Carolina
(800) 322-1871

Mid Norfolk
38 School Road
Reepham, Norwich NR10 4JP
England
Telephone: 1332 862972
Ferguson.

Mid-South Salvage, Inc.
Decatur, Alabama
(800) 325-7070

Mid-South Tractor Parts Inc.
Hwy. 62 E., Box 1790
Sikeston, Missouri 63801
(800) 325-7070

Mill Creek Valley Farms
3743 Mill Creek Road
Sidney, Ohio 45365
(937) 492-8702
They specialize in battery box sets for the entire Dubuque JD line (M - 430), and fender brackets (clamshell and two-cylinder flat tops).

Nampa Tractor Salvage
9055 Hwy 20
Nampa, Idaho 83687
(208) 467-4430
Lots of JD wheels, tractors, parts.

Nash Equipment
Route 26
Colebrook, New Hampshire
(603) 237-8857

North Alabama Tractor Salvage
Decatur, Alabama

Northwest Equipment
Utah
(801) 438-5343

Northwest Equipment
California
(707) 823-4048

Old Iron Auction
Web site: http://www.OldIronAuction.com
This licensed Internet auction site has parts, tools and tractors up for bid.

Olson Power & Equipment
Minnesota
(612) 674-4494

Osage Plains Eq.
Missouri
(417) 394-2541

Otto Gas Engine Works
2167 Blue Ball Road
Elkton, Maryland 21921
(410) 398-7340

Owen Sharman, Glen Innes
Australia
Telephone: 61 67 32 3079

Owyhee Tractor & Implement
2506 Highway 201
Nyssa, Oregon 97913
(541) 372-3410
Good source for Co-ops and Cockshutts.

P.D.Q. Parts
P.O. Box 3525
Des Moines, Iowa 50322
(800) 274-7334

Parts of the Past, Inc.
Lawrence, Kansas
(913) 749-5231

Patrick Edwards
Langley Farm, Langley Lane,
Oxford, England
Telephone: 1367 810259
Mainly Ferguson and Fordson.

Paynesville Tractor & Parts Co.
Box 231
Paynesville, Minnesota 30203
(800) 445-0061

Peglers
Ohio
(513) 423-4000

Pelican Tractor
Klamath Falls, Oregon
(503) 882-8809

Pete's Tractor Salvage
Rt. 1, Box 124
Anamoose, North Dakota 58710
(800) 541-7383
A very large salvage yard with great selection.

Rempel Tractor Parts
(800) 244-7662
All tractor types.

Restoration Supply Company
Dept G
Medway, Massachusetts 02053
(508) 533-4903

Rice Equipment
Clarion, Pennsylvania
(814) 226-9200

Rice Tractor Salvage
Sutherlin, Virginia
(804) 753-2114

Ridenours
413 West State Street
Trenton, Ohio 45067
(513) 988-0586
JD L/LA/LI specialists, also make reproduction sheet metal.

Rippee's Tractor
Missouri
(314) 431-5939

Robert Campbell
Route 1, Box 348
Newberry, Michigan 49868
(906) 293-3744

Rogue Valley Farm Equipment Repair
Oregon
(541) 772-1026
Magnetos, recommend for any tractor work.

Roydale International Ltd.
Alberta, Canada
(800) 661-9171

Russells Tractor Parts
Scottsboro, Alabama
(800) 248-8883

Rusty Acre
RR. 2, Box 181-a,
Austin, Minnesota 55912
(507) 433-0073

S. A. Fitts Salvage
Cascade, Virginia
(804) 685-7850

Schaefer Eq.
Illinois
(618) 833-5498

Schwanke Tractor
3310 S. Hwy. 71
Willmar, Minnesota 56201
(800) 537-5582

Sexsmith Used Farm Parts Ltd.
Sexsmith, Alberta
(800) 340-1192

Shoup Manufacturing Co.
145 Southwest Avenue
Kankakee, Illinois 60901
(800) 627-6137

Shuck Impl Co.
1924 E 1450 RD
Lawrence, Kansas 66044
(800) 654-5191

Skillings Tractor
North Hampton, Ohio
(513) 964-1486

Smith's Implement Co., Inc.
Hwy. 170
Downing, Wisconsin 54734
(800) 826-2806

South-Central Tractor Parts
Rt. 1, Box 1
Leland, Mississippi 38756
(800) 247-1237

Southeast Tractor Parts
Rt. 2, Box 565
Jefferson, South Carolina 29718
(888) 658-7171

Southern Counties Tractor Spares
137 Almondington Lane
Earnley, Chichester, W. Sus
United Kingdom
Telephone: 1243 512109
Ferguson and Fordson.

Spallinger Combine Parts
2325 County Road 28
Bluffton, Ohio 45817
(419) 358-8333

Staben Equipment
Oxnard, California
(805) 485-2103

Stamm Equipment Co
3450 12th Street
Wayland, Michigan
(616) 792-6204

Steiner Tractor Parts
G-10096 S. Saginaw Road
Holly, Michigan 48442
(810) 695-1919
Replacement parts, no used or OEM parts.

Stephens Equipment Co.
P.O. Box 89
(7460 E. St. Hwy. 86)
Frankton, Colorado 80116
(303) 688-3151
Greg Stephens is a John Deere dealer and is very knowledgeable and helpful. He regularly writes a column for Green Magazine. One of the largest inventories of NOS John Deere parts in the world.

Stevens Tractor
Route 1, Box 32-B
Coushatta, Louisiana 71019
(800) 333-9143

Storey Tractor
Bell Buckle, Tennessee
(800) 241-5671

Storey Tractor Parts
Midland, Tennessee
(615) 895-3041

Strojny Implement
1122 Hwy 153
Mosinee, Wisconsin 54455
(715) 693-4515
Specialize in Ford Ns.

Stromp's Dump
Spalding, Nebraska
(308) 497-2211

Stuckey Bros. Farm Supply
Hemingway, South Carolina
(803) 558-3330

Surplus Tractor
3215 W. Main
P.O. Box 2125
Fargo, North Dakota 58107
(800) 859-2045

The Antique Auto Battery Mfg. Co.
2320 Old Mill Road
Hudson, Ohio 44236
(800) 426-7580

The Old 20 Parts Co.
Cavendish Bridge,
Sharlow, Derby
United Kingdom
DE72 2HL
Telephone: 1332 792698
Most UK Tractors.

The Tractor Barn
6154 Highway 60
Brookline, Missouri 65619
(417) 881-3668

The Tractor Place
Knightdale, North Carolina
(919) 266-5846

Timber Tractor Parts
9624 S. Glasford Road
Glasford, Illinois 61533
(309) 389-5855
Ford specialist.

Tired Iron Salvage
Ohio
(419) 358-0390
JD and Farmall.

TMS
Ohio
(330) 669-3676
International Harvester.

Tony's Used Tractor and Combine Parts
Lidgerwood, North Dakota
(701) 538-4300

Tractor Implement Supply Co.
232 Lothenbach Ave.
St. Paul, Minnesota 55118
(612) 455-6681

Tractor Parts
8 Goshen Road
Bozrah, Connecticut 06334
(800) 344-PART

Truck & Trailer Parts
3114 East U.S. 30
Warsaw, Indiana 46580
(800) 825-7711

Used Parts Ranch
Ponoka, Alberta
(888) 877-7278

Van Noort Tractor Salvage
1003 10th Avenue
Rock Valley, Iowa 51247
(800) 831-8543

Vande Weerd Combine Salvage
RR 2, Box 49
Rock Valley, Iowa 51247
(800) 831-4814

Verle Decker
Route 2, Box 151
Hollenberg, Kansas 66946
(913) 337-2933

Vikel, Carroll
Tiffin, Iowa
(319) 645-2627
Oliver only.

Voskuilens' Service
Washington
(360) 354-2996
General tractor salvage.

Voyles Brothers Equipment
Parkin, Arkansas
(870) 755-2739

W. C. Littleton & Son Inc.
100 West Tenth Street
Laurel, Delaware 19956
(302) 875-7445

W. W. Grainger Inc.
5959 W. Howard St.
Chicago, Illinois 60648
(800) 225-5994

Wall Lake Used Parts
108 Center St.
Wall Lake, Iowa 51466
(800) 233-7107

Watertown Tractor Parts
2510 9th Ave. S. W.
Watertown, SD 57201
(800) 843-4413

Wayne's Used Parts
RR 1, Box 75
El Pasco, Illinois 61738
(309) 527-3125

Weller Tractor Salvage
Great Bend, Kansas
(800) 255-9235

Welters Farm Supply
Verona, Missouri
(417) 498-6496

Wenger's Farm Machinery Inc.
814 S. College
Myerstown, Pennsylvania 17067
(800) 451-5240

Westlock Tractors Parts Ltd.
Westlock, Alberta
(800) 563-011

Willard Equipment
Ohio
(419) 933-6791

Bill Williams
Rt. 2 91 CR5491
Baldwyn, Mississippi 38824
(601) 728-3747

Wilson Farms
20552 Old Mansfield Road
Fredricktown, Ohio 43019
(614) 694-5071
Primarily a salvage yard but some new parts.

Worthington Tractor Salvage
Rt.4, Box 14
Worthington, Minnesota 56187
(800) 533-5304

Worley Auction Service and Farm Salvage
Salem, Indiana
(800) 854-4313
Nationwide parts location service.

Yesterday's Tractors
P.O. Box 160
Chicacum, Washington 98325
Fax order number: (800) 250-5134
Web site: www.ytmag.com/store.htm
Specializes in parts for pre-1970 tractors.
Convenient on-line ordering system.

RESTORATION SERVICES
2 Cylinder Diesel Shop
Rt. 2, Box 241
Conway, Missouri 65632
(417) 589-3843
Specializes in two-cylinder John Deere
diesel engines.

Automotive Parts & Machine
(301) 663-8866
Rebuilds all types of engines, including any
tractor engine.

Branson Enterprises
7722 Elm Ave.
Rockford, Illinois 61115
(815) 633-4262
Carburetor and magneto restoration.

Burrey Carburetor Service
18028 Monroeville Road
Monroeville, Indiana 46773
(800) 287-7390

Central Fuel Injection
2409 Murray Road
Estherville, Iowa 51334
(712) 362-2212
Web site: http://www.CentralFuelInjection.com
Rebuilt diesel injection pumps and nozzles.

Dale Nickerson
8670 Glasgow Road
Cassadaga, New York 14718-9617
(716) 595-3260
Magneto Repair.

Denny's Carburetor Shop
8620 N. Fletcher Road
Casstown, Ohio 45326
(937) 368-2304
They also sell solid-state ignitions.

Fireball Heat Treating Co., Inc.
34 John Williams Street
Attleboro, Massachusetts 02703
(508) 222-2617
e-mail: webmaster@fireballht.com
Web site: www.fireballht.com
This firm can perform most any metallurgical process involving heat treating, stressing, case hardening, etc. Jim Thomson, one of the owners, is very knowledgeable and helpful.

Magneeders
Route 5, Box 505
Carthage, Missouri 64836
(417) 358-7863
Magneto restoration services.

Magneto Repair
800-MAG-NETO
Magneto restoration services.

Paper Pulleys, Inc.
810 Woodland Street
Columbia, Tennessee 38401
(615) 388-9099
They restore paper core belt pulleys.

RAM Remanufacturing and Distributing, Inc.
N. 604 Freya
Spokane, Washington 99202
(800) 233-6934
e-mail: RAMRemfg@aol.com
Web site: http://members.aol.com/RAMRemfg/
    Home/sales.html
The vintage Engine Machine Works Division can complete any type of engine machining you need for your antique tractor.

Robert's Carburetor Repair
Box 624
Spencer, Iowa 51301
(712) 262-5311
Also sells videos on how to do it yourself.

Tractor Steering Wheel Recovering and Repair
1400 121st Street W.
Rosemount, Minnesota 55068
(612) 455-1802
Steering wheel recovering.

RESTORATION SUPPLIES AND TOOLS
A-1 Leather Cup and Gasket Company
2103 Brennan Circle
Fort Worth, Texas
(817) 626-9664
Very good source of seals and gaskets. Custom-cut felt seals.

Joe Sykes
935 9th Ave NE
N. Tonawanda, New York
(716) 691-8519
Custom-made piston rings: Any size.

Jorde's Decals
935 9th Ave NE
Rochester, Minnesota 55906
(507) 288-5483
Very highly regarded source for John Deere decals.

K & K Antique Tractors
5995 M. 100 W.
Shelbyville, Indiana 46176
John Deere authorized source of vinyl cut decals.

Kevin Small
P.O. Box 92
Portersville, Pennsylvania 16051
Steam boiler hand hole gaskets.

Lubbock Gasket and Supply
402 19th Street
Lubbock, Texas 79401
(800) 527-2064
Custom and standard gaskets for antique tractors.

POR 15 Inc.
308 LockPort St.
Lemont, Illinois 60439
(800) 576-5822
Their gas tank sealing kit is especially effective.

TIP
P.O. Box 649
Canfield, Ohio 44406
(800) 321-9260
A very nice selection of quality sandblasting products.

Tires
M. E. Miller Tire
17386 State Hwy. 2
Wauseon, Ohio 43567
(419) 335-7010
Also sell memorabilia, tire putty, and parade lugs.

Tucker's Tire
844 S. Main Street
Dyersburg, Tennessee 38024
(800) 443-0802
This place is well liked and received among antique tractor enthusiasts.

INDEX